D0467584

ALL THE

PRESIDENTS'

WORDS

ALL THE PRESIDENTS' WORDS

*The Bully Pulpit
and the Creation
of the Virtual Presidency*

CAROL GELDERMAN

WALKER AND COMPANY
New York

First published in the United States of America in 1997 by Walker Publishing Company, Inc.

Published simultaneously in Canada by Thomas Allen & Son Canada, Limited, Markham, Ontario

Library of Congress Cataloging-in-Publication Data
Gelderman, Carol W.
All the presidents' words: the bully pulpit and the creation of the virtual presidency/Carol Gelderman.
p.   cm.
Includes bibliographical references and index.
ISBN 0-8027-1318-1
1. Presidents—United States—History—20th century.   2. Rhetoric—Political aspects—United States—History—20th century.
3. Speechwriting—United States—History—20th century.   4. United States—Politics and government—20th century.   I. Title.
E176.1.G35   1997
973.9′092′2—dc21   96-54067
CIP

Book design by Dede Cummings

Printed in the United States of America

2   4   6   8   10   9   7   5   3   1

To the other C.G.

May she, too, be fascinated by the workings

of our unique governmental system.

C O N T E N T S

Preface ix

Acknowledgments xiii

Prologue 1

[1]
POINT-TO-POINT NAVIGATION 11
Franklin Delano Roosevelt

[2]
HOLDING THE LINE 36
Harry S Truman
Dwight David Eisenhower
John Fitzgerald Kennedy
Lyndon Baines Johnson

[3]
THE VIRTUAL PRESIDENCY 76
Richard Millhous Nixon
Ronald Wilson Reagan

[4]
THE MESSAGE IN THE BOTTLE 116
Gerald Rudolph Ford
James Earl Carter
George Herbert Walker Bush

[VII]

CONTENTS

[5]
STRIKE UP THEIR BAND 156
William Jefferson Clinton

Epilogue *176*
Notes *181*
Index *213*

PREFACE

I TEACH in a university English department, which explains why I'm so frequently asked if I'm looking for literary values in what presidents say. Not at all, I reply, and then can't resist adding something that Ike is purported to have said when one of his own utterances was criticized as less than eloquent. If good writing was necessary for good leading, the country ought to turn to Hemingway.

But good leading is dependent on writing in another sense. No one can lead without first establishing direction. And there is no better way to determine direction than to be forced to marshal information into understandable and focused accounts, which is what writing does. Obviously presidents should take some part in the writing of their own words, but not all do. In fact, speaking the words that others have written is practically de rigueur in political circles, from the Oval Office to county headquarters.

Nor are politicians unusual in this respect. CEOs hire speechwriters; federal judges use clerks; syndicated columnists have research assistants who have been known to have written more than a few columns for their bosses. Even in the university, few college professors outside of English departments require regularly written essays as part of course work. Does anyone believe that students can learn to think—that is, sort out relationships among a plethora of facts—from memorizing for true-false, multiple-choice, and other types of computer-scored questions?

My concern about this nonchalance toward writing as a tool of thinking, coupled with a lifelong passion for politics and fascination with government, is the motivation for *All the Presidents' Words* and is the reason, probably, why no other book—at least none that I know of—articulates my particular "take" on the subject.

All the Presidents' Words is a behind-the-scenes scrutiny of the way presidential speeches are created and why the method of creation can have a tremendous effect on the success and failure of an administration. My focus is on how directly or indirectly the president and others are involved in the drafting and revising of speeches.

Speechwriting, whether by a president alone or with the assistance of aides, is a learning and synthesizing process. It provides an opportunity for the president and his advisers to discuss and refine ideas and to test conclusions before making them public. From Franklin Delano Roosevelt to Lyndon Baines Johnson, presidents openly used senior aides to help them write speeches. These aides also were actively involved in the policy decisions they helped communicate.

With Richard Nixon the collaborative process began to break down. For the first time ever, people primarily talented at writing were hired and put on the federal payroll as speechwriters. They needed neither policy expertise nor even knowledge about issues, since they were first and foremost wordsmiths, separated from the president and his policymakers. Divorcing the form of the presidential speech (structure and word choice) from its content (policy) has changed the function of the speeches—and, to some extent, the very nature of the presidency.

Not until this century did presidents speak directly to the public on a regular basis, but once they began, they spoke more and more frequently in each succeeding administration. This book begins with a prologue about Theodore Roosevelt and Woodrow Wilson, who brought into being what is today called the rhetorical presidency. Chapter 1 deals with FDR, and subsequent chapters cover Truman through Clinton. Presidents are grouped by similarity of their manner of managing their writers and not necessarily in the chronological order of their term in office.

ACKNOWLEDGMENTS

A BOOK about the way a president uses his speechwriters would be impoverished, if not impossible, without the cooperation of the speechwriters themselves. (Of course, cooperation should not be construed as approval.) First and foremost, then, I wish to acknowledge the willingness of the following writers to grant interviews: Donald Baer (Clinton), Aram Bakshian (Nixon, Ford, Reagan), Taylor Branch (helped with Clinton's 1993 inaugural only), Patrick Butler (Ford), Carolyn Curiel (Clinton), Mark Davis (Bush), Tony Dolan (Reagan), Jerry Doolittle (Carter), David Dreyer (Clinton), Terry Edmonds (Clinton), Bently Elliott (Reagan), Andrew Ferguson (Bush), Josh Gilder (Reagan), Robert Hartmann (Ford), Hendrik Hertzberg (Carter), Clark Judge (Reagan), James Keogh (Nixon), David Kusnet (Clinton), Eric Liu (Clinton), Harry McPherson (LBJ), Alison (Lissa) Muscatine (Clinton), Landon Parvin (Reagan), John Podhoretz (Reagan), Raymond Price, Jr. (Nixon), Jeremy Rosner (Clinton), David Shipley (Clinton), Gordon Stewart (Carter), Paul Theis (Ford), Michael Waldman (Clinton), and Carter Wilkie (Clinton).

Everyone's memory is subject to occasional lapses, so it was essential for me to match what I had learned from interviews (and books) with what each president's personal files, speech files, and daily diary showed, as well as the files and memos of the writers themselves, all the property of the National Archives and housed in the presidential libraries. I am grateful, then, to all the archivists at the presidential libraries, every one of whom was helpful, and especially to: Nancy Snedeker, Franklin Delano Roosevelt Library; Randy Sowell, Harry S. Truman Library; Dwight Standberg, Dwight Eisenhower Library; Moira Porter, John F. Kennedy Library; Linda Hanson, Lyndon B. Johnson Library; Mark Fischer, Richard Nixon Presidential Archives; William H. McNitt, Gerald Ford Library; Martin Elzy, Jimmy Carter Library; and Greg Cumming, Ronald Reagan Library.

I owe a special debt to Jay Tolson, editor of the *Wilson Quarterly,* who asked me to write an article on the subject of this book for the publication (spring 1995) and who suggested the title, *All the Presidents' Words;* and to Steve Lagerfeld, deputy editor, who skillfully edited my piece. Their encouragement and questions helped me immeasurably in narrowing my focus.

Thanks also to Burt Solomon of the *National Journal* for listening to my views on presidential rhetoric, thereby helping me to sharpen them, and for sharing his presidential expertise with me; to James Barnes, also of the *National Journal,* for his comments, especially about the Bush administration; to Theodore Sorensen for annotating the pages concerning President Kennedy; to Arthur Schlesinger, Jr. for advice and encouragement when I was considering whether to pursue this project; and to Stephen Ambrose whose friendship and books have been an inspiration.

Thanks to the National Endowment for the Humanities for a summer stipend in 1993 that I used to help defray costs of five months of research in the presidential libraries.

Thanks to William Rohde for his help with research; to Connie Phelps, Nancy Radonovich, and Gayle Barclay of the Interlibrary Loan Department of the University of New Orleans; to stalwart and always cheerful Tracy Deebs, who photocopied more presidential speeches than she wants to count and who typed the first draft of the manuscript; and to Elizabeth Arceneaux for retyping the final version.

Above all, I owe much to Jacqueline Johnson, my tactful, astute, hardworking, and expeditious editor; to Vicki Haire, the copyeditor (also industrious), to Marlene Tungseth, director of editorial production and design, and to Beth Caspar, the production editor, all of whom have tried their best to save me from myself.

Finally, I thank publisher George Gibson for believing in this project.

ALL THE
PRESIDENTS'
WORDS

P R O L O G U E

A SERIOUS student of politics and history, Theodore Roosevelt concluded that all presidents fell into two categories.
The first he called the Taft-Buchanan School. Its proponents
refused to act unless the Constitution specifically allowed the
action. The second, much smaller group, the Jackson-Lincolnites, believed the president had a duty to act unless the Constitution explicitly forbade the action. "The most important factor
in getting the right spirit in my Administration," Roosevelt
wrote, "was my insistence . . . that executive power was limited
only by specific restrictions and prohibitions appearing in the
Constitution or imposed by Congress under its Constitutional
powers." Acting on his theory, he set about establishing a direct
relationship with the American people through public speaking.
In his example lie the roots of twentieth-century presidential
leadership as it has come to be practiced.

Theodore Roosevelt was the first president to see the chief
executive's office as a "bully pulpit," by which he meant that
when he did not get his way with Congress he took his case to
the people. His theory of an active presidency exactly suited his
personality. He delighted in the spotlight. He had used "swings

around the circle," as he called his speaking tours, to get himself seen and his message heard by the electorate.

His most successful swing around the circle played a major role in the passage of the Hepburn Act, which tightened railroad regulation. For eighteen months, from the beginning of 1905 until its passage (despite the opposition of a majority within his own party) in mid-1906, he spoke to any group that would listen, which meant just about all. As a critic observed, Roosevelt had the "knack of doing things, and doing them noisily, clamorously; while he is in the neighborhood the public can no more look the other way than the small boy can turn his head away from a circus parade followed by a steam calliope."

Everything about the man attracted attention, from his pince-nez eyeglasses to his resonant tenor voice that rose to a shrill falsetto when he grew excited. While delivering a speech he paced back and forth, gesticulating and brandishing his manuscript at the audience. He both entertained and inspired his listeners, and in the process he showed Americans a new way of looking at and thinking about the presidency, as the voice for representing all of them and for promoting legislation on their behalf. Although his ebullient public speechifying did not directly influence much legislation other than the Hepburn Act, Roosevelt's model of the presidency as the bully pulpit led to a central and important change in federal governing in the twentieth century, namely, the shift of the seat of influence from Congress to the presidency.

Before Theodore Roosevelt, presidents did not speak about policy directly to the people but to other branches of government. The Constitution, which merely suggests that presidents talk to Congress from "time to time" about the state of the Union, does not mandate a single oratorical duty to the chief executive. The Founding Fathers looked with suspicion on presidential rhetoric directed toward winning over public opinion. Their fear was that popular oratory might undermine the rational and enlightened debate of the citizens' representatives that their system was designed to foster and on which it was thought to depend for its stability. Public presidential speechmaking was thought to lead to demagoguery.

Even during the extreme crisis of the Civil War, Abraham Lincoln fully affirmed the Founders' views on rhetorical matters by steadfastly refusing to discuss issues of the day in popular addresses. "Stressing the need to make his pronouncements on 'proper' or authoritative occasions, Lincoln recognized the need to rest his authority on the Constitution rather than upon raw popular will," political scientist Jeffrey Tulis observed in *The Rhetorical Presidency.* And for all Theodore Roosevelt's swings around the circle, he, too, felt the old constraints. Tradition still barred him from preempting Congress's deliberative duties, so he avoided public speech while the in-session Congress considered the Hepburn Act, for example.

Although Roosevelt placed an indelible stamp upon the presidency, only after Woodrow Wilson took office in 1913 did the bully-pulpit presidency take hold. Earlier in Wilson's career, as a professor of political economy at Princeton, he had developed a thoroughgoing critique of the Founders' idea of government, and Roosevelt was largely responsible. After a century of congressional dominance—with the exceptions of the Andrew Jackson and Abraham Lincoln administrations—the example of the former Rough Rider impelled Wilson to revise his initial view of the presidency as the useless fifth wheel. In *Congressional Government in the United States,* Wilson had argued for reform in the Congress as the way to more responsible government. After Roosevelt's revivification of the office, however, Wilson looked to the possibility of a dominant presidency, a view articulated in 1907 in his lectures at Columbia University and published in 1908 as *Constitutional Government.*

Wilson argued that the only national voice is that of the president; Congress represented merely local and sectional fragments of the nation, and partisan fragments at that. He acknowledged that Congress had been constitutionally endowed with formidable powers: the power of the purse, the power to override veto, to censure, even to impeach, the power to declare war and fix tariffs, among many others. But they could be overborne, Wilson reasoned, "only because the president has the nation behind him, and Congress has not. [The president] has no means of compelling Congress except through public opinion." Accordingly, after Wilson was elected he made persuasion the chief business of the U.S. presidency.

The Democratic convention of 1912 in Baltimore that launched Wilson's presidential bid was one of the nation's most suspenseful and, at its close, soul-stirring. The conservative and progressive contingents put the convention delegates on notice that they must choose between the two wings of their party. In ballot after excruciating ballot—forty-six in all—the Democrats ultimately chose the progressive wing, represented by Woodrow Wilson. As a result of a split in the Republican party—President William Taft, nominee of the regular Republicans, ran against former president Theodore Roosevelt, candidate of the just-formed Bull Moose contingent, as well as the Democrat—Wilson won the election with only 42 percent of the popular vote.

The new president delivered his Inaugural Address on March 4, 1913. That year, the heart and soul of progressivism, Democratic style, was the establishment of a free market. At the top of the agenda of domestic reform, then, was the first deep across-the-board downward revision of tariff rates since 1846. On March 17 the chairman of the House Ways and Means Committee notified Wilson that the tariff bill had been readied to go to the floor of the House, so Wilson called Congress into special session to deal with it. On March 26 he wrote a "message" he planned to present to Congress, and read it to his Cabinet two days later. On the evening of April 6, the twenty-eighth president "let it be known" that on April 8 he would *personally* read his message to Congress.

Members of the Senate and House professed "profound astonishment" at Wilson's decision to break a 113-year custom. The last president to appear in person before Congress was the nation's second, John Adams, who himself stopped going to Capitol Hill after his Fourth Annual Address on November 22, 1800, sending his final two messages to the legislature to be read by a clerk. All of Thomas Jefferson's messages went directly to the House's reading clerk. Twenty-four subsequent presidents followed Jefferson's example, and in so doing, seemed to have set adopted practice in stone.

Congress immediately started "delving into old records" to determine appropriate congressional procedure. "The town is agog," an amused president wrote a friend. The day before Wilson was due to speak, the Senate was in a frenzy of puzzlement and excitement about the propriety of a presidential visit to their domain. Two senators from Missouri, still smarting from the Baltimore defeat of their ally, Speaker Champ Clark, tried to sabotage the president's appearance through parliamentary tactics. They introduced argument after argument to persuade the Senate to adjourn without waiting for the House's resolution for a joint session the next day. After heated discussion, they succeeded in getting thirteen additional senators to vote with them for adjournment, an act in parliamentary terms tantamount to refusal to receive the president. Making matters worse, John Sharp Williams of Mississippi led a direct verbal attack. He referred to a presidential message delivered in person as a "speech from the throne, . . . a cheap and tawdry imitation of the pomposities and cavalcadings of monarchical countries." The chief executive of a democratic nation, he said, must never imitate the British custom of opening Parliament with a speech from the reigning king or queen.

Senate objections grew so sharp that Vice President Thomas Marshall, rather than submit the usual request for unanimous consent for the immediate consideration of the House's resolution, declared it a question of "highest privilege" on which unanimous consent was not required. The question of high privilege elicited more parliamentary wrangling, but Marshall's proposal carried.

On April 8 Wilson arrived at Capitol Hill at noon. Waiting crowds cheered him as he stepped out of the White House car. After acknowledging their exuberant greetings, he walked briskly to the Speaker's room to join the committee sent to welcome him. Soon after, Vice President Marshall led the Senate up to the main aisle of the House chamber. Marshall took his place next to the Speaker of the House behind what had formerly served as the reading clerk's desk, but today would accommodate the president.

The galleries had filled much earlier. Mrs. Wilson, her three daughters, and invited guests occupied the "president's pew" on the first row of reserved gallery space; behind them sat the town's diplomats and dignitaries. The public lucky or well connected enough to have gotten hastily issued passes took the remaining seats and standing room. At precisely 12:57 the doorkeeper stepped into the main aisle of the chamber and announced the president, who quickly made his way to the rostrum. After shaking hands with Speaker Clark, whom he had so narrowly beaten for the nomination only months before, and his vice president, Wilson turned to face the crowded room. He looked into the faces of many of the senators who had tried so hard to humiliate him just the day before.

"Gentlemen of the Congress," the president began. "I am very glad indeed to have this opportunity to address the two Houses directly and to verify for myself the impression that the President of the United States is a person, not a mere department of the Government hailing Congress from some isolated island of jealous power, sending messages, not speaking naturally and with his own voice—that he is a human being trying to cooperate with other human beings in a common service." Reading in a conversational tone, Wilson outlined the compelling reasons for tariff reform, thanked Congress for its courtesy in receiving him, and left the chamber to spirited applause, a short twelve minutes after he had entered.

Edith Wilson showed an instinctive grasp of the nature of her husband's brand of leadership with a remark she made in the car that took the Wilsons back to the White House on that memorable afternoon. She told her husband that his unexpected "going to the Hill" was precisely the kind of action that Theodore Roosevelt should have liked to have taken, "if only he had thought of it." "Yes," the president laughed, "I think I put one over on Teddy."

Newspapers across the country carried the short speech, whereby millions of Americans also "heard" what Wilson had said. No previous presidential speech had reached so many people. The country at large "was vastly interested, amused, impressed," Wilson biographer Ray Stannard Baker wrote, for "there was something new, bold, free about his leadership."

Editorial writers had a heyday with the Wilsonian innovation. "Is the national legislature to be held *in terrorem* in order to justify the self-assumed role of the All-Wise Teacher of the White House?" a reporter for the prestigious *Financial World* asked. The usually pro-Wilson New York *World* chided the president, saying the country "cannot afford to take the chance . . . of having his leadership rebuked as meddling." But overall, opinion was more favorable than not. A writer for *Harper's Weekly* spoke enthusiastically of Wilson's "new bossism." The *American Review of Reviews*'s editor enthused over the common sense of a president's taking charge of tariff matters, since congressmen had been elected to safeguard local interests, which, often enough, implied protection of a particular tariff. The *Outlook*'s editor praised the president's brevity and focus, and even the Republican *Chicago Tribune* noted Wilson's "dignity" and "impressiveness."

Every American, it seemed, had some opinion about the president's historic speech, but few understood its real significance. What Wilson had accomplished was enhanced publicity as a means of direct access to the public. Making personal appearances in Congress, a practice he continued through his two administrations, was *the* central element in his strategy for leading public opinion.

—

ALTHOUGH Roosevelt and Wilson wrote their own speeches, the plebiscitary presidency they introduced gave rise later to a new speechmaking machinery in the White House. A president who leads a nation rather than only the executive branch of government must be a loquacious president, and most recent ones have been loquacious to a fault, a change abetted (but not caused) by the rise of mass media, especially television. Gerald Ford, for example, averaged one speech every six hours in 1976 (including press conferences and announcements as well as formal speeches). Jimmy Carter addressed the country even more often, adding 9,873 single-spaced pages to the *Public Papers of the Presidents of the United States.* Ronald Reagan increased this bulk with another 13,000 pages, and Bill Clinton, in his first year as president, spoke publicly three times as often as Reagan did in his first twelve months. Recent presidents have had a staff of speechwriters efficiently producing words for them to say on every conceivable occasion. Once known as ghosts and hidden in the presidential closet, rhetoric makers since Franklin Roosevelt have been openly employed, some even becoming media celebrities.

Even in the earliest days of the Republic, presidents called on others for help with their speeches: Alexander Hamilton and James Madison helped George Washington draft his Farewell Address; Edward Livingston wrote Andrew Jackson's nullification proclamation; and George Bancroft composed Andrew Johnson's first annual message, to cite a few instances. But until recently, most presidents wrote their own words most of the time. Jefferson, the two Adamses, Madison, Monroe, and especially Lincoln were accomplished writers whose speeches are still a pleasure to read. In the twentieth century, William Mc-Kinley, Theodore Roosevelt, William Howard Taft, and Woodrow Wilson wrote for themselves.

The earliest presidential ghostwriters were invisible to the public. The idea of a president speaking with anything but his own words was unacceptable. Judson Welliver, the Oval Office's first "official" ghostwriter, wrote for Warren Harding. Hired as "literary clerk," he began White House service in 1921. Few Americans then or later knew anything about him or his job. He is remembered chiefly, if at all, for coining the term "Founding Fathers." Describing his career in *Who's Who in America,* Welliver wrote: "attached to White House organization, occupying confidential relation to presidents Harding and Coolidge until November 1, 1925, resigned." Herbert Hoover laboriously wrote his own major speeches, but he did employ ghostwriters, first French Strother, later replaced by George Hastings. They drafted minor addresses and performed editing duties. Surrogate speechwriting came fully into his own under Franklin Roosevelt. He never kept his speechwriters' literary activities secret. The public, knowing that he carefully directed and supervised the preparation of major addresses, began to take it for granted that speeches should be a composite product, that is, a collaboration.

Speeches are the core of the modern presidency. Presidents often are canonized or vilified not so much for what they do but for what they say they will do and how engagingly they say it. But who is putting the words in presidents' mouths? How much are contemporary presidents involved in acquiring information, sorting through issues, determining direction, and making decisions that form the basis for administration policies and national goals? What happens to policy when presidents barely know their writers' names? In their zeal to woo the public, how many presidents pander instead of lead? Does their perpetual going-to-the-public undermine the deliberative decision making essential to the system envisioned by the Founders?

Practical answers can be found and valuable lessons learned by exploring the evolution of the presidential speechwriting process and its effect on domestic and international policy, starting with Franklin Roosevelt, the undisputed master of the rhetorical presidency.

1

POINT-TO-POINT
NAVIGATION

Franklin Delano Roosevelt   1933–1945

F OR Franklin Delano Roosevelt, the essence of political leadership in a democracy was teaching. His radio talks to the nation that came to be called fireside chats did not preach or exhort, as his cousin Theodore Roosevelt's speeches did. FDR's explained in direct, simple, calm language a certain problem and what the administration proposed to do about it. These talks constituted a new genre in U.S. political literature, and they also fashioned a new relationship between the president and the people. The country's foremost civic educator called the room where he met reporters for his biweekly press conferences his "schoolroom," the budget, his "textbook," his speeches, "seminars."

Roosevelt understood that great presidents must be great teachers. Just as Lincoln had restored the Union, not the status quo antebellum Union but something vastly different, so too did FDR have to persuade the nation to replace laissez-faire economics with government initiatives. Using carefully crafted speeches to make revolutionary ideas feel familiar, he succeeded in shifting to Washington functions and concerns that had been the job of states or private groups since the founding of the Republic.

A political leader bent on getting the public to endorse a departure from accepted policy has to deal with public aversion to innovation; he has to study public opinion and make a strategic retreat when he is too far ahead of it. Speechwriter Samuel Rosenman quoted Roosevelt as saying, "It's a terrible thing to look over your shoulder when you are trying to lead and find no one there." His grasp of public opinion was the result of reading a variety of newspapers, hostile and friendly, as well as the daily digest of editorials prepared by the Commerce Department. He carried on an immense correspondence, sampled representative letters from the unprecedented volume that came to him, sent his wife to places he could not go himself, and placed great faith in her reports. He knew how to extract a maximum of information from each of the scores of experts who visited him.

When scientific polling (that is, the sampling method) came into use in 1935, he consulted that source of information about trends in public thinking. He regularly looked at Elmo Roper's column in the *New York Herald Tribune* that was based on Roper's *Fortune* surveys; he followed results from George Gallup's American Institute of Public Opinion polls; and he actually talked several times to Hadley Cantril, who founded the Office of Opinion Research at Princeton in 1939. Not once did President Roosevelt "change his mind," Cantril said later, "because of what any survey showed. But he did base his strategy a great deal on these results."

The reason Roosevelt expended so much energy in discerning the public's opinion of certain issues was not to figure out which way to veer but to discover how much and what kind of persuasion was needed to bring people along. In this way he determined what to emphasize, what illustrations to use to clothe the unorthodox in the garb of the familiar, what argument to employ to banish fear and rally the nation. Roosevelt's speeches were the prime instrument for his conduct of public affairs, the vehicle by which he set in motion social and moral forces that affected not only every American but people all over the world. "Roosevelt knew that all those words would constitute the bulk of the estate that he would leave to posterity," speechwriter and presidential troubleshooter Robert Sherwood said, "and that his ultimate measurement would depend on the reconciliation of what he said with what he did."

Roosevelt did not delegate speechwriting to others. He insisted on being involved in the construction, from start to finish, of all major speeches. Although crises followed one after another relentlessly during FDR's occupancy of the White House, the president set aside five or six nights a month to work on speeches. On these nights Roosevelt and his writers—over the years several different aides but always Samuel Rosenman— gathered at 7:15 in the president's study for drinks, which FDR mixed from a tray on his desk. Shoptalk was discouraged during the thirty-minute ritual; conversations usually consisted of gossip, funny stories, and reminiscences. At precisely 7:45, the men sat down to eat at a portable extension table that accommodated six.

Dinner over, the president moved to a sofa near the fireplace and read aloud the most recent draft, while a secretary sat ready to take his dictated revisions and addenda. Together he and his writers tightened and simplified phraseology, eliminated sentences, paragraphs, and often whole pages, and dictated fresh passages to take their place. The president often drew material from his own speech file, a collection of miscellaneous items that he had been accumulating for many years. It included items from his correspondence, notes from his reading, memoranda, clippings, and telegrams, as well as suggestions submitted by members of Congress and others. Sometimes a call went out to poet Archibald MacLeish, who served as librarian of Congress during the 1940s, or some other close adviser, to lend a hand.

After the president went to bed, Rosenman and Robert Sherwood and often Harry Hopkins, the speechwriting team during the 1940s, worked most of the night to produce another draft, which was placed on the president's breakfast tray the next morning. If there was time during the day, they conferred again and got further reactions and instructions from Roosevelt. In the evening, they resumed writing in another after-work session. The process continued day and night until they agreed on a final reading copy. Major speeches went through a dozen or more drafts, each of which the president had studied, added to, trimmed, read aloud, and subjected to searching criticism.

By the time he delivered the speech, Roosevelt knew it almost by heart and needed only occasional glances at the manuscript as he spoke. He was often persuasive and sometimes eloquent, displaying a power won in large part by his meticulous involvement in the writing process. Just as important, the men who helped him thoroughly understood his thought and rhetorical style, as well as his politics.

No leader's adviser ever had more influence than Harry Hopkins. He was the president's eyes, ears, and legs. During the war years he became the trusted go-between for Roosevelt and Winston Churchill; even Joseph Stalin showed uncommon respect for him. During FDR's first two terms, Hopkins had had a number of important jobs, among them head of the Works Progress Administration and secretary of commerce. Whatever was uppermost in Roosevelt's mind was what Hopkins worked on. He was privy to presidential secrets and papers. He enjoyed easy entrée to the president, living from 1940 to 1943 in Roosevelt's very house. He even had untrammeled access to that most heavily guarded area in the wartime White House, the Map Room, which was the nerve center of the Allied effort. As a (for a time *the*) key adviser, Hopkins made an ideal speechwriter. No policy, after all, can be fully shaped until it is put in words.

Samuel Rosenman did not live in the White House except for certain particularly frenzied speechwriting jobs, but he, too, had long been a part of Roosevelt's political life; in fact he had served FDR for a longer time than had Hopkins. Rosenman had been adviser and speechwriter to Governor Roosevelt. He introduced the words "New Deal," a phrase that became synonymous with FDR's name, in his draft of the governor's acceptance speech at the 1932 Democratic convention. Rosenman first suggested a brain trust, an informal group of advisers to contribute ideas and to help with speeches that went beyond the parochial concerns of one state. A Columbia University alumnus, Rosenman asked professors he knew there to become members of the group, principally so they could easily and inexpensively come and go between Albany and New York City and still tend to their scholarly duties.

At first Raymond Moley, Rexford Tugwell, Adolf Berle, and Lindsay Rogers, in addition to Roosevelt's former law partner Basil O'Connor, comprised the governor's "privy council," as he privately termed the men. Later others were added, so that eventually any FDR adviser came to be called a brain truster. Several of the original group went on to help run New Deal agencies, even while they maintained speechwriting duties. None, though, lasted as long as Rosenman, who served as speechwriter during all four presidential terms. Yet not until 1943 did he draw a federal paycheck. From the time of Roosevelt's first inauguration until then, Rosenman had served as judge on the New York Supreme Court, commuting to Washington on weekends and during summers at his own expense. Sheer physical exhaustion forced him to resign his judicial position in early 1943 and move to Washington to serve as the first special counsel to the president, a job especially created for the speechwriter.

When the brilliant young lawyer Thomas Corcoran,

brought in to help with speechwriting by original brain truster Raymond Moley in 1934, fell out of favor by the beginning of the third term, Rosenman and Hopkins looked for a replacement, especially as their duties expanded just before and during the war. Pulitzer-winning playwright Robert Sherwood joined the pair in 1940 to help with campaign speeches and stayed on as a close Roosevelt aide until the president's death in 1945. He, too, found himself juggling more and more duties as he became another of the chief executive's trusted troubleshooters. By early 1944, for example, Sherwood was spending considerable time overseas, trying to reorganize the Office of War Information, which Rosenman had set up in 1941. During the war, he and Rosenman, both New Yorkers, kept rooms at the Willard, a hotel directly across the street from the White House.

Clearly these men were more than mere verbal technicians; they were presidential aides deeply and continuously involved in high-level activities and associations. They had real policy responsibilities. Since every major speech of a president is in one way or another a policymaking speech, those who take part in its preparation while it is going through its many drafts are in a strategic position to help make that policy. They provide a sounding board for discussion of the best means of attaining certain of the president's goals. A naturally gregarious man who preferred talking to reading or writing, FDR liked to think out loud. Written speeches force an administration to make decisions, crystallize policy, impose discipline. The speech preparation process did exactly that for FDR.

Understanding the importance of preparing the public for big changes, he used his speeches to lead the public gradually, with a magnificent sense of timing. He knew when to use the bully pulpit and when to pull back. "I am like a cat," he once said. "I make a quick stroke and then I relax." Instead of introducing a piece of legislation and then trying to woo the public, the common practice of later presidents, Roosevelt slowly set about convincing the public first, so people could gradually come to accept his idea. A case in point is Social Security. Slowly, step-by-step, FDR persuaded the people that the economic assistance to be provided by Social Security did not undermine their ideal of self-reliance. He shaped public opinion through press conferences, a message to Congress, and two fireside chats, progressively moving toward his goal of legislation and culminating in a State of the Union Address.

Yet nothing exemplifies FDR's point-to-point navigation better than his success at shifting the country's mood from isolationist to internationalist by means of carefully constructed speeches delivered over a three-year period. From the Quarantine Speech of October 5, 1937, to the Arsenal of Democracy fireside chat of December 29, 1940, he "brought the people along" a "bite" at a time.

━

ALTHOUGH the United States had rejected the League of Nations, it had been basically internationalist in outlook, participating in foreign trade, attending world conferences, and signing international treaties. After the Japanese thrust into Manchuria in 1931, however, and the rise of Adolf Hitler in Germany, isolationist sentiment took hold in the United States. In 1933 the London Economic Conference that was convened to find answers to worldwide depression ended in failure; Germany resigned from the World Disarmament Conference; Germany and Japan quit the League of Nations. In 1934 the Nazis staged the infamous putsch that resulted in the murder of the Austrian chancellor, and Benito Mussolini invaded and conquered Ethiopia. The year 1936 brought the formal establishment of the Rome-Berlin Axis, the Spanish Civil War, and the Japanese and German Anti-Comintern Pact. When Italy joined in 1937, the Axis powers were united, causing England to rearm. Japan resumed its belligerent activities in China, now attacking the mainland. By July of 1937, the Sino-Japanese War, though undeclared, was on in earnest. As the specter of war grew more menacing, Americans became more isolationist. Hadley Cantril's poll of February 1937 showed the country to be overwhelmingly nationalist.

Like most Americans, Roosevelt wanted the United States to stay out of war, but he felt that maintaining isolationism ultimately would make the country more vulnerable than embarking upon some kind of international cooperation with the democracies. His personal correspondence as early as 1933 and continuing through the rest of the decade expresses this fear that public opinion was moving in a most unpragmatic direction. In a letter written just days before his first public move to change that direction, he acknowledges "the real perils of the international situation. I am disturbed by it and by its daily changing events. Soon I think the nation will begin to appreciate the ultimate dangers of isolating ourselves completely from all joint efforts towards peace."

The president deliberately chose Chicago, the heart of isolationism, as the site for his initial educative effort on October 5, 1937. He had assured the worried treasury secretary, Henry Morgenthau, Jr., that to accomplish his goal would be a matter of "longtime education, and I am not going to do anything which would require a definite response or action on the part of anybody." This explains Hopkins and Rosenman's failure, during the drafting process, to persuade the president to be more explicit about what he meant by quarantine, the key word of the speech; according to Rosenman, "he insisted on leaving it vague."

Following a jubilant morning ticker-tape parade down Michigan Avenue, FDR spoke of international cooperation, surprising everyone with his choice of subject matter. Since his ostensible purpose had been to dedicate the Outer Drive bridge, Chicagoans had expected a speech praising the Works Progress Administration, the agency responsible for building the span that linked the north and south sides of the city, but Roosevelt talked instead of foreign affairs. He warned Americans of the "present reign of terror and international lawlessness" that threatened the "very foundations of civilization." Peace-loving nations, he insisted, must make a concerted effort in opposition. "The peace, the freedom and the security of ninety percent of the population of the world is being jeopardized by the remaining ten percent who are threatening a breakdown of all international order and law." So rampant was this lawlessness, the president called it an epidemic: "When an epidemic of physical disease threatens to spread, the community approves and joins in a quarantine of the patients in order to protect the health of the community against the spread of the disease. . . . War is a contagion, whether it is declared or undeclared. It can engulf states and peoples remote from the original scene of hostilities." The president concluded by saying once again that there must be a concerted effort by the democracies to preserve peace. "America hates war. America hopes for peace. Therefore, America actively engages in the search for peace."

Although immediate reaction to the Quarantine Speech was more positive than negative—"I thought frankly that there would be more criticism," the president wrote former Wilson adviser Colonel Edward House—leading isolationists directed a vociferous and protracted attack in the press and over the radio. When FDR backed away from his hard-hitting statements on October 5, the public (and much later some historians) believed he had been "scared off" by the warmongering charges hurled at him. In fact, the president had drawn back because he feared the isolationists' confrontational hullabaloo might mislead public opinion. He had actually been encouraged by reaction to the speech to the point of telling Colonel House that "as time goes on we can slowly but surely make people realize that the threat of war would be greater to us if we close all the doors and windows than if we go into the street and use our influence to help curb the riot."

A mere week after the Quarantine Speech, the president addressed the nation in his tenth fireside chat since 1933. Because his purpose was to recall Congress to a special session to pass additional economic reforms owing to a persistent recession, he dealt with foreign matters in just four sentences: "I want our great democracy to be wise enough to realize that aloofness from war is not promoted by unawareness of war. In a world of mutual suspicions, peace must be affirmatively reached for. It cannot just be wished for. *And* it cannot be waited for."

The president's political instincts were on target. Despite his having made no foreign policy proposals, legislators were so nervous about the possibility of the United States being drawn into war that the special-session Congress almost passed the Ludlow Amendment. Representative Louis Ludlow, an Indiana Democrat, had been sponsoring a constitutional amendment that would require a national referendum before Congress could declare war. Senator Gerald Nye introduced a companion measure in the Senate. The Ludlow Amendment was defeated by a slim margin of 209 to 188, illustrating the strength of isolationist forces in Congress and giving a clear sign that the nation was not yet ready for a more active foreign policy.

If Roosevelt, as some suggested, had been planning to implement his Quarantine Speech by asking Congress to repeal the 1937 Neutrality Act, such a course no longer seemed feasible. It was abundantly clear to the president and to other internationalists that the Neutrality Act, which embargoed sales of munitions to any belligerent, unintentionally favored the aggressive nations, which had been rearming for years. When those nations blithely marched to war, fully equipped for battle, they easily vanquished their unprepared victims, denied the opportunity by law to buy U.S. munitions. But Congress was suspicious and rebellious because of a recession and bitterness about the pressure FDR had exerted to get Congress to pass a bill to increase the number of Supreme Court justices after the sitting nine judges had declared several key New Deal programs unconstitutional. As a result, Roosevelt's near-term prospects in seeking more control over foreign affairs had dimmed. In a letter at the end of the year to Joseph Tumulty, Woodrow Wilson's former secretary, the president complained about "Republican propaganda" for "talk [that] turned more and more to the 'peace at any price' theory. That is what I have to combat at the present time."

In his annual message to Congress on January 3, 1938, the president addressed domestic issues but managed to work in a warning to the nation that "much of the trouble in our own lifetime has sprung from a long period of inaction—from ignoring what fundamentally was happening to us, and from a time-serving unwillingness to face facts as they forced themselves upon us." The State of the Union Speech set the pattern for the year; the president always aligned matters at home with increasing danger abroad. His April 14, 1938, speech to the nation is typical. "Democracy has disappeared in several other great nations—not because the people of those nations disliked democracy but because they had grown tired of unemployment and insecurity, of seeing their children hungry." Even when England and France ignominiously bartered the liberty of the people of the Sudetenland to Hitler in return for the dictator's promise to end his expansionist policies, Roosevelt continued his go-slow policy. In early October, he did announce an increase of $300 million for national defense and directed the State Department to begin a drive for Congress to revise the Neutrality Act, but he stayed out of sight. He continued to confine himself to noncontroversial statements like the one he made on October 11 to the *New York Herald Tribune* Radio Forum. "There can be no peace," he said, "if the reign of law is . . . replaced . . . by sheer force; if national policy adopts as a deliberate instrument the threat of war."

Lawyers Benjamin Cohen and Thomas Corcoran, who often worked directly with the president on legislation, started helping Rosenman with speeches in 1938. They also took part in writing the 1939 State of the Union Address since they had been assigned to work on the "detailed estimates of what was needed for an adequate defense" that Roosevelt would promise in the speech.

Roosevelt delivered his annual message when Congress assembled on January 4, 1939. A calm but determined president described the menacing march of aggression overseas, spelled out its implications for the United States, and then dealt directly with neutrality. "Aggressive acts against sister [democratic] nations . . . automatically undermine all of us," he said. "When we deliberately try to legislate neutrality, our neutrality laws may operate unevenly and unfairly—may actually give aid to an aggressor and deny it to the victim. The instinct of self-preservation should warn us that we ought not to let that happen any more." A revision of the arms embargo provision of the neutrality laws as well as a defense buildup, the president concluded, were "measures short of war," the phrase by which the speech became known. Such measures would foster collective security among peace-loving nations.

Despite Senator Robert Taft's well-publicized complaint that implementation of the president's speech would lead the United States straight to the battlefields of Europe, Roosevelt persisted in his effort to get the arms embargo lifted. Three weeks later he met with the Senate's Foreign Affairs Committee. The intentions of the Axis powers are clear and have been for nearly three years, he began. There seemed to him at best a fifty-fifty chance that France and England could stop Hitler's advance. With Europe under the dictator's domination, Roosevelt continued, Africa was next and then Central and South America. The United States was likely to follow. Neutral or not, he concluded, it was in the country's best interest to arm France and Britain right away.

Publicly, the president said nothing like this, because he was still hoping to persuade Hitler to let the United States mediate between the Allies and the Axis. While communication between the leaders was ongoing, Roosevelt did not want to jeopardize the possibility, no matter how remote, of acting as neutral umpire. All hope died with the Nazi invasion of Poland and with France and England's declaration of war against Germany on September 3. That night the president spoke to the nation. He opened with a statement that "every effort of your government will be directed" toward keeping the United States out of war and then reviewed his own attempts to preserve peace. Echoing Woodrow Wilson's plea for neutrality in 1914, Roosevelt also asked for neutrality in deed if not in thought. "Even a neutral cannot be asked to close his mind or conscience."

In his struggle to effect repeal of the embargo provision of the Neutrality Act, he resorted to double-talk like this, but his real purpose in this speech was to make points with Congress, which had been called back to Washington for an "extraordinary" session. When it reconvened three weeks later, Roosevelt assured the body that a repeal would permit the sale of arms to the Allies, a "truer neutrality" than the present policy of aiding aggressors by default. Illogical as the argument appears, he had exactly captured the mood of the country: Support the Allies but stay out of war. He got what he asked for, even if the Allies had to pay in advance and provide their own transport.

Cash-and-carry arms turned out to be a short-lived stopgap, for France surrendered and England ran out of cash less than a year later, but even so, the policy energized isolationists for their last hurrah. Led by men like famed aviator Charles Lindbergh, Senators Bennett Clark, Gerald Nye, and Burton Wheeler, Congressman Hamilton Fish, and the Detroit radio priest Father Charles Coughlin, with the backing of Hearst's and Patterson's tabloids and Colonel McCormick's *Chicago Tribune,* they persuaded a sizable number of U.S. citizens that troubles in Europe were none of this country's business. Besides, they claimed, it was too late for the United States to catch up with the Axis powers' early start on munitions building. Roosevelt feared the "large funds at [the isolationists'] disposal for propaganda purposes." Moreover, he said, "they could command the services of a handful of U.S. senators who knew they had the power to filibuster, and who were willing to use that power, if necessary, to gain their ends."

To counter their strong emotional appeal, the president began his 1940 annual message to Congress by proclaiming the "vast difference between keeping out of war and pretending that war is none of our business. . . . Look ahead," he said, and figure out what kind of future American children might have if "the world comes to be dominated by concentrated forces alone," or if "world trade is controlled by any nation or group of nations which sets up that control through military force." Roosevelt offered principles without applications, because although the United States had power, until it had the will to act, he dared not utter a threat or offer a commitment for fear of political consequences. U.S. foreign policy, as a result, was ingenious rather than forthright, the best substitute the president could improvise for the more assertive policy he was debarred from following.

Only after the seismic shock of Hitler's advance far behind Allied lines did the president drop circuitous reasoning. From May 16, when he next addressed a joint session of Congress, until he achieved all-out, no-strings-attached aid to Britain, he used strong, blunt, direct language. In the preceding week Holland had surrendered to the Nazis, Belgium was in ruins, and France, supposed to have had the finest army in Europe, was close to giving up.

As the current writing triumvirate of Rosenman, Corcoran, and Cohen worked with the president on the important May speech, they had, according to Rosenman, "one eye on the war cables and the other on the message." All the while Roosevelt was in the process of making a momentous decision. Many in his inner circle were advising that the fight in Europe was hopeless, so he should keep all weapons at home for U.S. defense. Instead, Roosevelt called for making arms shipment abroad a priority to give the nation the time it needed to prepare adequately for its own defense.

Standing before the podium of the House, his leg braces firmly locked in place, Roosevelt waited for the 526 men and five women of Congress to be seated. "These are ominous days," he solemnly intoned. "The clear fact is that the American people must recast their thinking about national protection." Air-age technology had so shrunk the globe, the president reminded the nation, that aggressors abroad might suddenly imperil U.S. shores. The Atlantic and Pacific Oceans do not afford the protection isolationists claim, he continued. Detailing the advantage in armaments enjoyed by the Axis powers, Roosevelt asked Congress "not to take any action which would in any way hamper or delay the delivery of American made planes to foreign nations which have ordered them, or seek to purchase new planes. That from the point of view of our defense would be extremely shortsighted." Then he set a production goal of 50,000 planes a year, a figure that was ridiculed by the isolationists but was surpassed by a production of 90,000 in 1943. Next Roosevelt called for new appropriations for the armed services, and in a ringing conclusion, he proclaimed his faith in the dormant powers of an aroused democracy: "There are some who say that democracy cannot cope with the new technique of government developed in recent years by a few countries which deny the freedoms we maintain are essential to our democratic way of life. This I reject." The United States will require "a toughness of moral and physical fiber," he admitted, but herein lie "the characteristics of a free people, a people devoted to the institutions they themselves have built." A sustained ovation echoed throughout the chamber as the president, using a cane and an arm of a Secret Service man, made his way out of the room.

Ten days later Roosevelt talked to the nation in a fireside chat that Rosenman and Hopkins drafted. Speaking to announce his armament plans and to foster unity, he assured all groups that any speedup of the economy for defense purposes would benefit everyone equally. Crisis or no crisis, he said, New Deal labor reforms were here to stay.

The news from Europe worsened daily. Armchair strategists moved their colored map pins as commentators described panzer thrusts in northern Europe. Everyone in the United States knew what blitzkriegs were. Shortwave sets in Washington, D.C., picked up impassioned pleas from the French prime minister for America to intervene. On June 10, Italy declared war on France, then in extremis. "On this tenth day of June, 1940," the president said in a commencement address before his son's law school graduating class at the University of Virginia, "the hand that held the dagger has struck it into the back of its neighbor." The draft for this speech came from the State Department; Roosevelt inserted the sentence that so dramatically described Italy's infamy. On June 22, France capitulated and the Battle of Britain began. England alone stood between Hitler and his total mastery of Europe.

England's future was not promising at that moment. It was in dire need of ships, having lost so many of its own vessels to U-boat attacks. Roosevelt, at great political risk, traded fifty refurbished World War I destroyers for ninety-nine-year leases on British naval and air bases in the Western Hemisphere. Strictly speaking, the swap was not legal. It may not have been an outright gift, but it was certainly not cash-and-carry. Many Republicans and military men, fortunately, spoke up in favor of the trade, one calling it the greatest bargain since the Louisiana Purchase. On the other hand, the richest and most influential antiwar organization was created in direct response to the trade.

Founded by a Yale law school student, this organization— the Committee to Defend America First—chose General Robert Wood, chairman of Sears, Roebuck, to be its leader. Arguing that armaments must be kept at home for U.S. defense, the group attracted 800,000 members in its first six months.

Every isolationist on Capitol Hill, still a goodly number, enrolled in its ranks. The committee ran full-page advertisements in the nation's newspapers attacking Roosevelt's foreign policy.

There was now a curiously mottled, unstable quality to public opinion about foreign policy. America Firsters and other isolationist groups like Gerald L. K. Smith's committee of one million clashed with smaller, even more extreme groups. Ethnic isolationists like German- and Italian-Americans were resentful that most Americans harbored bitterness toward their former homelands, and Irish-Americans exhibited malevolence toward the English for two and a half centuries of persecution. There was also division within the ranks of the interventionists, including the best-known group, the Committee to Defend America by Aiding the Allies.

By way of visitors, polls, mail, newspapers, his own experts, and his intuitive political perception, Roosevelt picked up these soundings and took them to heart. His next speech called for a unified America. Hopkins and Rosenman worked on the September 11 speech with the president at his home in Hyde Park, New York, and in Washington, D.C. Speaking before the teamsters union convention, Roosevelt sought to rally not only the teamsters' support but that of "farmers and businessmen," factory workers, and, by implication, all Americans because "our mighty national defense effort in which we are engaged today" requires "a united people." Without union, "the morale of the people, as essential as guns and planes," is at risk. "Weakness in these days," the president said, "is a cordial invitation to attack. That's no longer a theory; it's a proven fact." And then forthrightly addressing the peace-at-any-price crowd, he said, "Let's have an end to the sort of appeasement that seeks to keep us helpless by playing on fear."

Not until October did Roosevelt publicly acknowledge that an election campaign was in progress, even though he was seeking an unprecedented third term. He had never even mentioned his opponent by name, but Wendell Willkie had been barnstorming the country, giving three or four speeches a day in which he accused the president of steering the nation toward social progress rather than toward preparedness. Supported by an overwhelmingly pro-Willkie press, the challenger began making headway in the polls by early October. Urged on by alarmed Democrats, the president announced five political speeches for the final two weeks before the election.

While assuming an above-the-fray role, the president had actually been stung by Willkie's charge. Roosevelt knew only too well how underprepared the United States was. Its army, which had languished in skeletal form since World War I, stood behind not only the armies of Germany, Britain, Russia, Italy, Japan, and China, but those of Portugal, Spain, Sweden, even tiny Switzerland. Congress had been engaged in a three-month debate over a proposed draft, the nation's first in peacetime, which passed in mid-October. Between the second and third of his campaign speeches, FDR returned to Washington to draw the first numbers under the Selective Service Act. In addition to the charge of slacker, Republicans had repeatedly and contrarily called him a warmonger, so he was careful in choosing words for the broadcast ceremony on October 16. Eschewing "selective service," "draft," "conscription," he hit upon "muster" to describe the new law, a fine choice that evoked memories of the farmers of Concord and Lexington taking their flintlock muskets down from fireplaces.

On October 28 he addressed a rally at Madison Square Garden in New York. On the grounds that the best defense in a weakened position is a strong offense, Roosevelt replied to Willkie's charges by using a favorite campaign weapon, ridicule of Republican inconsistency: "For almost seven years the Republican leaders in Congress kept on saying that I was placing too much emphasis on national defense. . . . Now always with their eyes on the good old ballot box, they are charging that we have placed too little emphasis on national defense. But, unlike them, the printed pages of the Congressional Record cannot be changed . . . at election time."

The record proved an effective counterattack. Quoting one statement after another made before 1940 by Republican leaders that the United States was spending too much for defense, Roosevelt compared their changed positions to "The Daring Young Man on the Flying Trapeze," a popular revival of an old song. The Republicans' capricious tenets, the president said, are like "somersaults or trapeze acts. On the radio Republican orators swing through the air with the greatest of ease, but the American people are not voting this year for the best trapeze performer."

Then the president moved from Republican statements to their voting records. (Roosevelt had told Rosenman and Sherwood, who had by this time joined the speechwriting team, to make a list of Republican votes.) His masterpiece of derision was a matter of rhyme and rhythm. First he cited chapter and verse on GOP leadership in opposition to administration defense measures. He concluded his lists of the various bills they had voted against with the specific votes of the three top Republican House leaders, Representatives Bruce Barton, Hamilton Fish, and Joseph Martin, Jr. (In the first draft, their names had been alphabetized, but during a speech session Rosenman and Sherwood suddenly perceived the more euphonious sequence of Martin, Barton, and Fish. The president repeated the sequence several times and indicated by swinging his finger how effective it would be with audiences.) Twice he used it at Madison Square Garden. The second time the crowd shouted the names with him, and the phrase echoed throughout the nation. In Boston a couple of nights later, when he cited yet more votes at cross-purposes to his own preparedness bills, the audience shouted Barton and Fish in reply to each mention of Martin. In spite of the fun the president had at his opponents' expense, he had actually tread very cautiously, fearing his policy of all-out assistance short of sending U.S. troops to Britain would be reversed.

On November 5 Roosevelt won the election with a healthy 449 electoral votes to Willkie's 82.

On the night of the election, the Luftwaffe unloaded tons of megabombs over London, the fiftieth consecutive night of Nazi air attacks. More than 900 RAF planes, many thousands of civilians, and the industrial heart of England had been lost in the raids. The very symbol of Anglo-Saxon democracy, the House of Commons, lay in ruins. U-boats had sunk so many merchant marine ships, the country's food supply was shrinking. The British government turned to the United States for help. England had been buying supplies from the United States, and according to the cash-and-carry terms specified in the Neutrality Act of 1939, had paid in advance and transported them across the Atlantic in its own ships. By the end of 1940, however, England was close to flat broke, and too many of its ships were disabled or destroyed to spare any for shipping even desperately needed munitions and food.

During a postelection Caribbean vacation on the USS *Tuscaloosa*, Roosevelt contrived a means of circumventing neutrality legislation so England could be saved. He had no idea how to execute his plan legally, he told Hopkins, but he knew he must find a way. The plan was Lend-Lease, the notion that the United States would send Britain munitions without charge and be repaid not in dollars but in kind after the war. The more he and Hopkins talked, the more buoyant the president became about his scheme.

Roosevelt returned to Washington on December 16. The next day he opened his 702nd press conference by offhandedly disclaiming "any particular news." For a while he casually talked about the inaugural and then carefully set about depicting himself as a reasonable middle-of-the-roader. With the extravagant claim that "a very overwhelming number of Americans believed the best American defense was aid for Britain," he made out that some of those people thought the United States should lend money and others that the country should give money for necessary weapons. He knew full well few people entertained such ideas, but he went on to describe this kind of hypothetical thinking as "banal."

"Now, what I am trying to do," he continued, "is to eliminate the dollar sign. That is something brand new in the thoughts of everybody in this room, I think." And then, as he had done so often before, he chose a homey metaphor to illustrate how he meant to get "rid of the silly, foolish, old dollar sign," and in so saying, he paved the way to Lend-Lease with his irresistible analogy of the garden hose.

> Suppose my neighbor's home catches fire, and I have a length of garden hose four or five hundred feet away. If he can take my hose and connect it up with his hydrant, I may help him put out his fire. Now what do I do? I don't say to him before that operation, "Neighbor, my garden hose cost me $15; you have to pay me $15 for it." . . . I don't want $15; I want my garden hose back after it is over. If it goes through the fire intact, he gives it back to me and thanks me for the use of it. But suppose it gets smacked up—gets holes in it—during the fire; we don't have too much formality about it, but I say to him, "I was glad to lend you that hose; I see I can't use it anymore." . . . He says, "All right, I will replace it." Now, if I get a nice garden hose back, I am in pretty good shape.

No one asked what use repayment "in kind" would be after the war and thus why his plan was not an outright gift of munitions. One perceptive reporter did point out a lack of ready U.S. war matériel to lend, but the president dismissed this inconvenient fact as unimportant. The moral of his simple and emotional metaphor was clear: By sending supplies to the British now, the United States would be abundantly repaid by the increase to its own security.

Highly engaging accounts of the press conference appeared

in newspapers across the country. "By the brilliant but simple trick of making news and *being* news," wrote historian Arthur Schlesinger, Jr., "Roosevelt outwitted the open hostility of publishers and converted the press into one of the most effective channels of public leadership." But news accounts of the press conference were only part one of Rooseveltian salesmanship. Part two was a radio speech to the nation that he announced would take place December 29.

The day after Christmas, speechwriters Samuel Rosenman and Robert Sherwood moved into the White House to collaborate on the speech with Hopkins, already living at 1600 Pennsylvania Avenue, and the president. With official Washington home for the holiday, the four men worked more or less uninterruptedly day and night. Hopkins provided the key phrase, "arsenal of democracy." All four writers agreed that it was to be as important a speech as Roosevelt's first on March 12, 1933, and so the president opened the speech with a reference to the earlier speech: "I tried to convey to the great mass of American people what the banking crisis meant to them in their daily lives. Tonight I want to do the same thing with the same people, in this new crisis which faces America." He then spoke of the impossibility of appeasing Hitler—"No man can tame a tiger into a kitten by stroking it"—of the need for an Allied victory to ensure U.S. security, of the dangers ahead if Britain were to fall. With a sure sense of geography, he showed how the Nazis could step from base to base right up to our borders. Worse, he continued, "if Great Britain goes down, the Axis powers could control the continents of Europe, Asia, Africa, Australia, and the high seas." Keeping in mind the fervent wish of Americans to stay out of war, Roosevelt justified aid to Britain on the grounds of self-interest. "The people of Europe who are defending themselves do not ask us to do their fighting. They ask for the implements of war, the planes, the tanks, the guns, the freighters, which will enable them to fight for their liberty and our security. . . . We must be the great arsenal of democracy."

The speech echoed like a clarion call to the world's remaining democracies. In the United States, more people listened to the president—76 percent—than had ever done so before. New York's theater owners and the nation's movie-house managers noted a drop in attendance on December 29. In London, citizens stunned after the bombing demolition of the square mile of the old walled city of London huddled around radios at 3:30 A.M. and cheered the vibrant voice coming to them from across the Atlantic; this, despite the loss of eight Christopher Wren churches, the ancient Guildhall, seat of the city's municipal government since William the Conqueror, and Old Bailey, the central criminal court. Huge fires had spread from Moorgate to Aldergate, from Old Street to Cannon Street. As the *New York Times* later reported on December 31, the Germans destroyed 500 years of English history in two hours.

German propaganda ministers had timed the dramatic assault to coincide with the president's radio speech in the hopes that stories of London's ruin would undermine the effect of the fireside chat. But Roosevelt's words buoyed up millions all over the world. The U.S. ambassador to Japan, Joseph Grew, commented that this speech would mark a turning point in history.

On January 6, 1941, Roosevelt formally presented his Lend-Lease plan to Congress as H.R. 1776. For the next two months a fierce and final battle raged between the isolationists and the interventionists about how to best protect the United States. Roosevelt's perspective triumphed. At the signing of Lend-Lease on March 11, 1941, he remarked, "The decisions of our democracy may be slowly arrived at. But when a decision is made, it is proclaimed not with the voice of one man but with the voice of 130 million." Looking back at this protracted battle against isolationism, speechwriter Hopkins later said, "Roosevelt had more to do than any man in his time in arousing the conscience of the civilized world to the menace of fascism and Nazism. And he did it by making speeches."

＝

FEW Americans then or now have grasped the genius with which Roosevelt made use of the bully pulpit. Clare Boothe Luce, for example, wife of publisher Henry Luce, made frequent fun of the president for what she called his continual shilly-shallying with impotent words. She mocked what she called his weakness and lassitude in the face of a disintegrating civilization by comparing the symbolic gestures that world leaders had come to be known by to a sign she thought fit for the president. Churchill had his fingered V for victory, she said; Hitler, a stiff arm raised above his head; Mussolini, a strut; and Roosevelt? She moistened her index finger and held it aloft to test the wind. She was clever, and she was accurate, but she had missed the point. As the president had explained in a letter to his friend Helen Reid, wife of the publisher of the Republican *New York Herald Tribune,* "You say you have been a pacifist all your life but you are now for universal service. From what extremes do the pendulums swing for us as individuals? Governments such as ours cannot swing so far or so quickly. They can only move in keeping with the thought and will of the great majority of our people. . . . Were it otherwise the very fabric of democracy . . . would be in danger of disintegration."

Roosevelt had sensed the danger coming as early as the mid-1930s. Despite initial praise, reactions to his blunt warning in the 1937 Quarantine Speech made him realize how unwilling Americans were at that time to act in concert with other nations, even other freedom-loving nations. Consequently, in 1938 and 1939, he softened his discourse on behalf of collective security; as war grew more imminent, he stepped up the tempo and directness of the rhetoric. As assistant secretary of the navy during the Wilson administration, Roosevelt had learned "the terrible responsibility of bringing a divided nation into war. He was going to be sure, very sure, that if the United States had to enter the war, it would enter as far as humanly possible a united nation." But when time ran out, and although barely 50 percent of Americans were willing to consider aid to Britain, the president urged the nation to become the great "arsenal of democracy." That speech alone, owing in large measure to its felicitous metaphor by which the speech is known, raised the percentage to 60.

Although Roosevelt died before the end of the war, his goal of making the United States the "arsenal of democracy" had been abundantly fulfilled. Between 1940 and 1945, the United States contributed 300,000 warplanes to the Allied cause. American factories produced more than two million trucks, 107,351 tanks, 87,620 warships, 5,475 cargo ships, over twenty million rifles, machine guns, and pistols, and forty-four million rounds of ammunition. This outpouring of war matériel was the dominant factor in winning the war.

Roosevelt's stunning success in mobilizing the nation rested on his notion of the purpose of presidential speechmaking. He had been "in the midst of a long process of education," he said in 1938, because "a nation has be educated to the point where [the goal] can be assimilated without spasms of indigestion." His strategy of gradually leading his countrymen from being neutral to feeling sympathy for the Allied cause to having the will to act had worked. Without doubt he was helped in achieving his goal by fostering close relationships with his speechwriting advisers and by granting them significant roles in policy decisions. "More than any other president," Samuel Rosenman said, "perhaps more than any other political figure in history, FDR used the spoken and written word to exercise leadership and carry out policies."

2

HOLDING THE LINE

Harry S Truman   1945–1953
Dwight David Eisenhower   1953–1961
John Fitzgerald Kennedy   1961–1963
Lyndon Baines Johnson   1963—1969

F RANKLIN Roosevelt left his mark on every subsequent president, and none more so than his first four successors, Harry Truman, Dwight Eisenhower, John Kennedy, and Lyndon Johnson. That influence was so dominant, in fact, that twenty-two years after Roosevelt's death, *Time-Life* correspondent Hugh Sidey could write, "You could stand on this Tuesday afternoon in February 1967 and look out over the faces in the East Room of the White House and suddenly understand that Franklin Roosevelt still owned Washington. His ideas prevailed. His men endured."

Three of the four presidents who succeeded Roosevelt were men whose careers he had advanced: Truman as his fourth-term vice president, Eisenhower as his supreme commander of the Allied Expeditionary Force in Europe, and Lyndon Johnson as his congressional protégé. John Kennedy had first gained familiarity with Washington when Roosevelt named his father to high office. And like Roosevelt, Presidents Truman, Kennedy, and Johnson gave their legislative initiatives thematic unity as in the Fair Deal, New Frontier, and Great Society. Even Eisenhower, the lone Republican of the four, managed to persuade his party to accept New Deal ground rules for the economy and internationalism.

All four presidents followed in Roosevelt's speechwriting footsteps. They adopted his collaborative method by choosing writers from among their top advisers and by recognizing the connection between writing and policymaking. Policy is made of words, they understood, and words shape thought.

Finally, in dealing with a growing recalcitrance on the part of the Soviet Union, all four adopted the theory that if the United States held the line long enough, the Soviet Union would collapse from within. Each articulated this policy in a crucial speech to the American people. Truman led the way with what has become known as the Truman Doctrine speech.

AFTER a brief and uneventful vice presidency during which the president was almost continuously absent from Washington, Harry S Truman had been catapulted into the top job when FDR died on April 12, 1945. Uninformed about and unprepared for the Herculean tasks of ending a World War and keeping peace, the new president turned instinctively to old Missouri friends for help. One of these, Commodore James Vardaman, became the president's naval aide. A few months later Vardaman brought from St. Louis a young lawyer friend, Clark Clifford, to be his assistant. When Vardaman moved to the Federal Reserve, Clifford, still in the Naval Reserve, became naval aide. He was assigned to the White House Map Room, a place so secret that Truman himself did not learn of its existence until right after Roosevelt's inauguration. Informed that the president had left Washington for a secret conference with Churchill and Stalin at Yalta, Truman was told to send only "absolutely urgent" dispatches through the Map Room.

Not once, though, during his eighty-two-day vice presidency was he admitted to its exclusive precincts. When he did gain access, he declared the place a marvel, providing as it did an up-to-the-minute military and political picture of the world.

Clifford, too, had been dazzled and somewhat over-whelmed by its plethora of inside information about all that had taken place since the U.S. entry into the war. Depending on twenty-eight-year-old George Elsey, the Map Room's junior officer since 1942, he mastered as much of the material as he had time for, since his new position required him to work also with Sam Rosenman, who had stayed on in the White House for a few months to help ease Truman's transition from quasi-private to first citizen by assisting with speechwriting. Right away Clifford grasped the unusual opportunity afforded a speechwriter to sway the course of an action. "Here was a man sitting in the White House working on presidential speeches and taking part in the determination of presidential policy," the naval aide later told an interviewer. When Rosenman left gov-ernment service in early 1946, Clifford had his eye on the speechwriting job. "Somebody had to work on the speeches," he mused. "Somebody had to serve as liaison with Cabinet members; somebody had to be in close contact with the Justice Department all the time." That somebody came to be Clark Clifford when Truman selected him for the Rosenman position on June 1, 1946. Not surprisingly, Clifford chose his Map Room mentor, George Elsey, to be his assistant.

Before long Clifford was spending more time with the pres-ident than any of his other advisers, beginning each day at Tru-man's early-morning staff conference and ending it with a branchwater-and-bourbon highball in a private evening meet-ing in the Oval Office. Of course, he conferred regularly with Elsey. With years of immersion in communications between FDR and the Allied leaders, Elsey proved indispensable to Clif-ford and, through him, to Truman. Helping to prepare the pres-ident for the Potsdam Conference that took place only three months after he had assumed office consumed the greater portion of Elsey's time in his new job. Even so, he continued producing the daily digest of the many messages and reports that still arrived day and night from commanders around the world. Soon Clifford and Elsey were handling everything that the not-yet-created National Security Council subsequently managed. Their most far-reaching policy initiative, from which emanated all of Truman's foreign policy speeches, occurred early in the administration.

George Kennan, at the time the scholarly chargé d'affaires at the U.S. Embassy in Moscow, sent an 8,000-word telegram to the State Department late in February 1946. Ever after referred to as the "long telegram," it warned of the dangers of Stalinism. Two weeks after the Kennan message, Winston Churchill delivered his famous Iron Curtain speech at Fulton, Missouri, in which he cited instances of Soviet expansionism.

> From Stettin in the Baltic to Trieste in the Adriatic, an iron curtain has descended across the continent. Behind that line lie all the capitals of the ancient states of central and eastern Europe. Warsaw, Berlin, Prague, Vienna, Budapest, Belgrade, Bucharest, and Sofia, all these famous cities and the population around them lie in the Soviet sphere and are all subject in one form or another, not only to Soviet influence but to a very high and increasing measure of control from Moscow.

Truman gave no overt indication of disagreement with Churchill, but he wrote his family in Independence, Missouri, saying he was not ready to abandon the era of wartime cooperation with the Soviet Union. He even sent a cable to Stalin inviting him to the United States to speak directly to the country. The Soviet leader responded by refusing to withdraw troops from the region of northern Iran known as Azerbaijan, as he had promised Roosevelt and Churchill he would do after the war. Soviet defiance of past accords continued throughout the spring and summer, provoking Truman to reconsider this earlier conciliatory position.

"The Russians are trying to chisel away a little here, a little there," the president said at the regular morning staff meeting on July 12, 1946. He told Clifford to assemble a list of Soviet violations. "I want to be ready to reveal to the whole world the full truth about the Russian failure to honor agreements," the president added. Clifford passed the assignment to his assistant, who argued for a broader study. What was needed, Elsey said, was a report on the totality of Soviet-U.S. relations.

No one in the administration could better probe such a subject. Elsey's close reading of Soviet behavior during the preceding four years from the secret confines of the Map Room uniquely equipped him to do the necessary research for an all-inclusive interagency foreign policy review. Although Clifford got most of the credit, Elsey did the work, an exhausting, all-consuming, eight-week project. From every government agency and department that dealt with the Soviet Union, he sought copies of agreements that the United States and USSR had signed, as well as commentaries about Soviet implementation or violation of each. Follow-up questions elicited more comment. Elsey also delved into the papers of Roosevelt, of Harry Hopkins, and of Admiral William Leahy, appointed by FDR to keep him informed on day-to-day details of the war. He searched texts, obtained by the Central Intelligence Agency, of Radio Moscow broadcasts, summaries of *Pravda* stories, and reams of other material.

In the end, Elsey had brought together for the first time facts and opinions that had been delivered to the White House piecemeal over a period of years—but what had never been said before, according to Clifford, was that the United States needed to create "an integrated policy and a coherent strategy to resist the Soviet Union." Elsey's depiction of Soviet activity since the war turned out to be consistent with Kennan's analysis and Churchill's speech. Moreover, based on his findings of Soviet arms buildup and espionage, he concluded that the United States should neither disarm nor fail to support freedom-loving nations in their struggles to resist communism. He finished his lengthy report by mid-September. Clifford read and edited the document, and then, because Truman wanted to distribute it to high-ranking Cabinet members and officials who did business with Russia, sent it to the print shop.

Truman got his copy on September 24. Very early the next morning he telephoned Clifford to find out how many copies had been printed. "Twenty," the special counsel answered. The president instructed Clifford and Elsey to keep their copies and to lock the others in his personal safe. Impressed by the comprehensiveness of the study, the president thought it too "explosive" for distribution.

Although alarmed, Truman took no action for five months. When Great Britain announced its withdrawal from Greece and Turkey, the president sensed that the time to act had arrived. With Soviet aggrandizement in central and eastern Europe in mind, he fully apprehended the danger. Since the time of the czars, Russia had lusted after an outlet to the Mediterranean Sea for its navy, which domination of the Dardanelles, currently under Turkish control, would provide. Moreover, if the Soviets could get hold of Iranian oil, most of which lay buried in the Azerbaijan province in the north, in an area that adjoined the Soviet republic of the same name, they would upset the world's balance of raw materials. Obviously the loss of Greece and Turkey would be serious enough, but worse, there were other Mediterranean nations whose shaky postwar economies made them just as susceptible to communism. Truman decided that the United States must fill the vacuum of power that was about to be created by Britain's exit from the region and help Greece and Turkey contain what was certain to be another instance of Soviet expansion.

On February 27, 1947, the president, Secretary of State George Marshall, and Undersecretary Dean Acheson met with the congressional leaders to spell out for them the ramifications of what they perceived to be the coming crisis. Senator Arthur Vandenburg, the Republican chairman of the Foreign Relations Committee, promised support if and only if President Truman personally argued the case for aid to Greece and Turkey and linked it to the survival of the West. The president announced his willingness to "lay it on the line." Eschewing further study, he directed key State Department advisers to begin drafting such a statement as the basis for a speech before Congress. "It's funny how a pending speech will clear the air on policies," he said.

To clear the air, the president's advisers had to resolve a heated dispute over the scope of the speech's underlying justification. Acheson clearly acknowledged the dilemma faced by the officers chosen to take part in the drafting process. Could the administration expect a Republican, budget-conscious, once again isolationist-minded Congress to approve military and economic assistance without putting it in a context of preventing further Soviet expansion? On the other hand, the policy that justified aid had such staggering global implications, involving the United States for the first time in its history in other countries' peacetime affairs, surely Congress and the American people would balk at its open-endedness. After all, the rationalization for aid to Greece and Turkey very probably would extend elsewhere; countries other than these faced similar problems. Where would U.S. support end?

Acheson pushed for a strong all-out statement that clearly illuminated Soviet intentions. Kennan, surprisingly, objected, fearing an overaggressive Soviet response. Simply ask for aid, he advised, and avoid alarming Stalin. Most views on how to present the policy ranged between Acheson's and Kennan's. Unfortunately, the multiplicity of outlook showed up in draft after draft, resulting in a hodgepodge of conflicting points. Wisely, Acheson put Joseph Jones of State's public affairs office in charge of writing, so subsequent attempts might at least sound coherent.

Between March 2 and March 6 Truman made a state visit to Mexico, the first to that country by a sitting president. Back in Washington the morning of March 7, he read State's latest draft, which he said sounded like an "investment prospectus [with] all sorts of background data and statistical figures." He wanted a straightforward "declaration of general policy," he told Clifford. The next day the special counsel summoned Joseph Jones to his office to suggest changes. Jones's fifth revision ended the State Department's active participation in the process.

At first Elsey had argued against an "all-out" speech on the grounds that it was being planned too rapidly and also that the Soviets had not yet taken overt action, thereby making the situation in Greece and Turkey still somewhat abstract. Since an all-out speech would be "the most significant speech in the president's administration," it could prove to provoke the Soviets unnecessarily, he concluded. When Clifford pointed out the unlikelihood of congressional approval of aid without justification on national security grounds, Elsey threw himself into making the speech "the opening gun in a campaign to bring people the realization that the War isn't over." Once committed, he became more aggressive than anyone else in translating Truman's ideas about the Soviets into a firm cold war policy.

All day Sunday, March 9, Truman in the Oval Office and Clifford and Elsey in the Cabinet Room refashioned the final State Department draft. By the end of the day "hardly a line [remained] of the working text that wasn't criss-crossed by either Clifford's or Elsey's corrections." At noon on the tenth, Clifford took the latest version to the president, and Elsey circulated it to key members of the White House staff. Later everyone assembled in the Cabinet Room for the usual round-the-table session. Truman read aloud, and staffers suggested revisions. Truman wanted still more "punch." Yet another revision appeared in late afternoon, which the president approved and sent to Acheson and Jones for their blessing. Their changes became part of the March 11 draft, finished in time for a last scrutiny at the regular morning staff meeting. Just before 1:00 P.M. the much-revised final message of 2,200 words was frozen for posterity. Within a span of just two and a half weeks, from the time of Britain's announcement of withdrawal to Truman's March 12 delivery, the executive branch had coordinated a consensus, developed a program that signaled a major turning point in U.S. policy, built a case, and devised a message of breathtaking about-face. As Acheson remarked, when President Truman "had made a decision, he moved fast."

Riding to Capitol Hill for the reading before Congress in the early afternoon of March 12, Truman went over the speech with Clifford one last time, underlining sentences that needed emphasis, especially the no-hedging, no-double-talk three that announced what was thereafter called the Truman Doctrine:

> I believe that it must be the policy of the United States to support free peoples who are resisting attempted subjugation by armed minorities or by outside pressures. I believe that we must assist free peoples to work out their own destinies in their own way. I believe that our help should be primarily through economic and financial aid, which is essential to economic stability and orderly political processes.

The Truman Doctrine, as seminal a document as the Monroe Doctrine in 1823 and FDR's Lend-Lease speech in 1941, guided the country's foreign policy, for better and for worse, for the next forty-two years. It was embraced by every one of the president's successors until the cold war ended in 1989. Its first application, the requested $400 million to bolster the hard-pressed Greek and Turkish governments against Communist pressure, became law in May.

Because the written word is the point of subsequent reference, policymaking possibilities abound right up to the final version. The brainstorming behind the Truman Doctrine—a major effort involving scores of key people in the military, in the State Department, on the White House staff, and the president himself, "right in the middle from the ground up," as Elsey put it—kept refining policy as each session produced a new draft. Proponents and opponents of the policy or its specific language argued their case, and Truman settled on the final word. The day-by-day process reminded Clifford of his experiences as a trial lawyer. Truman sat as judge, determining what course the speech should take and what language used. The president retained from the first much of the spirit and some of the language of Elsey's Russian report. Even so, the speechwriter modestly referred to his September 24 document as a mere "consolidation," disavowing any function in the policy formulation. But dismissal of his role is disingenuous. As one of Truman's principal writers, he helped to select and control the flow of data to the president. As Clifford had observed, the writing of major presidential speeches is "where the moving and shaking [goes] on in the White House."

DWIGHT David Eisenhower was more aware than most that the speechwriting process is of necessity kaleidoscopic, involving the participation of myriad individuals from relevant departments and staff. As a former speechwriter for General Douglas MacArthur, Eisenhower knew from experience that defining policy inevitably sets off debate and that without a "chief of staff" of drafting, the policymaking process can go on endlessly. Yet even with a chief of drafting, preparation for what came to be called the Atoms for Peace Speech lasted for most of the first year of Eisenhower's presidency.

On March 5, 1953, barely six weeks after Eisenhower's inauguration, Joseph Stalin died, affording an opportunity for the president to make conciliatory moves toward the Kremlin's new leaders. Since the Soviet Union had detonated its first atomic bomb four years earlier, the United States and the USSR had been hurling charges at each other and building and stock-piling nuclear weapons. With new leaders in both countries, the time was ripe, Eisenhower believed, to try to build mutual trust in order to reduce nuclear arms or at least stop the buildup.

His first public attempt in this direction, over the objections of Secretary of State John Foster Dulles, was a speech before the American Society of Newspaper Editors on April 16, 1953. Eisenhower directed two of his aides to write this speech: C. D. Jackson, his special assistant for cold war strategy and "a key figure in [his] creative idea department," according to Chief of Staff Sherman Adams; and Emmet Hughes, a campaign speech-writer who had moved to the White House staff after the inau-gural. The former general monitored every line of every draft, "often providing them with imagery and telling phrases," ac-cording to Eisenhower biographer Stephen Ambrose. The three men worked on the speech for two weeks. In it, Eisenhower asked the Soviets for "a chance for a just peace." During that time Dulles had been out of Washington. Returning shortly before it was to be given, he read the final draft with strong disapproval, not only because of its content but also because he could do little to effect change so close to delivery time. He learned a lesson. Seeing the preparation of speeches as insepara-ble from the development of policy, he told the writers that henceforth he must clear each draft page by page when it related to foreign policy.

The application of Dulles's stringent speech policy to the preparation of Atoms for Peace added to Jackson's drafting headaches, since Eisenhower had appointed him to take charge of the speech. For over seven months Jackson circulated dozens and dozens of drafts among senior advisers in the Atomic En-ergy Commission, the State Department, Pentagon, and on the National Security Council.

Eisenhower's original purpose in making the speech was to

alert Americans to the perils of ongoing nuclear proliferation and to seek their support of the administration's attempts to curtail it. Not everyone in his administration shared his view, most prominently his secretary of state; always deal with the Soviets from overwhelming strength summed up Dulles's rigid anti-Communist position. Bolstered by the early-spring report on the horrors of a nuclear holocaust submitted by J. Robert Oppenheimer, director of the development of the atomic bomb, the president determined to move forward in the face of contrary advice from men like Dulles.

The initial phase of the drafting, which started in late April 1953, was called Operation Candor. With the advice and help of others, principally Admiral Lewis Strauss, chairman of the Atomic Energy Commission, and fellow writer Emmet Hughes, Jackson turned out scores of drafts, collectively characterized by the word "bang" because they so graphically pictured the potential devastation to the United States from Soviet attack. Eisenhower dismissed them all with the remark: "We don't want to scare the country to death."

A second round of drafts started circulating in July. Scarier than the first batch, they were dubbed "bang bang." Added to the nuclear horrors that could be visited upon the United States were those upon the USSR if and when the Americans retaliated. After dozens of drafts had been shuffled all over Washington, the president read the finished paper, shook his head, sighed, and said, "This leaves everybody dead on both sides, with no hope anywhere. Can't we find some hope here?" Understandably, Jackson felt frustrated. He, too, wanted to put an end to the arms race, but trying to forge some sort of consensus out of a plethora of perspectives had so far proved to be impossible. The Candor Speech "shows every appearance of being loused up. I am afraid [it] is slowly dying from a severe attack of committee-itis," he complained. Eisenhower said to keep trying. Then, in early August, the Soviets exploded their first H-bomb.

The president got the news while vacationing in Denver. He began to "search the impasse to action," he wrote in his memoirs. "One day I hit upon the idea of actual physical donations of isotopes from our then unequaled nuclear stockpile to a common fund for peaceful purposes. This would have to mean donations by both Russia and the United States, with Britain also in the picture at least in a minor way. I wanted to develop this thought in such a way as to provide at the very least a calm and reasonable atmosphere in which the whole matter could be considered." He sent a message to Strauss and Jackson through his special assistant for national security affairs, General Robert Cutler, to meet him in New York on August 19 to discuss the matter. They arrived at the appointed hour with an outline of ideas they had come up with, to which Eisenhower added his own.

During September, highest-level top-secret discussions produced little of value. The president summoned all participants to the White House for a breakfast meeting on Saturday, October 3. He no longer wanted objections, he said. He wanted practical suggestions to make his idea work. Since the international pooling of fissionable material took precedence over but did not replace educating the American public about the perils of the nuclear age, the drafting process took on a new code name. Operation Candor became Operation Wheaties, because the shift in focus had taken place at the breakfast meeting. For much of October, Dulles and Secretary of Defense Charles Wilson met with Strauss and Jackson to try to make Eisenhower's plan feasible, but an exasperated Jackson phoned Cutler on the seventeenth to report the lack of progress. Jackson said the speech process "was getting off the rails again thanks to Foster [Dulles], who give[s] every appearance of deliberately sidetracking me." Cutler must have set things right, because when the men met with the president early in November, Eisenhower only criticized the candor section as still "too truculent and heavy." Jackson told Emmet Hughes, by this time back with his former employer, Time, Inc., in New York, that "the project is firmly on the rails for the near future. Whether or not we will run out of track . . . God knows! I have been taking extraordinary measures to limit this to the absolute minimum number of top characters."

Jackson's optimism at this point stemmed from a November 6 memo Strauss wrote. In it he outlined every basic of the plan, including a method of ensuring the safety of pooled fissionable material from sudden seizure. Although Atoms for Peace had become essentially an Eisenhower-Strauss-Jackson act, dissenters continued to voice misgivings. A beleaguered Jackson wrote in his daily log, "red lights blinking all over the place," referring to a November 25 meeting in Dulles's office. Two days later the speechwriter was near despair: "Reprise in Foster's office. . . . Real problem is very deep and goes beyond any disagreement on wording or technical details. Real problem is basic philosophy—are we or are we not prepared to embark on a course which may in fact lead to nuclear disarmament? Soldier boys and their civilian governesses say no." Three days later, which he called Black Monday, he related his reactions to a Wheaties meeting with the president. "Two agonizingly awful hours. All negative suggestions with Dulles straddling the fence. Meeting broke up with the president promising to re-read Wheaties that night." Jackson dashed off an urgent message to Sherman Adams about the "danger of frittering away what is probably the greatest opportunity we have yet had to stop the arms race." Not until December 3 did Eisenhower declare unequivocally his firm intention of delivering Atoms for Peace.

In its beginnings in late April, the speech had been designed for a domestic audience. No one then dreamed the drafting would have taken so long, but its lengthy evolution turned out to be fortuitous. The day after his final decision to make the speech, Eisenhower had to fly to Bermuda for a Big Three Conference with English prime minister Winston Churchill and French premier Joseph Laniel. On his December 8 return,

ALL THE PRESIDENTS' WORDS

the General Assembly of the United Nations would be winding up its year's business. Why not deliver Atoms for Peace before the "perfect world audience," aides suggested. By careful maneuvering, Eisenhower could attend the conference, explain his atomic pooling plan to Churchill and Laniel, and still get to New York in time to address the UN. Accordingly, the U.S. representative to the UN, Henry Cabot Lodge, Jr., advised Secretary-General Dag Hammarskjöld that the president would be pleased to honor the standing invitation to speak before the UN that had been extended to him at the time of his inauguration.

Jackson worked on Wheaties draft seven on the way to Bermuda. After the American party got to the Mid-Ocean Club the afternoon of December 4, Lodge phoned to confirm Hammarskjöld's "invitation," so Eisenhower showed the current draft of the speech to Churchill and Laniel. By Sunday the sixth, Jackson had revised and rewritten it and labeled it Bermuda draft two. Between conference sessions, Eisenhower read it and made further changes. On December 7, the State Department notified all its ambassadors worldwide to get word to the foreign ministers of their respective countries that the president's speech the next day was to be taken with the utmost seriousness. The ambassador to the Soviet Union personally delivered the message to the Kremlin: Eisenhower was about to make a major policy announcement on which he solicited the support and cooperation of the Soviets, Charles Bohlen told Foreign Minister V. M. Molotov. In Washington, the United States Information Agency was primed for an important release so that its international broadcasters could publicize the president's proposal. Meanwhile Jackson studied Eisenhower's newest edits and started in on Bermuda draft three, which he did not complete until 5:30 A.M. on December 8.

Busy with meetings until departure, Eisenhower never looked at this draft until airborne. Every passenger aboard the *Columbine* worked throughout the three-and-a-half-hour flight to New York. Eisenhower, Dulles, Strauss, and Jackson sat in swivel chairs around the table in the president's compartment giving each page a line-by-line edit. They worked feverishly and harmoniously, somewhat surprising Jackson, who later commented that "Foster's client having made up his mind, Foster hitting on all 16." Page by page, the copy was passed to Press Secretary James Hagerty. After reading the insertions and deletions from a newspaperman's point of view, Hagerty took the copy page by page to a secretary at the stencil-cutting typewriter in the forward compartment. There two electric typewriters, one to cut mimeograph stencils and the other with jumbo typeface for the president's reading copy, and a mimeograph machine had been put in place in Bermuda. As the secretary finished typing a page, she passed it across the aisle to another secretary at the jumbo typewriter. While Hagerty walked back to the president's compartment for the next page, the secretary read the stencil of the last page and handed it to the army staff sergeant, who cranked the duplicating machine.

The finished document filled nine stencils. The sergeant ran off 500 copies of each. From Bermuda to New York there was not a quiet spot or idle moment aboard *Columbine.* Hagerty going in one direction passed Secret Service guards going the other way, lugging copies from the whirling duplicator to the *Columbine's* front compartment behind the pilot's cabin, there to be stacked in proper order on two long tables. The plane arrived over New York with the assembly line inside still running full tilt. The pilot had to circle for thirty minutes and then taxi slowly on the runway after he had landed so the job could be finished. Even as the plane was rolling to a stop, the president underlined on his jumbo copy words he wanted to emphasize, while the secretary of state, chairman of the Atomic Energy Commission, and the president's two special assistants collated and stapled together nine-page sets of the mimeographed copies for distribution to the press at the airport. The hardworking group deplaned, jumped in waiting limousines that followed a motorcycle escort to Manhattan, sirens screaming, and arrived at the UN a few minutes before five. The president walked immediately to the General Assembly podium to read the just-completed speech.

In somber tones he set forth the potentialities for destruction opened up by the mastery of the atom. Next he made it plain that the United States wanted to use atomic energy not for destruction but for peace. Finally he put forward his dramatic new proposal, "the core of the speech," he said.

> The governments principally involved [could] . . . begin now and continue to make joint contributions from their stockpiles of normal uranium and fissionable material to an international Atomic Energy Agency. . . .
>
> The more important responsibility of the Atomic Energy Agency would be to devise methods whereby fissionable materials would be allocated to serve the peaceful pursuits of mankind. Experts would be mobilized to apply atomic energy to the needs of agriculture, medicine, and other peaceful activities. A special purpose would be to provide abundant electrical energy in the power-starved areas of the world. Thus the contributing powers would be dedicating some of their strength to serve the needs rather than the fears of mankind.

Eisenhower challenged the Soviets to join an international effort to aid underdeveloped nations, and he did so in front of the whole world so there could be no mistake about his offer. If they were really interested in peace, the president had given them the chance to demonstrate their commitment. The Soviet refusal to respond hardened his attitude toward them. His generous and sincere proposal had been rebuffed, and the chief goal of his administration, nuclear disarmament, died. Indeed, the tragedy of the Eisenhower years was the ultimate failure of Atoms for Peace, as evidenced by the forty-plus years of nuclear arms frenzy that were to follow.

Even so, the speech was a resounding strategic success. While holding out the olive branch of peace, Eisenhower recognized that the USSR was not likely to change its nuclear-stockpiling goals overnight. So the two "peace" speeches that he delivered during his first year in the presidency had worthwhile secondary goals. In each one the president probed Soviet intentions in the light of the changed leadership. Specifically in the case of his greatest presidential speech, Atoms for Peace, the United States won a great psychological victory by showcasing the nation as a peace-seeking one. It was no accident that the president's assistant for cold war strategy was also the principal drafter of Atoms for Peace.

This momentous speech was, indeed, a collaboration. The input of Dulles, Hughes, Jackson, Strauss, and others provided prewriting brainstorming. Their debate helped bring the issues and the possible consequences into clear focus for the president. Atoms for Peace illustrates why the presidential writer (or writers) must be a trusted aide with ready access to the Oval Office.

As speechwriter Emmet Hughes pointed out in *The Ordeal of Power,* the confrontationalist attitudes of Dulles and others in Defense and State, which vied with Eisenhower's leanings toward rapprochement with the Soviets, might have prevailed without Jackson's wholehearted commitment to Eisenhower's viewpoint. Had Jackson not occupied—by presidential order—the command post for writing Atoms for Peace, he could never have exercised the leverage he did. He determined the timing of consultations, deadlines, and the final periods of review. Throughout the long process of preparation, that he was the president's personal representative carried clout. (Speaking on his own, he would have been shut out of the debate very early on.) In a sense, Jackson controlled the debate by controlling its written record, minutes of meetings, notes from consultations with the principal figures involved in the debate, relevant interagency information, and the like. The president carefully reviewed that record before making his final decision to go ahead with the speech on December 3. Although Atoms for Peace was Eisenhower's idea and decision, it was Jackson who had kept it from sinking for seven and a half wearying months. Yet, it was the former general's commanding supervision that synthesized the debate, leading to a decisive speech and a coherent foreign policy.

—

JOHN Fitzgerald Kennedy's special counsel and principal speechwriter, Theodore Sorensen, did not have the luxury of seven and a half months to nurture the president's response to the Soviet installation of nuclear missiles in Cuba in the fall of 1962. While still president-elect, Kennedy had had to deal with Cuba. When he met with Eisenhower on January 19, 1961, the day before his inauguration as the thirty-fifth president, Cuba had loomed large in their discussion of the principal trouble spots of the world. Just three months later, on April 17, Kennedy's first Cuban crisis flared up. Backed by the Central Intelligence Agency, Cuban exiles from Fidel Castro's revolution failed in their attempt to invade their homeland—at the Bay of Pigs—and overthrow the dictator. The plan behind this invasion had sounded sensible enough to the new president when put to him by Allen Dulles, the CIA director and holdover from the Eisenhower administration, but unbeknownst to Kennedy, every step of the plan had been based on shaky and even false information. The CIA had underestimated Castro and the strength of his popular support, made erroneous assumptions, and misrepresented the plan of the invasion to the White House. Although Kennedy had approved the continuation of the CIA project, when the invasion went awry, he refused to send in U.S. troops on the grounds that the USSR might retaliate in West Berlin, another sensitive trouble spot, and in so doing set off World War III. But Soviet premier Nikita Khrushchev told his aides this showed Kennedy to be weak, timid, and indecisive. He wondered "whether anyone who had abandoned the Cuban invading forces on the beaches would have the will to launch a nuclear attack."

Because of the failure at the Bay of Pigs, Kennedy pushed for a summit meeting between the superpower leaders. "I have to show [Khrushchev] we can be just as tough as he is," he told his aide Kenneth O'Donnell. But after the Vienna meeting in June, Kennedy was still convinced of Khrushchev's condescending view of him. As the president confessed to James Reston of the *New York Times:* "I think [Khrushchev] thought that anyone who was so young and inexperienced as to get into the mess [Bay of Pigs] could be taken. And anyone who got into it and didn't see it through had no guts. . . . I've got a terrible problem. If he thinks I'm inexperienced and have no guts, until we remove those ideas we won't get anywhere with him. So we have to act."

Kennedy's "terrible problem" came to a head with his second Cuban crisis. It began on October 16, 1962, when photographs taken by a U-2 aircraft provided indisputable evidence of Soviet deployment of nuclear missiles in Cuba, and ended on October 28, when news came by Moscow radio of Khrushchev's compliance with U.S. demands to remove the missiles. During those thirteen days of October, the world for the first time faced the very real possibility of nuclear war and the consequent extinction of the human species.

The Kennedy administration had known that the Soviets had been shipping arms and men to Cuba at increasing rates since summer. Surface-to-air missiles, fighters, bombers, and thousands of troops had been sighted in late August. Every missile, plane, troop, and technician sent to Cuba, Khrushchev repeatedly assured a concerned Kennedy, was to defend Cuba against an expected second invasion by the United States. Accepting the view of his Soviet experts that Khrushchev never stationed nuclear missiles outside Soviet territory, Kennedy told the American people that the missiles in Cuba were short-range antiaircraft weapons but would be closely monitored nonetheless.

The Republican campaign committees in the Senate and

House announced that Cuba would be the dominant issue of the 1962 campaign. Republican congressmen had repeatedly warned of the dangers of Soviet arms shipments to Cuba. Senator Kenneth Keating of New York called Kennedy a "do-nothing" president. To defuse the issue, Kennedy gave notice to the Soviets on September 4 that if they introduced offensive ground-to-ground missiles into Cuba, they would suffer serious consequences. On October 10, Senator Keating claimed "100 per cent reliable" evidence from Cuban exiles that nuclear missile bases were under construction. But Keating was not president. Despite the claims of Cuban refugees that contradicted Khrushchev's statements, the president required indisputable evidence. Such proof did not exist on October 10. An authorized U-2 mission over Cuba was delayed until October 14, because of bad weather. All day October 15, military and intelligence men from the National Photographic Interpretation Center developed, scrutinized, and analyzed the October 14 photographs. When they spotted medium-range ballistic missile sites, they notified top CIA officials, Defense Secretary Robert McNamara, and National Security Adviser McGeorge Bundy. Bundy took the photographic evidence to the president the morning of October 16.

"We're probably going to have to bomb them," an alarmed president said at first. Then he ordered daily U-2 flights to blanket the entire Cuban landscape and summoned his closest and most trusted advisers to the Cabinet Room for an 11:45 meeting. This group made up the executive committee of the National Security Council, an ad hoc, top-secret body that Kennedy assembled to manage the crisis, consisted of fourteen senior officials. Others who intermittently met with ex comm included UN ambassador Adlai Stevenson, Truman's secretary of state Dean Acheson, and Vice President Lyndon Johnson. In a television interview at the end of December 1962, the president said that two of the fourteen, his brother Attorney General Robert Kennedy and his speechwriter Theodore Sorensen, deserved much of the credit for the successful outcome of the crisis. Of all his advisers, Kennedy felt most at ease with these two. He had always been close to his brother and grew so to Sorensen, his legislative assistant and sole writer during his Senate career. Sorensen's word counted for a bit more than other advisers', for he was the most thoroughly attuned to Kennedy's ideas, beliefs, and style.

The core group met dozens of times during the next thirteen days. As speechwriter, Sorensen made a summary of most meetings, which the president read. Entrusting this responsibility to a single person, Sorensen later said, was the only way to ensure that Kennedy got a clear sense of an emerging policy. Because the president believed that whichever side made the first announcement of the missiles would dominate the politics of the crisis by framing the world debate, he made it clear at the initial meeting that he had to be the one to do so. Thus secrecy was of the utmost importance.

As the men of ex comm shuttled between meetings practically around the clock in Undersecretary George Ball's conference room on the seventh floor of State, in the Old Executive Office Building, and in the White House, they took care to arrive at different gates and at different times to dampen suspicions among the press that something big was up. To the same end, the president kept up regular activities, including campaigning for congressional Democrats. As the week wore on, U-2 pictures gave an even greater sense of urgency to the deliberations. More medium-range and intermediate-range ballistic missile sites were spotted. New networks of roads appeared almost daily, and thousands of tents went up to house the Soviet troops and personnel that kept arriving. That time was running out dominated discussions, yet there continued to be sharp divisions over how to respond. "Each of us changed his mind more than once that week on the best course of action to take," Sorensen wrote three years later, "not only because new facts and arguments were adduced but because in the president's words, whatever action we took had so many disadvantages to it and each . . . raised the prospect that it might escalate the Soviet Union into a nuclear war." Khrushchev had himself said publicly on September 11 that any U.S. action against Cuba would unleash nuclear war.

As early as the first meeting on October 16, a half-dozen potential courses of action had been identified. At one extreme was to do nothing at all. Neither Kennedy nor McNamara thought the Soviet missiles did much to harm U.S. security, since the country was already living under the shadow of Soviet missiles that could be launched from Soviet territory or submarines; therefore, there was no real change in our situation that required drastic action. And both men knew it was hard to argue that the United States should refuse to tolerate Soviet missiles in Cuba when U.S./NATO intermediate-range ballistic missiles (IRBMs) in Turkey faced the Soviet border. They also realized that had Kennedy successfully consummated the Cuban invasion of April 1961, he likely would not now be faced with a crisis that risked nuclear holocaust. But the president had issued an unambiguous pledge to the American people on September 13 at his forty-third news conference when he said that if Khrushchev moved strategic (long-range) missiles to Cuba or in any other way made the island "an offensive military lease of significant capacity," as commander in chief he would "do whatever must be done." Now that he found himself in the very situation he had described, he really had to do *something* to get the missiles off the island. "It can be argued that in the fall of 1962 and the hot political climate over Cuba," historian Michael Beschloss wrote, "Americans would never have tolerated nuclear missiles in Cuba and that anyone who was president would have felt compelled to demand their removal." But JFK had "locked" himself into a fairly "specific course of action," Beschloss reasoned. Small wonder that the president commented to his brother that to do nothing was to be impeached.

Attention soon centered on two of the remaining five alternatives: air strike and blockade. Both had serious drawbacks. The ideal air strike would be "surgical"—that is, a single air sortie would go in and take out the missiles—but air force experts said such a plan was not feasible. Many sorties would be required, Soviet troops and technicians would be killed, and even then there could be no assurance of getting every missile. Moreover, to achieve success, the strike should be sudden and unexpected. A surprise attack looked too much like Pearl Harbor, Robert Kennedy argued, and it ran counter to U.S. tradition and principles. Discussion then turned to an announced strike, but the problem of warning the Soviets proved unsolvable. No one could devise a message to Khrushchev that would not give him a propaganda advantage. Unlike the fait accompli of an air strike, a blockade offered a prolonged and agonizing approach, giving Soviet technicians time to make the missiles operational, if they were not so already. Yet the blockade was a more limited, low-key action that gave Khrushchev options and thus was less menacing than an air strike.

On Thursday October 18, Soviet foreign minister Andrei Gromyko arrived at the White House in the late afternoon for a previously scheduled meeting with the president, during which both leaders kept up their respective deceptions. Ex comm had still not arrived at a consensus. Finally at 9:00 P.M. "we took a vote," Robert Kennedy told his brother. "It was eleven for blockade, six for bombing." But Friday morning General Maxwell Taylor (chairman of the Joint Chiefs of Staff), Dean Acheson, and McGeorge Bundy were waiting for the president when he came down to the office. They urged him to order an air strike. Time was running out, they argued, and even if an order were given that moment, it could not be executed until Monday October 22. But the number of sorties the air force wanted to do the job had risen to 800! Just before leaving Washington to campaign in Illinois and Ohio, Kennedy had told Sorensen and his brother to pull the group together quickly. He wanted to act on Sunday. The attorney general promised to call the president back to Washington as soon as a consensus held. The president's last instruction was to Sorensen to write two speeches, one announcing a naval blockade of Soviet ships carrying the missiles and the other calling for an air strike against the missile sites.

Sorensen first tackled the blockade draft, his preference. But he soon realized that before he could write, he needed answers to several questions: how to relate the blockade to the removal of the missiles, what to say about the U-2 surveillance that revealed indicting pictures of Soviet activity, what to tell Khrushchev. When ex comm reconvened Friday afternoon, Sorensen offered them questions instead of a speech draft. "As the concrete answers were provided in our discussion," Sorensen said, "the final shape of the president's policy began to take shape." The air strike was abandoned, so Sorensen went back to work on the blockade after the meeting broke up. He worked until 3:00 A.M. on Saturday. "By answering those questions and having those answers translated into speech form overnight," Sorensen said later, "the group did become more persuaded of the logic and rightfulness of the blockade course."

At 9:00 A.M. Saturday, ex comm reviewed, amended, and generally approved Sorensen's draft. Robert Kennedy called the president, who flew back from Chicago, arriving at the White House for a meeting with ex comm at 2:30 P.M. Once again the full ramifications of both courses were put before the president. McNamara presented the argument for a quarantine—Franklin Roosevelt's 1937 term "quarantine" was borrowed as less bellicose than "blockade"—and Bundy the bombing position. When Roswell Gilpatric, the normally taciturn deputy defense secretary, said that "essentially, Mr. President, this is a choice between a limited and an unlimited action," Kennedy decided on the quarantine approach. Still uneasy, however, he checked one more time with the Air Force Tactical Bombing Command to make absolutely certain that a truly limited air strike was not feasible.

On Saturday night, Sorensen redrafted and circulated his quarantine speech. Although Kennedy had wanted to make the speech Sunday night, he agreed to wait until Monday to allow time for notifying the relevant persons and for readying the military. The navy deployed 180 ships to the Caribbean. The B-52 bomber force was ordered into the air fully loaded with atomic weapons; as one plane completed its shift and landed, another took its place in the air. The First Armored Division started to move out of Texas late Saturday night and headed for embarkation ports in Georgia. Five other divisions were placed on alert. Kennedy's congressional liaison director, Larry O'Brien, rounded up bipartisan leaders of Congress, scattered all over the country campaigning, and provided military transportation for them back to Washington. Press Secretary Pierre Salinger coordinated information policy with his counterparts in the State Department, USIA, and the Pentagon.

On Sunday, the State Department drafted forty-three letters to heads of government, including Mayor Willy Brandt of West Berlin and Khrushchev, to be delivered with a copy of Kennedy's speech. Explanatory telegrams went out to U.S. ambassadors around the world at 6:00 P.M. The president informed former presidents Hoover, Truman, and Eisenhower.

By Sunday afternoon, Sorensen had written four drafts, and still questions remained, all answered at a subsequent meeting of the National Security Council. Minor changes kept being made throughout Monday morning. Each change was rushed to USIA translators and to State for transmission to U.S. embassies. At noon on Monday October 22, Salinger announced the president's speech for that night.

At 7:00 P.M. the president recounted the evidence of the Soviet buildup for the American people. He enumerated Soviet protestations that the arms shipments were defensive, and after each he said, "That statement was false." (This was reminiscent of Franklin Roosevelt's Day of Infamy Speech to Congress declaring war, which Sorensen had read before completing the final draft.) Aggressive conduct, Kennedy continued, "if allowed to go unchecked and unchallenged, ultimately leads to war." He then listed steps the United States was taking, beginning with quarantine. The president emphasized that any missile launched from the bases in Cuba would be regarded as an attack by the Soviet Union "requiring full retaliatory response," and he called on Premier Khrushchev to "halt and eliminate this clandestine, reckless, and provocative threat to world peace." Thus, the speech was a combination of the blockade and air strike approaches, because it contained not only the quarantine element but also the warning that an attack by one of the Cuban missiles would be regarded as an attack on the United States by the Soviet Union. It also included a warning that construction on the Soviet missiles would have to stop or the United States would take further action, implying that an air strike would be part of that action. Finally, the speech called for diplomatic action in the UN and Organization of American States and reassured the Cuban people that the quarantine was not aimed at them.

Ex comm kept meeting for the next six days. Each Khrushchev response—five letters in all—required a carefully worded reply. Once again Sorensen played a major role. Not until 9:00 A.M. Sunday, October 28, when Moscow Radio broadcast a final Khrushchev letter, did ex comm disband. The Soviet leader stated that he had ordered work on the missile sites halted, the missiles crated and returned to Russia, and the action to be verified by the United Nations. In return, he asked for the blockade to be lifted and for the United States to pledge not to attack or invade Cuba. The deal was made. If Khrushchev had not had much respect for Kennedy's determination before this confrontation, he did now.

The Cuban missile crisis, historian and Kennedy aide Arthur

Schlesinger, Jr., said, provided "relief from the pressures of the Cold War." It taught the superpowers that the exercise of national sovereignty was limited in a nuclear war. The Soviet Union never went to nuclear alert in all the years of the cold war; the United States never did again after this crisis. Nor did the United States and the USSR ever again confront each other directly. Khrushchev had gambled and lost because, as Vice President Lyndon Johnson put it, the president "plays a damn good hand of poker. I'll say that for him." What no one in the administration knew until it was revealed at a 1989 conference that brought the Soviet and U.S. missile-crisis participants together in Moscow was that the Soviet forces in Cuba during the missile crisis possessed far more nuclear power than the CIA had estimated. They had one- to three-megaton hydrogen warheads for twenty medium-range ballistic missiles that could have been targeted on U.S. cities as far north as Washington, as well as warheads for short-range tactical artillery rockets that the Soviet field commanders in Cuba were authorized to use against a U.S. invasion force.

Kennedy's use of a handpicked inner circle to work on the speech in response to the Cuban missile crisis helped him keep his deliberations secret and gave ex comm a forum for top-level debate. Although ex-comm participant Dean Acheson gave low marks to Kennedy's consensus-style decision making, he did credit the president for keeping his speechwriter intimately involved in the decision-making process, because, he said, a major speech like this one is "where policy is made, regardless of where it is supposed to be made." As if in corroboration, Sorensen told a *National Journal* reporter ten years later, "The answer in the Cuban missile crisis was not resolved until it . . . was . . . effectively worded."

THE principal writer for Lyndon Baines Johnson's historic March 31, 1968, speech on U.S. policy in Vietnam was Special

Counsel Harry McPherson, a native Texan who had worked
for Johnson in the Senate and had then served at the Pentagon
during the Kennedy administration. This dramatic speech illustrates how the drafting process forces decisions on policy. As
drafts circulated through the State, Defense, and Treasury departments, and to the Joint Chiefs of Staff, and as all their various points of views clashed, were absorbed or eliminated, a new
Vietnam policy emerged. Once McPherson started drafting, "it
was as if the lead end of a reel of unseen film had been slipped
into a projector," journalist-historian Theodore White said, and
"it would unwind from the first frame to an unknown climax
in the weeks ahead."

The speech had its origins in Johnson's need to respond to
the Vietcong's massive attacks on Saigon and thirty-six provin-
cial capitals that began during the Tet (the Vietnamese New
Year) holiday at the end of January and continued well into
February. When the assault was over, the Vietcong, the Communist insurgents supported by North Vietnam, had hit five of
the six largest cities in the South and one quarter of its 242
district capitals. In Saigon a Vietcong suicide squad blasted a
hole in the wall surrounding the U.S. Embassy compound and
entered the grounds. The Communist forces held the ancient
imperial city of Hue for twenty-six days. When a final body
count revealed that more Vietcong had been killed than Americans and South Vietnamese soldiers, Johnson announced the
assault's failure. But in size and scope, the Tet offensive, as the
attack came to be known, made a mockery of the president's
statement as well as of the military's optimistic progress reports.
General William Westmoreland, commander of the U.S. military in South Vietnam, had assured the president and the country just before Tet that "the end begins to come into view."
Public support of Johnson's handling of the war plummeted to
a low of 26 percent. In March the president would be challenged by two Democratic senators, Eugene McCarthy and
Robert Kennedy, who would run against him in the primaries

for the 1968 Democratic presidential nomination as antiwar candidates.

Drafting of the speech, designed to put Tet into perspective and to steady the nation, began in the first week of February. The first draft promised more of the same policy of escalation. Later, McPherson summarized its message in an interview: "We shall not give up; we shall not be defeated by this latest outbreak of aggression and driven out of South Vietnam; we shall put in the men who are necessary to stem the tide of this aggression; we have no desire whatever to take a foot of North Vietnam, nor to change their government; and we want to settle this thing in the worst possible way at the peace table."

The number of men and women necessary to stem the tide turned out to be a staggering 206,000 (added to the 525,000 already in Vietnam), according to General Earle Wheeler, chairman of the Joint Chiefs of Staff, who had returned from a fact-finding trip to South Vietnam on February 28. Never questioning whether troops should be sent, Johnson named a task force to determine which units could be called, what the mix of army, navy, and marines should be, and how to absorb the economic impact the additional troops would create. Clark Clifford was sworn in as secretary of defense, succeeding Robert McNamara, in time to direct the task force. Now heading the department he had helped to create while serving in the Truman administration, Clifford turned the task force meetings into an inquiry into overall Vietnam policy.

The new secretary of defense had already begun to reassess his former hard-line position on the war. The preceding August, the president had sent him to the nations of Southeast Asia that had been contributing small numbers of troops to the war effort to ask them for a bigger contribution. Not perceiving the Communist threat that had become a U.S. obsession, they flatly refused to send more men to war. If this was a war to save Asia from communism, Clifford reasoned, and Asians saw no Communist threat, maybe U.S. policy in this corner of South-

east Asia was a misapplication of the Truman Doctrine he had
helped to formulate. Thus a more skeptical Clifford was less
willing to accept military assessments than he had been in the
past. He carefully cross-examined the generals, asking them
how they would go about winning the war, what their strategy
would be if they got the requested 206,000 troops, how long it
would take to achieve victory, whether they could estimate the
cost, and if the enemy had lost the Tet offensive, as the president
and the military claimed, how the administration should explain
the need for so many new troops. When the military was unable
to provide an acceptable rationale for the increase, Clifford realized that "the main field of battle was not the Vietnam task
force but the president's mind."

McPherson, too, had been questioning the wisdom of the
administration's war policy, and like Clifford, he appreciated the
difficulty in expressing these doubts to the president. As an adviser who had worked closely with Johnson for twelve years, he
thought he understood the president's abhorrence of changing
direction.

> When you've spent as much time laboring with this thing as
> he had, when so much that was in you was invested in this,
> when it had seemed the only decision to make, and when the
> judgment of history on his administration was riding on . . .
> whether it had been right to escalate in Vietnam, . . . the idea
> of opening this yawning issue, this chasm under your feet, is a
> horrible thing. Imagine! Christ, you put five hundred and fifty
> thousand Americans out there; you've lost twenty-five thou-
> sand of them dead! What if it's wrong? . . . He must have
> thought I'm not going to be the Democratic president pushing
> liberal social legislation who's letting go of a part òf Southeast
> Asia that my predecessor John Kennedy and his predecessor
> Dwight Eisenhower said was critical to the free world.

Not mentioned by McPherson was the Cuban missile crisis, still
fresh in Johnson's (and Secretary of State Dean Rusk's) mind,

accounting for the president's fear of lessening his hard line. "The Communist menace was palpable" to him, Clifford accurately observed.

Although McPherson had not attended the task force meetings about operational details, he was kept informed because Johnson had made it clear from the start that as coordinator of the speech, McPherson was to serve as everyone's conduit. The chief writer kept drafting while the meetings took place, producing five more drafts much like the first. They spelled out a tough and uncompromising stand: a refusal to consider a bombing halt without clear reciprocity, a call-up of reserves (the number of which kept changing), and a demand that Congress pass a surtax to pay for the increase.

Clifford had not realized how close his and McPherson's views were until he phoned the speechwriter after the fourth draft and asked him point-blank. After realizing he had an ally from the president's inner circle, Clifford said, "Old boy [McPherson was in fact much younger than Clifford], we have a lot of work to do together. And I think we're going to pre-vail." Later the defense secretary wrote that McPherson became "one of my most deeply trusted associates—virtually the only man on the White House staff with whom I could talk freely."

Encouraging for the two allies was the gradual whittling down of the number of troops from over 200,000 to just under 15,000, "the guts of the Vietnam decision," according to McPherson. "That was more important than the decision on the bombing limitation." Clifford disagreed, calling the smaller deployment "a major step to the insiders but to no one else. From a de-escalation standpoint, it offers nothing. From a negotiating standpoint, it still offers nothing."

The war in Vietnam had sparked a host of controversies, and some of the sharpest centered on the bombing of the North. From the time the bombing had started early in 1965, it had been interspersed with pauses and offers to suspend the attacks altogether if the enemy stopped infiltrating troops into the

South or showed some willingness to negotiate. But infiltration continued, and there was no negotiation. The crux of Johnson's March 31 speech, then, notwithstanding McPherson's statement about troop reduction, was to be about getting the North Vietnamese to lay down arms and turn to the conference table, a goal that might be achieved by promising a no-strings-attached bombing halt.

"Well we could stop the bombing during the rainy season in the North," Secretary Rusk suggested on March 4. It would not cost much militarily, he continued, since air sorties "were way down at that time anyway." Conceding "serious political and military risks" even then, he concluded that "major peace proposals aren't promising unless there is a cessation of bombing."

"Get on your horses on that," the president said. "Staff it out."

"So during March," the secretary told an interviewer, "we prepared a plan for the cessation of the bombings except up north to the twentieth parallel accompanied by an offer to have talks with North Vietnam." Others in the administration had also made proposals to halt the bombing, including George Ball and most notably Robert McNamara (in a lengthy memo on November 1, 1967), but the record shows that Rusk's was the first to spur serious debate. Yet only a week into the deliberations, the secretary appeared before the Senate Foreign Relations Committee and said: "It is quite clear from our recent contacts with Hanoi that they would not accept a partial cessation of the bombing as a step toward peace in any way, shape, or form. That does not mean that as we move into the future, that we don't consider examining that and all the other proposals that we can get our hands on and we can think up ourselves."

Clifford believed, with some warrant, that Rusk had made his proposal primarily as a public relations ploy in order to justify an intensification of the war after its failure. "The fact is we actually had it in the draft at one time," Clifford said, "that the president would stop bombing north of the twentieth parallel and State came along saying that was too clear-cut and would be too clear a signal."

From March 22 until the night of the speech, events moved quickly. On that day Johnson called his inner circle to the White House to consider, once again, limiting the bombing. This group consisted of McPherson, Rusk, and Clifford; Walt Rostow, the national security adviser; William Bundy, the assistant secretary of state for East Asian and Pacific Affairs; and George Christian, the president's press secretary. Rusk said a limitation to the twentieth parallel was the best that could be offered, but that past experience showed the Communists would abuse a bombing cessation. He reminded everyone that the North Vietnamese always said, "You have got to stop bombing all of North Vietnam before we'll talk," but to do so would endanger Americans in the demilitarized zone, an area through which North Vietnamese troops and supplies had to pass. For this reason, the president insisted that there be no halt without matching restraint from Hanoi. The meeting ended on this dilemma.

Although there had been no agreement by the end of the meeting on Friday the twenty-second, McPherson wrote a memo for the president on Saturday the twenty-third in which he refined the bombing-halt proposal by suggesting that it be communicated to the enemy only as a first step in de-escalation, to be followed by others if a corresponding de-escalation was observed by the other side. "If it doesn't work, if we don't get talks," McPherson concluded, "at least we will be in a better posture toward the world." The president showed the memo to Rusk, who made no recommendations but said that Mc-Pherson's ideas were similar to the ones he had been working on since March 4.

On Monday and Tuesday, March 25 and 26, the president conferred with his unofficial advisers, the so-called Elder Wise

Men. This group of veterans of government service included, among others, McGeorge Bundy, an architect of the Vietnam policy under Kennedy and Johnson; Dean Acheson, secretary of state in the Truman administration; Cyrus Vance, former deputy defense secretary and a Johnson troubleshooter; George Ball, undersecretary of state in the Kennedy and Johnson administrations; Arthur Dean, President Eisenhower's Korean war negotiator; Douglas Dillon, secretary of the treasury under Kennedy; and three retired generals, Omar Bradley, Maxwell Taylor (also a former ambassador to South Vietnam), and Matthew Ridgeway. After two full days of briefings and meetings, Acheson summed up the majority view. "We can no longer do the job we set out to do . . . and we must begin to take steps to disengage." The previous fall, almost without exception and with Clifford a participant, they had backed the president's policy. But in the wake of the Tet offensive, most had had a change of heart. When Acheson spoke of the impossibility of achieving military victory, General Wheeler interrupted. "We were not seeking a military victory in Vietnam," he said, "only helping the Vietnamese avoid a Communist victory." "Then what in the name of God are 500,000 men out there doing—chasing girls? This is not a semantic game, General," the infuriated former secretary said. "If the deployment of all those men is not an effort to gain a military solution, then words have lost all meaning."

That night at dinner with McPherson, Acheson gave the speechwriter an editorial that had appeared in the *Winston-Salem Sunday Journal and Sentinel*. It was written by the paper's editor and publisher, Wallace Carroll, and represented the secretary's views.

> The war has made us—all of us—lose sight of our national purposes. We need to stand back and get our priorities right. Enemy no. 1 is Russia. Enemy no. 2 is China. The vital strategic areas, in their proper order, are Western Europe (partic-

ularly Germany), Japan, the Middle East, Latin America—and
only then Southeast Asia. The most crucial priority of all, of
course, is the home front.

McPherson sent the editorial to the president.

On March 28, McPherson, Clifford, Rostow, and William
Bundy met in Rusk's office. McPherson called the meeting
"the best I ever went to." There the advisers turned their attention to draft number seven, still a hard-line defense of the war.
The teeth-clenching, see-it-through statement announced that
15,000 more troops would be sent to Vietnam. It made a pro
forma plea for peace at the negotiating table and said nothing
about cutting back the bombing.

"This speech as presently written," Clifford said, "is wrong.
The speech is more of the same. The American people are fed
up with more of the same . . . because more of the same means
no win and only a continual long drag on American resources."
Clifford continued in this vein for a full hour. Bundy, who was
sympathetic to Clifford's view, worried that whatever Johnson
said, he should not imply that the United States might get out
of Southeast Asia altogether lest everything that had been
gained would be lost. Rostow and Rusk raised questions but
did not speak against Clifford's statement. Even so, McPherson
had no idea where Rusk stood. "Dean Rusk is a curious man,"
he said later, "and perhaps reserves his deepest views for the
men he serves and for no other company, but on many occasions, at many meetings when the meeting called out for Rusk
to make a statement of his position, he passed."

During lunch in Rusk's dining room, Clifford suggested
that McPherson write a new, softened draft along the lines of
their morning discussions, and let the president choose between
the two speeches. Before McPherson set to work on alternate
draft one, he and Clifford conferred by phone for an hour. Rostow called the White House to tell the president about the new
draft and to ask for a group meeting at 6:30 P.M. The speech-

writer dispatched the new draft to Johnson at 6:00 in time for him to read it before 6:30. Although Johnson and the advisers discussed alternate draft one for an hour, the president gave little indication of what he thought. Even so, McPherson wrote alternate draft two and sent it to the president later that night.

If Johnson's stern public statements were indicative of his current state of mind, there appeared to be little hope of any change in policy before the March 31 address, only three days hence. A week earlier he had derided those who would "tuck our tails and violate our commitments" in Vietnam. Frequently he lashed out at critics with one of his pet phrases, that he was "hunkering down like a Texas jackrabbit in a hailstorm." But privately, the president was deeply divided and undecided. He had struggled over each draft, trying to fix on the right course of action. Assistant Special Counsel Larry Temple had observed his anguish firsthand. Early each morning he went to Johnson's bedroom as a sort of high-level courier between the president and members of his staff. During the weeks of drafting, Temple observed, "the speech was uppermost in [his] mind. On occasion he'd hand the speech to Mrs. Johnson" for her criticism.

> I think that, if I am correct in the way I was reading the president at the time, he was using the drafts of the speech to make up his mind what he was going to do. It wasn't a matter that he had made up his mind and he was trying to formalize it verbally with a speech. I think he was using the draft of the speech as the vehicle by which he made up his mind what he was going to do. . . . I don't think that when he first decided to make the speech he knew exactly what he would say in that speech. . . . It was only toward the end that he did make the decision that we ought to pull back on the bombing.

That decision came on March 29. Johnson quietly phoned McPherson with revisions to alternate draft two. It was an uncharacteristically low-key way to announce to McPherson what surely was the most difficult decision of his presidency. McPherson told Clifford; they had "pre-vailed," Clifford said exultingly.

On Saturday March 30, the president, Nicholas Katzenbach (acting for Rusk, who was en route to Asia), Clifford, Wheeler, William Bundy, and George Christian examined every word in three additional alternate drafts that McPherson had written. They worked throughout the day and into the night, finishing at nine. Their toughest job was choosing language to describe the geographic limitation on the bombing. McPherson eventually came up with the following: "Tonight, I have ordered our aircraft and naval vessels to make no attacks on North Vietnam, except in the area north of the demilitarized zone where the continuing enemy buildup directly threatens allied forward positions and where the movements of their troops and supplies are clearly related to this threat." On Sunday March 31, Johnson and White House assistant Horace Busby wrote the peroration. During rehearsal, the president made twenty additional changes in the language of the speech.

This was modern presidential speechwriting at its best. For two months, top advisers, military experts, and the aptly named Wise Men had reasoned together in what had amounted to a kind of exalted brainstorming to bring forth a speech and policy of major national concern. Because all information and opinion were funneled through McPherson, the process worked. As McPherson said later:

> One of the things I've learned in government, to my surprise, was that very frequently you can't tell when something is happening. You have a meeting; it's called for the purpose of developing a policy; you finish the meeting and you're not really sure whether the policy is any different from what it was when you walked in the room or not. And the only thing that gives you a sense of finality about the meeting is the assignment to some person to draft up the sense of the meeting. When that's done, you can usually get the sense that something's happened.

That the final speech represented a shift of 180 degrees from the first version was startlingly dramatic in itself. But that was nothing compared with the excitement generated by the speech's completely unexpected conclusion: "I shall not seek, and I will not accept, the nomination of my party for another term as your president."

The first time anyone in his inner circle had any inkling of the surprise announcement was the afternoon before the speech when Johnson told McPherson, in Clifford's presence, not to worry about writing a new ending for the speech. He winked and said, "I may have one of my own." Privately, Johnson had been agonizing over whether to run for reelection or not, off and on since the beginning of the year. In the hour before the speech, aides phoned Cabinet members to inform them about the impending announcement.

Lyndon Johnson had used the fourteen drafts of his speech, which seven weeks of discussion had yielded, to make a decision that reversed his former position on Southeast Asia. On March 31, 1968, the bombing halt went into effect over North Vietnam, except in the area near the demilitarized zone. Six weeks later, delegates from Hanoi and Washington began meeting for preliminary talks in Paris. And six months after that, on October 31, the president extended the bombing halt to all of North Vietnam as another step in mutual de-escalation, and as an incentive to negotiations, negotiations that remained in stalemate long after the end of the Johnson administration.

McPherson's role in that decision was considerable. Because he deliberately moderated the language characteristic of Johnson's previous war pronouncements, he was able to moderate policy. "You can't separate words from policy that easily," he said. "The phrase does shape the content; rhetoric tilts the significance."

Writers for the major speeches of Presidents Truman, Eisenhower, Kennedy, and Johnson were their senior aides, who had regular access to them. Because the intricate and intimate relationship between speechwriting and policymaking blurs the line between a speechwriting assignment and policy assistance, the writer should be at the nexus of decision making. Since writing is the most exact form of thinking, it could hardly be otherwise. And yet, President Johnson was the last president to use writers in this manner. In the future, speeches written by people not in close and continuous contact with the president and his policymakers became the norm, transforming the rhetorical presidency into something quite different from its original manifestation.

3

THE VIRTUAL
PRESIDENCY

Richard Milhous Nixon   *1969–1974*
Ronald Wilson Reagan   *1981–1989*

I N the modern presidency," Richard Milhous Nixon wrote
in his memoirs, "concern for image must rank with concern
for substance." In reality, shaping the image took precedence
over substance during his presidency. Most modern presidents
had paid some attention to their public persona, but none to the
extent of the thirty-seventh president. Domestic adviser John
Ehrlichman estimated that "Nixon spent half his working time"
on image making. "I have watched Nixon spend a morning
designing [TV anchor] Walter Cronkite's lead story for that
evening, then send Ron Ziegler [press secretary], Henry Kissinger [national security adviser], and me out to a press briefing
to deliver it in such a way that Cronkite couldn't ignore it."

By the time Nixon first ran for president in 1960, fourteen
years into "his public life," he had developed an unwavering
conviction that the perceived image of what a president is and
does is far more important than what he actually is or does.
When he became president he had very specific opinions about

the public images of his predecessors. Scattered throughout his presidential memos to H. R. Haldeman, his chief of staff, are comments like: "Taft infinitely more effective than Teddy Roosevelt, but Roosevelt had personality"; "Ike had been distant and all business but appeared warm and kindly"; "JFK did nothing but appeared great while LBJ did everything and appeared terrible"; "Teddy Roosevelt and JFK both well-born charmers sliding by on personality"; "Kennedy was colder, more ruthless than [Nixon], but look at his PR"; "Kennedy blew practically everything and still got credit."

Determined to put Richard Nixon in the best possible light, he made himself an architect of his presidential image, served by advertising and public relations men, most notably Haldeman, a former vice president of J. Walter Thompson. Nixon's 1968 campaign illustrated how his image was shaped. Former *New York Herald Tribune* editor and staff speechwriter Raymond Price, Jr., carefully spelled out strategy.

> We have to be very clear on this point: that the response is to the image, not the man, since 99 percent of the voters have no contact with the man. It's not what's there that counts, it's what's projected—and carrying it one step further, it's not what he projects but rather what the voter receives. It's not the man we have to change, but rather the received impression. . . . [W]ords are important—but less for what they actually say than for the sense they convey, for the impression they give of the man himself. . . . All this is a roundabout way of getting at the point that we should be concentrating on building a received image of RN. . . . It suggests that we take the time and money to experiment, in a controlled manner, with film and television techniques, with particular emphasis on pinpointing those *controlled* uses of the television medium that can *best* convey the *image* we want to get across.

Accordingly Nixon's campaign staff, which included Harry Treleaven of J. Walter Thompson and Frank Shakespeare of

CBS, as well as Price, filmed Nixon before live audiences and then carefully edited out the best segments for later TV broadcast. With no reporters present who might ask hard questions, Nixon relaxed and came off as sincere in these segments.

These men understood better than most in the late 1960s that on television, appearance and manner count more than substance. Political reality need not correspond to objective reality; a new image was all the reality that counted. If reality was no longer objective, it was subjective. The reality of Richard Nixon, then, became what Nixon and his aides said it was. The campaign strategy worked like a dream. The press responded to it by calling the candidate the new Nixon, not noticing that the new Nixon was not new; a "new" Nixon had been proclaimed in the 1950s and again in the early 1960s, each time he ran for office. But this time the tactic worked. This Nixon became the thirty-seventh president on January 20, 1969.

Right from the start of his presidency, Nixon bombarded Haldeman with memos that dealt with staff efforts to "create a more friendly image of the P," as Haldeman routinely referred to the president. "We don't do an adequate job of selling our story," the president wrote in May 1969. "Real problem is we don't have a real PR operator, at a very high level, who really works at this all day, every day." A year and a half later he wrote Haldeman that "we've totally failed in our real PR." Yet it was Nixon himself who exercised centralized control over the government's public relations network. He had set up a promotional apparatus unprecedented in White House history. He created the Office of Communications, an entirely new public relations arm of the White House to coordinate a "line of the day," an orchestration of all segments of the executive branch to send one thematic message. "The problem with government was that everybody went off on their own way," said Herbert Klein, Nixon's first director of communications. "We set up weekly meetings with the people assigned to public affairs in each department of government, so that the same song was singing through each department."

The Nixon administration also established the Office of Public Liaison to feed local, regional, and specialty news organizations outside the Washington press corps. The office regularly sent material to 3,000 editors, arranged briefings for news executives, wrote stories and editorials for submission to newspapers and magazines, set up a speakers bureau, and taped and made available radio reports to local broadcasting stations, many of which put them on the air without disclosing their origin.

The efforts of Liaison, a quasi–press office in effect, coupled with the president's deliberate withholding of selected news from his press secretary diminished the power of that position. Nixon preferred to make his own press statements in the White House Briefing Room so that he and not the television and print reporters determined what news of the administration to broadcast or publish. "He insisted that he be given one hundred words," a tight television news bite, speechwriter David Gergen said. "And we had to count them. We had to put up in a corner of the page how many words were on this paper. He would go out and deliver one hundred words, and then he'd walk out. He knew that the reporters had to use what he wanted to say because if you gave them five hundred words, they would select part of it and determine what the point of the statement was. It was a very rigorous system." Consumer advocate Ralph Nader started referring to the White House press corps as a "mimeo machine" for Richard Nixon's pronouncements.

Press conferences did not appeal to Nixon. He held fewer than any of his predecessors. By the end of his first four years, he had had twenty-eight press conferences. (FDR, who averaged two a week during his twelve and a quarter years as president, had reached twenty-eight by his third *month* in office.) Nixon insisted that his public appearances take place under the most controlled circumstances. Accordingly, his chosen public forum was the television address to the nation.

Speechmaking stood at the apex of his image making; he considered it the most essential duty in his job as chief executive, since it afforded him the opportunity to make his point before the largest number of voters. "He was the supreme prime time president," wrote former Kennedy speechwriter Arthur Schlesinger, Jr. "In his first eighteen months Nixon had been on television at prime time more than Eisenhower, Kennedy, and Johnson combined in their first eighteen months. Returning from China, he lay over at Anchorage in Alaska for nine hours simply so that he could descend on Washington at 9:00 P.M., the primest of prime hours."

To script his effort to "establish the mystique" by providing material needed by the Communications, Liaison, and Press offices, the president established the first formally structured White House speechwriting office, called the Writing and Research Department. Its writers and researchers, whose ranks fluctuated from twelve to fifty, were the first Americans to be listed as such on the payroll of the executive branch. Nixon lumped the writers with staffers in Communications and Liaison, referring to them in toto as the "PR group."

In addition to drafting speeches, they analyzed public opinion polls, drew up lists of remarks for the president to use "extemporaneously" in public appearances, and took on a variety of hidden-hand tactics like composing letters to the editor under real and assumed names, scripting the entire 1972 Republican convention, and assembling "assault books" on the president's enemies and political opponents. They even collected and indexed anecdotes for the so-called Richard Nixon Human Interest Program. (Under "Strength in Adversity" was filed a vignette about Nixon as a young father falling on the ice while keeping two-year-old Tricia safe in his arms.)

Yet for all this, the writers rarely assumed a consultative role in policy matters. Unlike their predecessors from Rosenman to

McPherson, Nixon's writers had no regular access to the Oval Office; they dealt instead with Haldeman as intermediary. James Keogh, the former executive editor of *Time* magazine who had managed speechwriting during the campaign of 1968, became the department's first head. Raymond Price, Jr., William Safire, and Patrick Buchanan did most of the writing with the help of Bryce Harlow, who had done writing for Eisenhower, and Lee Huebner, who later became editor and publisher of the Paris *Herald Tribune*. The writers, especially Buchanan, complained about their lack of access to Nixon. Despite the high professional caliber of their writing talent, they saw themselves as members of a service department rather than a locus for policymaking. This galled them because each understood that policy develops in the preparation of a speech. "I left at the end of 1970 because I was not happy with this situation," Keogh says today. "I thought we did not have enough access. Everything went through Haldeman, and as a result I thought we weren't as effective as we could have been. Obviously Nixon wanted it that way or it wouldn't have been that way. I made several suggestions for changes that were not taken, so I departed."

Price assumed Keogh's position as chief, even though he knew firsthand how rarely he would speak directly with the president. In his diary entry of January 9, 1970, Haldeman described Nixon's not atypical reaction to Price's speech drafts: "Reviewed Price's first real draft of State of the Union, . . . a complete disaster. . . . Led to a new harangue for speechwriter who can write a Nixon speech. Hard for Ray to hit it right when he has no direct contact with P and no real guidance."

Domestic adviser John Ehrlichman reported on a similar scene that took place the following year at the same time and with the same writer working on the State of the Union Address.

> On January 12, 1971, I had a series of Sunday phone calls from the president as he worked on the SOTU he would give

later that month. He had just received a proposed draft from Ray Price, the writer he'd assigned to help with that speech, and Nixon was not happy. His first call was to tell me that the proposed draft was terrible and that if *he* was to have to do this speech work, unassisted by competent writers, then we couldn't expect him to do any other chores around the office. "Tell everyone there's to be no further contact with the president for the next two days. Tell Henry [Kissinger] and Bob [Haldeman]. Henry wants to resign again. Tell him I just can't see him. I'm going to have to do this speech."

Despite the frustration of working in the dark, Price today defends the system because Haldeman was an "honest doorkeeper, an honest broker of others' ideas; my ideas always got to the president intact." Although the speechwriter had advised and written for Nixon before and during the 1968 campaign and had worked on both Inaugural and the State of the Union addresses, he did not get more access to the president until the start of the second term when he resigned as head of Speechwriting to become what he called " 'house philosopher,' [to] bring in new ideas from around the country and [to] pull disparate elements" of Nixon's philosophy of government into a rhetorical whole.

David Gergen, whom Price had hired straight out of the navy, became the department's third chief. At this time the intermediary to Nixon was General Alexander Haig, who took Haldeman's place after his forced resignation. Unlike Haldeman, Haig had his own agenda, says Price, and thus was a less honest doorkeeper to the speechwriters. Nixon himself controlled the shape and content of every major speech, although he incorporated material from his writers. "Each major speech takes a week at least, of off-and-on, but regular, hard lonely work," the president's secretary Rose Mary Woods said in describing the boss's speechwriting labor, "outlining on pads of yellow paper, dictating drafts, polishing. It's hard, slow work."

Hard work was essential, the president believed, because

"thinking a speech through helps a leader think his policy through." Such an essentially rhetorical man understood instinctively that the act of writing is the act of learning. But Nixon's speechmaking process differed from those of earlier presidents who did their own writing mainly because of Nixon's perception of the purposes of presidential speech. He frequently wrote speeches (and thus made policy) in response to data supplied by his researchers and pollsters. In a memo to Haldeman he made it clear that "it has always been my view that polls should only be taken when they provide information . . . that will be a basis for changing policy." By contrast, Franklin Roosevelt and his immediate successors used the speechwriting process to formulate policy and attain "so much of it as will receive general support by teaching." Nixon employed it chiefly to manipulate public opinion. His November 3, 1969, speech on Vietnam, his "most significant on foreign policy" he declared, is a case in point.

The war in Vietnam overshadowed all other policy issues, foreign and domestic, during his first administration. After a political honeymoon of a few months, the antiwar movement again began to gather momentum. A nationwide day of protest was planned for October 15, 1969, to be followed on November 15 by a protest march on Washington. Although Nixon had declared that "under no circumstances" would he be influenced by these activities, few believed him, especially after he announced on October 13 a major speech on Vietnam to be televised on November 3. The three-week notice was in itself unusual, and the positioning of the speech between two antiwar demonstrations suggested politicizing. The November 3 speech merely enunciated policies that had been in effect at least since Nixon's June meeting with South Vietnam president Nguyen Van Thieu on Midway Island. Specifically, these policies aimed to avoid precipitate withdrawal of U.S. troops, to keep the withdrawal timetable secret, to maintain a non-Communist government in Saigon by the gradual transfer of military efforts to the South Vietnamese armed forces under the supervision of a reduced U.S. occupation force, and to foster negotiation. The only "new" element in the November 3 speech was its ending.

> And so tonight—to you, the great silent majority of my fellow Americans—I ask for your support. I pledged in my campaign for the presidency to end the war in a way that we could win the peace. . . . The more support I can have from the American people, the sooner that pledge can be redeemed; for the more divided we are at home, the less likely the enemy is to negotiate at Paris. Let us be united for peace.

The term "silent majority" so delighted the president that after he wrote it in a November 1 draft at 4:00 A.M., he called Haldeman to announce, "the baby's been born."

The peroration was widely thought to have been a deliberate attempt to polarize by dividing the nation into a tiny minority of noisy protesters deliberately obstructing peace and a large majority of quiet patriots. William Safire said this had been Nixon's point exactly. "He wanted to draw the battle lines between us and them—of the folks versus the elitists, of the 'mute masses,' in [Theodore] White's alliterative phrase, against the noisy minority."

Everything about the November 3 speech had been designed to stiffen the public's resolve in pursuing what had been government policy, Nixon said, since Eisenhower's administration. He began by comparing himself, favorably, with his predecessor. "Many believe that President Johnson's decision to send American combat forces into South Vietnam was wrong. And many others—I among them—have been strongly critical of the way the war has been conducted." He proceeded to discuss how the United States got involved in the war, instead of addressing the burning question of how to get out. He persisted in justifying his administration's snail-like pace of troop withdrawal by reiterating the time-worn (and to many by 1969, the questionable) domino theory. And finally, after throwing a conciliatory bone to dissenters by admitting that some may be idealists, he took it away by castigating them as a misguided "vocal minority" who try to impose "their point of view" on the majority. In short, Nixon appeared more eager to end dissent against the war than the war itself. Clearly he had written off the peace movement and appealed instead to what his own young assistant attorney general had referred to as the emerging Republican majority. Among this emerging majority were the ten million Americans who had voted in the 1968 election for independent George Wallace, and whose support Nixon needed in order to win in 1972. The overwhelmingly positive public response to the speech indicated that Nixon was onto something big.

Not one to leave anything to chance, he set into motion what Nixon biographer Stephen Ambrose called the "Nixon Big Charge." White House staffer Charles "Colson organized a supposedly spontaneous support from veterans across the nation," Ambrose wrote. "Others organized a supposedly spontaneous telegram barrage of support to the White House. The president piled them up on his desk and called in the photographers. 'The great silent majority,' he said, 'has spoken.' " Nor was this all. He directed that hundreds of copies of the speech be printed and delivered to friendly congressmen, governors, and staffers "who might be speaking on this subject," as Nixon wrote in a memo to Haldeman, "and who need to have a line on it." Haldeman organized "strike forces" of staffers to answer any negative comment emanating from network anchors and print reporters of the *New York Times*, the *Washington Post*, and the newsmagazines. Staffers who had solicited favorable remarks *before* the speech "released" them through the Office of Liaison immediately after. Staffer Alexander Butterfield began organizing a second barrage of wires to arrive at the White House two weeks later. Small wonder the *National Journal* later observed how "obsessed with the cosmetics of public relations" this administration appeared to be.

Closest to Richard Nixon's heart in all the promotional folderol was his need to show Americans how hard he worked on speeches. He urged the PR group not to emphasize "the substance [of] the November 3 speech . . . as important but the method—the hours of preparation involved." Referring to himself in the third person, as he frequently did, he dictated instructions for Ehrlichman about what to say and whom to "contact" concerning his manner of preparation for the November 3 speech. "The President has curious work habits," Nixon recorded. "He reads, works, talks to the staff on the phone until midnight. . . . The president has slept only four hours a night. He goes to bed at eleven or twelve, then awakens at two and works from two to three. That's when he does his clearest thinking. Then he sleeps until seven-thirty." Despite continuous complaining about the "incredible hours alone" that solitary writing entailed, Nixon was inordinately proud that "no one except Theodore Roosevelt and Woodrow Wilson" had worked so "completely" on major speeches.

Beginning with a weekend at Camp David on October 24, the president had labored on his speech an average of twelve hours a day until November 3. In preparation he had studied position papers from Defense, State, and the National Security Council, but he wrote the speech himself, all twelve drafts of it. Up to delivery time, only Henry Kissinger, his national security adviser, whom Nixon had consulted far more than Secretary of State William Rogers, and Rose Mary Woods, who typed it, knew what the president planned to say. This was partly because of Nixon's "strong predilection for secretive and isolated decision-making," according to Kissinger, and partly because of his love of surprise. "Surprise will increase the size of the audience and massively expand the impact of the speech," he said. He was right on both points: The speech attracted seventy-two million listeners, and comment on it lasted for weeks, principally owing to the efforts of his PR group to keep the speech in the news.

Even though the speech covered a major national issue, Nixon had not consulted with Congress, the Cabinet (not even the secretaries of defense and state), or with his staff. White House aides were not "channels of communication," as they had been for previous presidents. Unlike earlier presidents who had "organized the most searching canvas of possible alternatives," Nixon withdrew behind his chief of staff to shield himself from criticism. He rarely saw the men he had enlisted to aid him. Even telephone calls from senior-level assistants and Cabinet secretaries were automatically switched to Haldeman's office. Their memoranda, too, were routed to the chief of staff, who decided whether to pass them on to the president. Staffers who did challenge him were sorry later. In a book about his White House years, Safire cites instances from his own experience. "When I objected to the torrent of interviews given by the president in early 1971, . . . I was ostracized for three months. When I volunteered a suggestion in a Vietnam speech draft that no more draftees be sent to fight, I was promptly taken off the speech entirely, and was less inclined to do that again." As Arthur Schlesinger, Jr., reminded readers of *The Imperial Presidency,* LBJ might have angrily resisted opposition, but eventually "his own complex antennae kept him, in the end, in unwilling and indignant touch with reality. The rising protest in the executive branch, in Congress, in the press, and on the streets . . . eventually persuaded him that he could go down the [Vietnam] road no farther." Not so for Nixon, who at decision time retreated into his regal isolation. He deserted the Oval Office for working offices in the Old Executive Office Building and at Camp David.

On April 20, 1970, the president surprised everyone, even Secretary of Defense Melvin Laird and Secretary of State William Rogers, when he announced the withdrawal of 150,000 troops from Vietnam. Surprise at the higher-than-expected number most assuredly "massively expanded the impact" of the speech, more so than Nixon could have hoped. The Vietnam

Moratorium Committee, which had spearheaded the mass demonstrations that sandwiched the speech of November 3, 1969, let it be known that it was going out of business. Yet Nixon had fallen far behind his own self-imposed timetable for ending U.S. troop involvement. The April 20 announcement had actually been an admission that even a full year in the future—April 1971—more than a quarter of a million combat soldiers would still be in Vietnam. (He had campaigned two years earlier as having a "secret plan to end the war.") Still, by the last week in April 1970, the steam had gone out of the peace movement. But when President Nixon delivered his Invasion of Cambodia Speech on April 30, that brought it back to life with a vengeance.

April 1970 had been a terrible month for the president. First his nomination of Judge G. Harrold Carswell for the Supreme Court had been turned down by the Senate, his second rejected Supreme Court nomination. Then the Senate Foreign Relations Committee voted unanimously for repeal of the Gulf of Tonkin Resolution (which Johnson had used as the legal basis for his escalation of the undeclared Vietnam War) as a reminder to Nixon that he was limited constitutionally as to how far he could go in directing the nation's foreign affairs. In the middle of the month, an explosion in the service module of Apollo XIII had forced the astronauts to abort a planned lunar landing and initially jeopardized their eventual safe return to Earth. Worst of the month's bad news was that fighting had spread in Cambodia, South Vietnam's bordering neighbor.

In mid-March, the pro-Western general Lon Nol had seized power when Cambodia's ruler Prince Norodom Sihanouk was in the Soviet Union. Lon Nol planned to increase the size of his army in order to rid Cambodia of the country's North Vietnamese and Vietcong troops who inhabited sanctuaries that had been established with Sihanouk's acquiescence along the South Vietnam–Cambodia border. (At the same time, Sihanouk looked the other way at U.S. bombing raids of the sanctuaries.)

In a memo the day after the coup, Nixon told Kissinger that he wanted the CIA "to develop and implement a plan for maximum assistance to pro-US elements in Cambodia." When CIA director Richard Helms, William Rogers, and Melvin Laird advised against aid, Nixon held back, but very reluctantly. A month later, on April 16, he went ahead anyway, ordering the CIA to give all-out support to Lon Nol by turning over captured enemy arms and by sending money. But he wanted even bolder action. In a rare meeting with the National Security Council on April 22, he asked for their ideas about how to do more. Laird and Rogers preferred doing nothing, Kissinger suggested attacking the sanctuaries with South Vietnamese troops, and the Joint Chiefs of Staff advised using U.S. troops as well.

On Thursday April 23, Nixon told Haldeman to cancel all appointments "so he could concentrate on [the] Cambodia decision," and left the next day for Camp David to work on the speech that would announce that decision. For this speech he chose Pat Buchanan to help him with the writing. "This was not the time, the President was sure, for Ray Price's uplift," Safire said, because this was a speech that Nixon meant to give to the people "with the bark on." For the next seven days the president alternated between Camp David and his hideaway speechwriting office in the Old Executive Office Building. He worked for hours each day on eight successive drafts, using them and those supplied by Buchanan, in addition to ongoing discussions with Kissinger, to choose which option to pursue. "But in the days before announcing this most fateful decision," the national security adviser wrote in his memoirs, "Richard Nixon was virtually alone, sitting in a darkened room in the OEOB, the stereo softly playing neoclassical music—reflecting, resentful, collecting his thoughts and anger."

On Saturday April 25, Kissinger went to Camp David to urge the president not to cut Laird and Rogers out of the decision-making process. "You can't ram [your resolution] down their throats without their having a chance to give their views." The president had already decided what course he would follow and knew that neither the secretary of state nor the secretary of defense would approve of it, but he reluctantly agreed to meet with them the next night in Washington. To avoid unpleasantness at the Sunday meeting, Nixon conducted it as if it were a briefing. Rogers and Laird sat mute as Kissinger, Helms, and General Earle Wheeler, chairman of the Joint Chiefs of Staff, talked. As soon as everyone had left, the president recalled Kissinger and ordered him to write a directive authorizing an attack by U.S. forces into Cambodia, a move Kissinger had come to support several days earlier. The president told Kissinger he planned to dictate a summary of events leading to his decision that would record the contrary views of his senior advisers; however, later he said he "was shocked and disappointed when an apparently intentional leak to the press revealed that Bill Rogers and Mel Laird had been opposed to my Cambodian decision."

On Thursday April 30 at 9:00 P.M., Nixon spoke to the nation from the Oval Office to justify what he had called "my most controversial foreign-policy decision." The speech began with a false statement. Because Cambodia had been "a neutral nation since the Geneva Accords of 1954, . . . American policy since then has been to scrupulously respect the neutrality of the Cambodian people." The United States, the president continued, had never "moved against the enemy sanctuaries because we did not wish to violate the territory of a neutral nation," although, he added, the North Vietnamese had not respected its neutrality. The truth was that the U.S. Air Force had been hammering Communist bases in eastern Cambodia for over a year. On orders from the White House, B-52s had conducted 3,620 secret raids on the jungle sanctuaries during that time.

Since the point of the speech was to announce and justify the administration's intention of overtly violating that neutrality by invading Cambodia with ground troops—Americans still knew nothing about the year-long secret Cambodian bombing—Nixon referred to a map of Southeast Asia to illustrate how close North Vietnamese forces were to Saigon, especially those at the sanctuaries at Parrot's Peak (thirty-six miles) and Fishhook (fifty miles). He argued that the protection of U.S. forces in Saigon demanded "cleaning out major North Vietnamese and Vietcong territories," and promised that "once the enemy forces are driven out of these sanctuaries and once their military supplies are destroyed, we will withdraw." At the time, there was considerable evidence that the enemy was already evacuating the sanctuary areas and moving farther away from the South Vietnamese border, yet Nixon insisted on sending in the infantry anyway. "Tonight," he said, "Americans and South Vietnamese units will attack the headquarters for the entire Communist military operation in South Vietnam. This key control center has been occupied by the North Vietnamese and Vietcong for five years in blatant violation of Cambodia's neutrality."

There was no such entity as a "key control center," and Nixon knew it. What he said implied a Pentagon-like command post, or at any rate, a controlled bastion, but Hanoi preferred a floating network of leaders who moved from one place to another, hidden by the lush overgrowth of the Cambodian jungles. When Secretary Laird read the speech, only hours before delivery, he urged the president at the very least to remove the statement that the chief purpose of the Cambodian invasion was to capture "the headquarters for the entire Communist military operation in South Vietnam." Nixon refused. To lessen the effect of certain criticism over this point, Kissinger briefed reporters an hour before airtime, cautioning them not to expect that the illusory and elusive headquarters could actually be captured.

For the second time in six months, Nixon had discarded the advice of his foreign policy advisers and taken a hard rhetorical line that pleased him, Haldeman, Attorney General John Mitchell, friend Bebe Rebozo, but few others. Even Buchanan made it clear that "it was the old man's speech. He knew just what he wanted to say." Despite this disclaimer, Buchanan seems to have gotten a large share of the blame for the speech's hard line, since he did not work on speeches for Nixon again. Henceforth, he handled the daily news summary, and for a time in late 1970, he was assigned to Vice President Spiro Agnew.

What Nixon wanted in the Cambodia speech was to put Hanoi on notice that "we will not be humiliated. We will not be defeated." Having ignored warnings that his listeners would see the speech as an enlargement of the war, he went out of his way to show he was still intent on seeking military victory: "If, when the chips are down, the world's most powerful nation, the United States of America, acts like a pitiful helpless giant, the forces of totalitarianism and anarchy will threaten free nations and free institutions throughout the world. It is not our power but our will that is being tested tonight."

The president ended on a note most commentators found self-pitying. Despite his having made this decision in the same room in which Wilson, Roosevelt, Eisenhower, and Kennedy had made their great decisions, Nixon said, his policies, unlike theirs, were immediately assailed by "counsels of doubt and defeat from some of the most widely known opinion leaders in the nation." More specifically, he compared his Cambodian decision to Kennedy's during the Cuban missile crisis, which was why, he said, he had not consulted Congress. But the Cambodian situation was no sudden emergency. The president admitted as much in the speech when he said the North Vietnamese had been in Cambodia for five years.

Debate within the executive branch might at least have ameliorated his hard line, but the president ignored everyone except those whose views bolstered his own. He was essentially a loner in policymaking matters. He repeatedly left his top officials uninformed; consequently they could not consent or oppose or give advice. He kept everyone at bay, even the Cabinet. He regularly bypassed the State Department, using Kissinger as his back channel for information and implementation, and the Defense Department, preferring to deal directly with the military. "Nixon gets very little firsthand," a former presidential staffer explained. "He doesn't read the papers raw very much." His chief of staff was an important source of outside opinion, but he "served only to stiffen [Nixon] in his lone-wolf stance, . . . encourage his anger, . . . tell him he is right and everyone else is wrong."

Finally, claiming to be above politics, as he had also done in the November 3 speech, Nixon said, "I would rather be a one-term president than a two-term president at the cost of seeing America become a second-rate power and see this nation accept the first defeat in its proud 190-year history."

Right after the speech, Haldeman met with the White House senior PR staff to distribute a National Security Council packet that served as the basis for the usual "game plan to sell the making of a decision." Highlighted on page one was the only rationalization any of them could hope to get away with in light of the president's "misstatements." "Only the president has all the facts on this situation. He must act in what he considers to be the best interests of our country and our troops." "All the people who talk to people," as Nixon sometimes called the PR group, met every day for the next several days. Three days after the speech, on Sunday, Nixon wandered into one of their meetings to update the "PR game plan."

"Don't worry about divisiveness," the president exhorted. "Having drawn the sword don't take it out—stick it in hard, because for people to go squealing around while a combat operation is under way, undercutting the very purpose of the action where good men are losing their lives—that's beyond the pale. Hit 'em in the gut. No defensiveness."

What was beyond the pale was Nixon's deliberate pumping up of the rhetoric. He could have described the Cambodian invasion as the simple, temporary rearguard incursion into enemy territory that it was, but instead he employed emotionally charged, cataclysmic language. Either the United States invades Cambodia, he declared categorically, or no young American "can have a chance to grow up in a world of peace and justice." This was bombast, pure and simple, and nearly every senior adviser, staffer, and congressional leader commented on it, describing the speech as excessive and bellicose. It also sounded like another attempt to rally the silent majority he had so effectively wooed in the November 3 speech.

The depth and breadth of public reaction surprised him. The Vietnam Moratorium Committee sprang back to life and joined with the National Student Association in calling for a nationwide student strike. Several dozen college presidents appealed to the president to consider the dangers of the unprecedented alienation of the country's youth. The Senate's Foreign Relations Committee castigated Nixon for "conducting a constitutionally unauthorized, presidential war on Indochina [that is, Cambodia, Laos, and Vietnam] without the consent of Congress." Four days after the speech, national guardsmen in Ohio fired their rifles into an angry crowd of undergraduates at Kent State University, killing two demonstrators and two onlookers. Hundreds of colleges signed the strike list. In California, Governor Ronald Reagan closed down the state university system with its 280,000 students. Even the stock market reacted by falling to its lowest level in seven years.

On May 30, Nixon announced that the incursion had met its objectives; by June 30, the last U.S. troops had left Cambodia. "The operation," Nixon said, "had been a complete success." In fact, the Cambodian invasion had resulted in a few enemy deaths but did little, if anything, to stem the flow of supplies to the Vietcong and North Vietnamese. Moreover, it added yet another country the United States had pledged to defend; it revived the antiwar movement; it led to the killing of four college students; and it hardened Congress in its resolve to more closely monitor a president's foreign policy moves in the future. It had been anything but a success. (Ironically, exactly five years after the April 30 speech, on April 30, 1975, the South Vietnamese government announced its unconditional surrender to the Communists and reported that the name of Saigon was changed to Ho Chi Minh City. The Lon Nol regime also fell to the Khmer Rouge in April of 1975, and the disastrous American involvement in Indochina ended.)

Speechmaking like Nixon's, with its public relations emphasis, draws listeners' attention away from issues and to the speaker, his ability to speak, and his style of presentation. This is upside down from the speechmaking practice of presidents like Harry Truman, who said, "Make good policies, and good relations will follow." But with Nixon, as historian Henry Steele Commager wrote in the *Washington Post* on May 27, 1973, "great issues of war and peace, of wealth and commonwealth, are to be decided not on their merits but through the manipulation of public opinion and the purveying of false information even by the president, who himself appears and sounds more and more like the head of a giant public relations firm."

Even Nixon loyalists commented on "the purveying of false information," albeit more euphemistically. Nixon's failure, William Safire believed, stemmed from his being "concerned too much with how he would be perceived, creating a mask that became the man." David Gergen also admitted that the president's obsession with image resulted in too much distance between public rhetoric and deed.

When speeches play so strongly to public opinion, a gap between public words and deeds is frequently the result. How different Nixon's speechmaking was from that of the president he served as vice president, who strongly believed, as speechwriter Emmet Hughes put it, that "to affirm the word passionately, then fail to give it testimony in deed is self-defeating." In his own words, Eisenhower said, "The job is to convince, not to publicize."

The thirty-seventh president had changed not only the nature of presidential speeches but also the function of a chief executive's writers. In pre-Nixon days, speechwriters were a few close aides who had policy responsibilities and ready access to their presidents and for whom speechwriting was a secondary assignment. Throughout the Nixon administration and after, speechwriters served first and foremost as wordsmiths with little or no access to the Oval Office.

Nixon's predecessors had shown that a full collaboration with speechwriters produced cognitive benefits, at least as well as solitary speechwriting once did. In fact, in a country as populous and diverse as this and in a world as dangerous and complex, collaborative efforts may be essential. As a rule, subsequently, the more contemporary presidents have avoided working closely with their speechwriters (even when, like Nixon, they did a lot of their own writing), the more they tended to find themselves in various kinds of political trouble.

—

THE true heir to Richard Nixon's synchronized approach to rhetoric was Ronald Wilson Reagan. Between Reagan's election in November 1980 and his inauguration in January 1981, Nixon speechwriter David Gergen, aided by Republican pollsters Richard Wirthlin and Richard Beale, drew up the Initial Action Plan, a memo that outlined every presidential action and speech to be taken or given during the first 100 days of the new administration. Beginning January 20, Reagan's first-term communications team set about executing the proposed agenda. Members of the team were James Baker, the chief of staff; Richard Darman, Baker's chief assistant; Michael Deaver, the deputy chief of staff; and David Gergen, the communications director. They relied on the amply staffed Offices of Communications, Public Liaison, and Public Affairs, all Nixon innovations. Each morning at 8:15, the team met, determined the line of the day, and prepared a set of index cards for the president. The cards listed the day's schedule and scripts of speeches and of jokes to tell visitors at both casual and formal ceremonies. Then the line of the day passed to Press Secretary Larry Speakes, who went into action.

Speakes made daily conference calls to press secretaries of other executive agencies, played host to regional broadcasters and editors, and computerized the story line for mass marketing, sending out instructions on how to plug electronically into prepared press statements and audio- and videotapes to 10,000 newspapers and radio and television stations. Because the strategists made television *the* organizing framework for the entire public relations package, the Press Office videotaped the White House version of the news and beamed it via satellite to 900 television stations outside Washington. To a large extent, the Reagan White House functioned like a giant television studio.

And herein lies the reason Reagan was the "great communicator." He was to television what FDR was to radio. In a book about his experiences in the Reagan and Bush administrations, Richard Darman devoted a chapter to showing that Reagan's masterful use of television, albeit at the expense of substance and formal argument, was the reason for his popularity. Understanding more clearly than any president before him how completely the television medium dominates American life, Reagan and his speechwriters designed his rhetoric specifically for the video camera by turning issues into snapshots with stories.

Reagan's speech at Notre Dame University in March 1988 is an example of the presidential made-for-television speech and his flawless performance in executing it. The president went to the university to dedicate a stamp honoring its famous football coach Knute Rockne. Reagan appeared to be late, because when the proceedings began, he had not joined those on the dais. Scenes from the 1940 movie *Knute Rockne,* which featured the young actor Reagan as George Gipp, played on a large screen. In one of the scenes, a priest ends the eulogy of the coach with the words "ask the president of the United States." At this moment the film stopped, the band struck up "Hail to the Chief," and Reagan bounded to the platform to deliver an upbeat speech praising morality-based education like Notre Dame's. At the end, he tossed a football to the cheering students, ensuring a big play on the nation's nightly newscasts.

His speech at Moscow State University in May of 1988 provided an even more memorable photo opportunity. This was one of several speeches he made on what was his first trip to the land he called the "evil empire." Reagan made the trip to sign two modest arms-control agreements. But his real aim was to make a case for democracy and freedom before the Soviet people.

Speechwriter Josh Gilder flew to the Soviet Union on a "pre-advance" to check out venues for the various addresses the president would make and to absorb atmosphere and background. He inspected the auditorium at the university, the locality for what was to be the principal speech of the trip, the one that the Soviets had agreed could be telecast around the world. From the standpoint of television, the setting seemed all wrong to Gilder. Behind the speaker's podium was a gargantuan head of Lenin lighted from above, giving the Bolshevik leader a demonic look, and an even larger bright red mural of the revolution, complete with hammers and sickles, behind Lenin. Gilder asked to have the bust, conveniently on wheels, removed and the mural covered. As a shaken guide—almost in tears, Gilder remembers—set about covering his country's most patriotic symbols, the speechwriter had second thoughts. Leave Lenin and the mural untouched, he said, and the relieved Soviet guide was left to ponder the situation. Later Gilder fashioned words for Reagan that skillfully wove the verbal and visual to encapsulate the point of the speech. "Standing here before a mural of your revolution, I want to talk about a very different revolution that is taking place right now, quietly sweeping the globe without bloodshed or conflict." The president went on to talk movingly about entrepreneurs, "the explorers of the modern era," who make technological progress possible, comparing them to government planners who will never outdo the "millions of individuals working day and night to make their dreams come true."

In video-age image making, the picture takes precedence over the word. New language, such as "the art of the back-drop," became part of the administration's regular discussions. "We wanted to control what people saw," Gergen said, "which made daily priorities crystal clear—the network evening news, the morning shows, cable news network, and local regional news programs." The impresario of visual choreography, Michael Deaver, designed each presidential action as a one-minute or two-minute spot on the evening network news. "We would go through the president's schedule day by day and hour by hour," Deaver said, "and figure out what we wanted the story to be at the end of each day and at the end of each week. And that worked 90% of the time." Deaver made Reagan an abiding presence in the nation's living rooms. Countless times cameramen pictured this most photographed of all presidents jauntily striding to or from the helicopter, while reporters, kept at an administration-approved safe distance away, shouted questions at the smiling, thumbs-up figure. Hundreds, probably thousands, of hazy telephoto shots of Reagan on horseback or clearing brush on his California ranch conveyed the message that this oldest of American presidents was exceptionally vigorous.

Late every afternoon, as close as possible to story deadline, Gergen phoned reporters to give the White House slant on the day's news. "As opposed to Kissinger and Haldeman and that crowd, whose view was that you could control media by giving them bits and pieces [of information]," Deputy Press Secretary Leslie Janka said, "the Reagan White House came to the totally opposite conclusion that the media will take what we feed them. . . . They've got to write their story every day. You give them their story, they'll go away. As long as you come in there every day, hand them a well-packaged, premasticated story in the format they want, they'll go away. The phrase is 'manipulation by inundation.' You give them the line of the day, you give them the facts, access to people who will speak on the record. . . . And you do that long enough, they're going to stop bringing their own stories, and stop being investigative reporters of any kind."

No Broadway show or Hollywood film was ever so carefully staged as the public governing of the Reagan administration. Reagan supplied the vision, voice, stage presence, and good looks while an inner circle of advisers managed the nation's affairs. According to Donald Regan, who became chief of staff during Reagan's second term, these advisers treated the president like a "supreme anchorman whose public persona was the most important element of the presidency." Reagan's fourth and last chief of staff, Kenneth Duberstein, admitted that the president required a "very strong stage manager–producer-director," but whatever he was given to say and do, he "played to the emotions of his countrymen" like the professional he was.

The emphasis on speeches for TV annoyed some of the staffers. Even political strategist Lee Atwater grew tired of it. "I can't think of a single meeting I was at for more than an hour when someone didn't say, 'How will it play in the media?' " By media, Atwater meant television, which is the medium of news for most Americans.

To test how well the speeches would play on television, pollsters also had a prominent role in the Reagan White House communication process. Although Reagan's pollster Richard Wirthlin never joined the president's staff, he sat in on weekly strategy meetings. His firm, Decision Making Information, Inc., pretested public attitudes before the president spoke on any issue. Since the firm had 250 telephone links for rapid polling, the pollster could do national polls on hot issues in a day. Wirthlin's chief tool, however, was the focus group, which consisted of twenty people chosen to represent the demographic characteristics of the country at large. Focus groups, which operated all over the country, helped to fashion appealing and believable messages by listening to a Reagan stand-in read a proposed speech while they fingered computerized dials. A printout listing the text on one side and a word-by-word audience response on the other went to the speechwriters so they could identify "power phrases." The speechwriters were then expected to emphasize words that had elicited the most positive responses and eliminate less evocative words in subsequent drafts.

The writers objected to the presence of pollsters in speechwriting. In a book about her two years as a Reagan writer, Peggy Noonan described a meeting of the writers with Wirthlin in Donald Regan's office shortly after the 1986 State of the Union Address. According to Noonan, Wirthlin made it clear that he had a better "read" on what the public wanted than the writers. He had analyzed the responses of focus group members. Wirthlin pointed out that early in the speech when the president said "reach for the stars," they pressed buttons to indicate positive responses. The word "free" is a good word, he said, especially "free man from nuclear terror. . . . When you speechwriters talk about reform, that is good," he continued. "It's pro-family, pro-jobs, pro-future, pro-America. Pro is positive." The parts of the speech that did not work, he said, were those that were not positive in some way. He singled out a section in which the president spoke about the freedom fighters in Afghanistan, Angola, Cambodia, and Nicaragua. "The listeners didn't know where these countries are," Wirthlin groused, "and anyway it sounds like we're launching a four-point war. Part of the problem seems to be that the language was so powerful it put people on edge. It made them feel 'down.' It wasn't positive."

"This isn't writing," Noonan scrawled in a note she passed to head speechwriter Bently Elliott. To her it was more like "where's-the-beefization of mankind."

On at least one occasion Reagan delivered a major policy

speech the principal premises of which had been widely tested before focus groups but *not* subjected to policy review. The March 23, 1983, speech announced the Strategic Defense Initiative, popularly dubbed Star Wars. In utopian theory, energy beams capable of destroying Soviet missiles after their launch but before their warheads deployed were to be mounted on orbiting platforms to provide a space shield or "superdome" over the United States. When the president first heard about the theory, he embraced it wholeheartedly but did not probe for details.

Although SDI was a radical departure from the doctrine of nuclear deterrence by which this country and the Allies had been defended since World War II, Reagan told the nation that "after careful consultation with my advisers, including the Joint Chiefs of Staff," he was proposing a plan to reduce and even eliminate nuclear weapons from the world. The facts are that not a single meeting of the National Security Council was held to discuss this issue; the Joint Chiefs of Staff met with the president only once to listen to the president's idea in the broadest sense but had no idea that Reagan meant SDI as an imminent policy move; no one in State or Defense had been consulted. Only NSC adviser William Clark was as enthusiastic as Reagan, so he enlisted fellow NSC member Robert McFarlane and three staffers, including John Poindexter, to devise a proposal. SDI became a crash project that deliberately avoided technical debate because the president wanted to make the announcement as soon as possible. Objectors might stop the idea before it got going, so "we didn't tell anyone what we were doing," Poindexter said. Aram Bakshian, the assigned speechwriter, was as clueless as everyone else about SDI; at the last minute he was told to write a generic address on peace and national security. McFarlane privately wrote the short insert that announced SDI.

Despite the deliberate secrecy, word of the speech spread through the executive branch less than forty-eight hours before delivery. As a result, the speech started circulating throughout the departments. Reaction was unanimously negative. The Joint Chiefs strongly recommended postponement. Richard Perle, top Pentagon civilian thinker on arms issues, seconded their counsel. What exactly did Reagan mean by SDI? everyone asked. Was he talking about a defense against all nuclear weapons or just ballistic missiles? Was SDI to be land-based, permissible under the 1972 ABM Treaty, or a space-based defense, clearly forbidden by the treaty? What about cost, time frame?

"We don't have the technology to do this," Secretary of State George Shultz exclaimed after reading the speech. His "flabbergasted" senior aides called the idea a "pipe dream." Shultz met with the president several times over the next two days, arguing for toning down the rhetoric, at the very least. "It's too sweeping. It's a revolution in our strategic doctrine." Moreover, he added, "we need some very precise Qs and As to handle the difficult and tricky questioning that will inevitably follow. Without this, people will say we don't know what we're talking about." Undersecretary Lawrence Eagleburger wondered what SDI might mean for the latest stealth technology. "If a new defensive system could not be penetrated by offensive weapons, then the stealth technology was already obsolete," he pointed out. "If a new defensive system could be penetrated by stealth, the statements the president proposed to make were far too extravagant." Privately he suggested the "president seems to be proposing an updated version of the Maginot line." When Shultz learned that SDI applied to ballistic missiles only, he redoubled his effort to persuade Reagan to lessen the exaggeration of his rhetorical claims, saying over and over that "the idea and the rhetoric don't fit together."

No one, however, could deter Reagan, belying the widespread notion that his "handlers" had turned him into a willing ventriloquist's puppet. Speechwriter Landon Parvin speculated that Reagan believed so strongly in American ingenuity that he felt certain the experts would one day be proven wrong. Had he not been so aloof from his staff and detached from policy discussions, Parvin added, he probably would have been less inclined to follow his grandiose vision. Reagan went ahead with a somewhat toned-down speech, secure in the knowledge that the public loved SDI because Michael Deaver had arranged for extensive testing before focus groups and reported solid support for a "space shield." (Deaver admitted that those queried had no idea how such a shield would work, but they liked the "concept." His own view, cheerfully confessed to investigative journalist Mark Hertsgaard, was "he didn't know or care whether SDI would actually work.")

RONALD Reagan's theatrical use of the bully pulpit was unparalleled. Over the eight years of his presidency fourteen uncommonly talented writers scripted his stage-managed public appearances. When he first arrived at the White House in January of 1981, he delivered a packet of his past speeches to the Speechwriting Office with the instruction that the writers learn to imitate his style and substance.

In many ways Reagan was the most literary of contemporary presidents. Words flowed smoothly from his pen. Like FDR, he knew how to reduce complex issues to simple narratives, like parables. Not incidentally, he was a great admirer of Roosevelt, having come to maturity during the Roosevelt era listening to the president's fireside chats and memorizing some of their best passages. And he looked to his predecessor to teach him how to reach people effectively.

During his six terms as president of the Screen Actors Guild and eight years as a General Electric spokesman, Reagan had written hundreds of speeches. Over that period he moved from ardent Roosevelt Democrat to a leading advocate for what was called in the mid-1960s the New Right. In 1964, he gained national political visibility by making a televised sales pitch for Republican presidential candidate Barry Goldwater called "A Time for Choosing." "The Speech," as it has come to be known, consisted largely of anecdotes and characterizations of heroes and villains. All of them illustrated the struggle between good and evil, which to Reagan was the conflict between the United States and the Soviet Union and between the individual and big government. He stayed on the right and repeated "the Speech" in one form or another for the rest of his life.

After he became president he charged his speechwriters with the task of elaborating on "the Speech's" core ideas—that a centrally administered government tended to weaken a free people's character and that abroad the source of all evil was the Soviet Union—and applying them to multiple situations. Anthony Dolan, who had served on two separate occasions as head of the Speechwriting Department, called the 1964 speech " 'seminal.' I believed in the things Ronald Reagan believed in." Writer Allan Meyer, a former career military officer, called "the Speech" and his department's interpretation of it "the conscience of the presidency." Bently Elliott, the department's director from May 1981 to June 1986, prepared for his speech-writing job by spending "three weeks reading all [Reagan's] speeches and making sheaves of notes—on war, on blacks, on rhetoric, on the economy. And I just absorbed his way of expressing things." Landon Parvin concurred. "Reagan was easy to write for because he had a definite philosophy and a consistent voice." No one misunderstood where he stood, for he was rhetorically consistent throughout eight years of his presidency. From the night of his acceptance speech for his first nomination in Detroit's Cobo Hall to the day he turned over the Oval Office to George Bush, he stuck to a few simple themes and repeated them with force and conviction.

"Ronald Reagan had a superior gift for the spoken word," Elliott told an interviewer. "He got to the heart of his message in one line, a kind of exclamation point to the whole speech, and sometimes in a few words. When he spoke of the 'magic of the market' and the 'evil empire,' people remembered. He was only practicing what he preached, that 'specificity is the soul of credibility.' " Above all else, Reagan understood the elemental power of storytelling. He made his vision concrete in heartwarming anecdotes, tales of saints and sinners who, even if they did resemble Norman Rockwell paintings, were far more memorable than cold bare facts. A typical example of this quality was his prophetic address to the members of the British Parliament at the Palace of Westminster on June 8, 1982. In it Reagan accurately predicted that Poland, "magnificently unreconciled to repression," would openly rebel, leading to a "global campaign for freedom" that would prevail in Eastern Europe and the Soviet Union.

> We're approaching the end of a bloody century plagued by a terrible political invention—totalitarianism. Optimism comes less easily today, not because democracy is less vigorous, but because democracy's enemies have refined their instruments of repression. Yet optimism is in order, because day by day democracy is proving itself to be a not-at-all fragile flower. From Stettin on the Baltic to Varna on the Black Sea, the regimes planted by totalitarianism have had more than 30 years to establish their legitimacy. But none—not one regime—has yet been able to risk free elections. Regimes planted by bayonets do not take root. . . .
>
> I've often wondered about the shyness of some of us in the West about standing for those ideals that have done so much to ease the plight of man and the hardships of our imperfect world. This reluctance to use those vast resources at our command reminds me of the elderly lady whose home was bombed in the Blitz. As the rescuers moved about, they found a bottle of brandy she'd stored behind the staircase, which was all that was left standing. And since she was barely conscious, one of the workers pulled the cork to give her a taste of it. She came around immediately and said, "Here now—there now, put it back. That is for emergencies."
>
> Well, the emergency is upon us. Let us be shy no longer. Let us go to our strength. Let us offer hope. Let us tell the world that a new age is not only possible but probable.

Speechwriter Anthony Dolan had cogently articulated Reagan's precise feelings and beliefs about the evils of communism. It was Dolan, in fact, who in a later speech called the Soviet Union the "evil empire," which came to epitomize Reagan's view.

Although Reagan had shown himself to be a fine writer, he was only minimally involved in speechwriting in the White House. In the early weeks of his first term, the writers met with the president on Friday mornings, but very soon meetings trailed off and then stopped. After that, the writers dealt with David Gergen and when he left in 1983, with Richard Darman, Baker's top aide. Gergen or Darman had the final say on what went to the president. "Dave is a consensus person," Elliott says today, "so he let most everything go through and pushed back only on some of our more vivid phrases like 'the Soviet Union is the focus of evil' and on abortion matters. There was friction, but a lot that was good in the speeches got in to the president. When Darman arrived on the scene, our words got scrutinized more carefully, so there was more friction. But in some ways Darman helped us by making a speech stronger, more coherent."

"In the end, all substance and tactics came down to the drafting of words," Darman said, "whether you're talking about a law, a regulation, an order, or a speech. My job frequently involved mediating about words." When Regan was chief of staff, his aides did the mediating, especially David Chew, who took over Darman's old job. At this point the writers were cut off from all access to the president and to the policy people.

With Reagan removed from the process, someone had to have the final word because fights between the writers and the policy people were unavoidable. After an assigned writer had completed a draft, it left the Speechwriting Department for fact-checking and policy-adjusting at all pertinent federal agencies and among important members of the White House staff.

Noonan recounted her frustration at having her prose go through a twenty-five-station review. "It would come back tapioca." The writers dismissed those who quashed their words as bureaucrats and blamed them for the unending attempt to separate words from policy. "A bureaucrat from State who was assigned to work with the NSC on the annual economic summits," Noonan complained, "used to come into Speechwriting and refer to himself and his colleagues as 'we substantive types' and to the speechwriters as 'you wordsmiths.' He was simply saying, we do policy and you dance around with words. We would smile back. Our smiles said, 'the dancer is the dance.' "

Precisely so, especially when the writer is a close presidential aide, for he or she influences the president, who has the last word. But in this administration the policy people worked apart from the writers. Whenever the writer made policy, it usually was inadvertent. Since speeches were scheduled long before they were delivered, sometimes the writers had to do a draft before they knew what the issue would be, so they would create an issue for the speech. Even after reviewing a researcher's collection of past presidential remarks on an agreed-upon subject, the writer was often in a quandary. "What *is* the policy on conservation?" Noonan wondered before starting a speech on that subject. "Lacking certainty, we intuit." As she herself readily admitted, often she "would use the 'hand grenade' technique. I would write a statement embodying an unambiguous, history-making commitment, throw it into the policy-making machinery, and sooner or later someone would knock it down or pick it up."

For the most part, the president stayed aloof from the factions warring over "his" words. He never sat down with his writers to hammer out policy decisions, as Noonan knew only too well. "I can't write well without hearing the person I'm writing for talk in conversation," she told Elliott. "If you think he sounds stale, it's because the speechwriters haven't met with him in over a year," she complained to Darman. But the president rarely conferred with aides either. He had set the course years before becoming president; others charted it and made policy to execute it. "As long as his A-team was in charge of the White House staff, things worked," onetime chief writer Aram Bakshian said, alluding to the first-term troika of Baker, Edwin Meese, and Deaver. Reagan saw himself not as the originator of policy but as its chief marketer. Thus, he did not need to attend meetings. When he did, he rarely asked questions. A major speech only reached him in the penultimate draft, in essence the policy transaction, and that is when he got involved. His editing was excellent, and often extensive, as attested to by all the speechwriters, but it was still just editing; substance had been set by others. His editorial changes constituted the final draft. No president, certainly in recent memory and maybe ever, had delegated as much decision making, which is what speechmaking essentially is.

Reagan's lack of involvement in the substance of speechwriting can be readily discerned right from the beginning of his first administration. The director of management and budget, David Stockman, described the preparation of the September 24, 1981, speech on his economic plan in a book about his White House years. His account shows the president as notably absent.

> The TV speech was scheduled for Thursday evening. . . . Six different drafts of the speech were now circulating inside the White House. But as of Tuesday evening, *no one* knew what the contents or thrust of the message would be. . . . By late afternoon [of delivery day] the president's speech was still being chopped, scissored, and pasted together in the Roosevelt Room. This was unusual to say the least. Ordinarily, nationwide presidential addresses are wrapped up days ahead of time. Gergen, Deaver, the speechwriters, and I were all shouting and throwing papers around, trying to make it come together. . . . [The speech had] strong words, but they were a caricature of the truth, and they marked a profound turning

point. . . . The Reagan Administration went into hiding from
the massive fiscal disorder it had unleashed.

The "fiscal disorder" Stockman was referring to resulted from
Reagan's massive across-the-board income tax cut and con-
comitant defense buildup that brought about the clearest failure
of this administration. During Reagan's watch, the cumulative
national debt tripled from $900 billion to $2.7 trillion, leaving
taxpayers with $200 billion per year in interest payments to ser-
vice the debt. "No one, over the years, taught people more
emphatically to hate a Government deficit," writer Garry Wills
said in a *New York Times* story on Reagan's economic policies,
"and no one ever gave us bigger ones to hate."

Reagan's minimal involvement in the writing of his presidential words moved communications scholar Kathleen Hall
Jamieson to ask whether "President Reagan's reliance on
speechwriters . . . played a role in his disposition to accept information about Iran-Contra dealings uncritically and to trust his
aides to act in his best interest. . . . Why should we expect
someone who embraces the words of others to suddenly become an active, inquiring, scrutinizing manager of information
when offered a plan for aiding the Contras?"

The Iran-Contra operation involved the selling of arms to
Iran in an attempt to gain the freedom of U.S. hostages being
held there, even though it conflicted with Reagan's publicly
stated policy against bargaining with terrorists. It was orchestrated by NSC members Robert McFarlane and John Poindexter, NSC staffer Lieutenant Colonel Oliver North, and CIA
director William Casey. "Ultimately the guy behind it, who got
it going, and the only guy who can stop it, was and is Ronald
Reagan," Shultz said when he learned what had been secretly
transpiring. The same group then diverted profits from the arms
sales to the Contra forces who were fighting a guerrilla war
against the pro-Soviet Sandinista government of Nicaragua,
contrary to the law. (In October 1984 Congress had banned

governmental aid to the Contras.) Not until November 4, 1986, fully eighteen months after the arms-for-hostages plan had been put into effect, did the story begin to unfold in the press. En route to Vienna at the time, Shultz fired off a cable to Poindexter warning him that "the only way to contain damage is to . . . get everything out in the open, and fast." Poindexter responded that he planned to "stonewall" whatever news of the illegal operation became public. "I was amazed," Shultz later wrote, "that despite the revelations and immediate uproar in the country, Congress, and press, Poindexter and the White House-NSC staffs were apparently intent on plowing ahead with what sounded to me like *more* 'arms-for-hostages' swaps."

Back in Washington, Shultz met with the president and the responsible NSC group and tried without success to persuade them that "Iran is playing us for suckers, and we are paying extortion money to them." A press release describing the meeting was prepared and passed by Shultz for his approval. It concluded with the president's statement "that our policy of not making concessions to terrorists remains intact." "That's a lie," Shultz said in disgust. "It's Watergate all over again."

Because the Iranian operation continued to dominate the news, Reagan spoke to the nation on November 13, 1986, claiming that the charges were "utterly false." Patrick Buchanan crafted the speech largely from information from Oliver North. North and Poindexter, who was later convicted of lying to Congress, had been lying to administration officials and to the writers who were trying to make a credible case for Reagan's actions. The factual inaccuracies in the speech affected the president's delivery, which biographer Lou Cannon described as "carping, angry, defensive."

Secretary Shultz was discouraged about the prospects of turning the president around on this issue.

The president's speech convinced me that Ronald Reagan still truly did not believe that what had happened had, in fact, happened. To him the reality was different. I had seen him like this before on other issues. He would go over the "script" of an event, past or present, in his mind, and once that script was mastered, that was the truth—no fact, no argument, no plea for reconsideration, could change his mind. So what Ronald Reagan said to the American people was true to him, although it was not the reality.

And the public seemed to sense this; few believed in the factuality of what the president had said, so on November 19 he held a press conference. He said that there would be no further arms shipments to Iran, that what he did was right, and that "we're going to continue on this path." He followed with a list of incorrect statements, so many in fact that his secretary of state instructed an aide to get a transcript of the press conference and "list one by one all the erroneous points he had made," then show this list to the president. The president's press conference remarks as well as his written opening statement were almost word for word from two NSC reports. The first was a seventeen-page chronology Poindexter wrote that had as its objective, McFarlane claimed, a distancing of Reagan from approval of arms sales, and the second was a November 18 memo that McFarlane wrote, which he later acknowledged "was not a full and completely accurate account."

Hoping to have put the matter behind him, Reagan was disappointed when further reports asserted that profits from arms sales had been diverted to the Contras. Once again, the president addressed the nation. On December 2, 1986, he conceded that illegal acts might have occurred. "If actions . . . were taken without my authorization, knowledge, or concurrence, this will be exposed and appropriate, corrective steps will be implemented." He appointed an investigative commission to be headed by former Texas senator John Tower. The Tower board, which took testimony and reviewed documents during January 1987, then issued its report on February 26. Nothing linked Reagan directly to illegal acts, the report stated, but owing to his lax "management style," zealous subordinates probably "duped" him. As historian Michael Schaller wrote in his summation of the Reagan years, *Reckoning with Reagan,* the "conclusion portrayed the president as a well-intentioned, laid-back fellow not always sure of the facts. At worst a fool, but not a knave."

Forced to report to the American people, the president called on Landon Parvin to write the speech. Parvin had been a member of the Speechwriting Department until 1983, and when he started his own writing consultancy, the Reagans became his first clients. They had chosen well, for Reagan had put himself in the unenviable position of having to admit culpability or incompetence. In a masterpiece of image rebuilding, he delivered a speech to the nation on March 4, 1987, managing to avoid both alternatives. He cast himself as a firm and unflinching foe of precisely what he had been caught doing: dealing with a terrorist state. "A few months ago I told the American people I did not trade arms for hostages. My heart and my best intentions still tell me that's true, but the facts and evidence tell me it is not." Then he proceeded to talk about being "angry" over "activities undertaken without my knowledge." Referring to the whole sordid story as an antecedentless "it," he said, "it was a mistake." He gave no indication throughout that "it" was his mistake. He ended with a peroration that told his listeners how to deal with problems. "Now what should happen when you make a mistake is this: You take your knocks, you learn your lessons, and then you move on. That's the healthiest way to deal with a problem. . . . You know . . . you've made plenty of mistakes, if you've lived your life properly. So you learn. You put things in perspective. You pull your energies together. You change. You go forward."

Reagan did not play much of a role in drafing his semi-apology. As Parvin said, Reagan's real message was, "I didn't do it, and I promise I'll never do it again." According to Reagan biographer Lou Cannon, the task of persuading the president to make a public admission, orchestrated by Mrs. Reagan, fell primarily to speechwriter Parvin and to John Tower. Political adviser Stuart Spencer also helped by recommending that Tower's role be kept secret, since it appeared unseemly to advertise that the man who had passed judgment also assisted in writing a response to it. Yet only Tower had the facts, which Parvin needed. Despite his halfhearted admission, Reagan remained convinced that he had not traded arms for hostages. As the fifth of his six national security advisers, Frank Carlucci, remarked, "Once he had something fixed in his mind that was the way it was." Spencer summed up public response. "The Iran-Contra thing went away awful fast. The people all thought he was guilty. He made a goddamn mistake, now let's go on."

———

IT was commonplace for Reagan's principal advisers to find the president inattentive, unfocused, and incurious, uninformed, even about current events, and notoriously loose with facts (Richard Darman said that Reagan tended "to remember only the evidence that reinforced his ideological predilections"). Whatever his shortcomings Reagan's vision of America was for him the central purpose of his presidency. As Dolan said, Reagan understood that governing is not "about meetings, conferences, phone calls, rules and decisions; ideas were the stuff of politics, . . . the great moving forces in history." Above all else, Reagan succeeded in reviving public confidence, which was at low ebb when he took the nation's helm. The Republican party today is his party. He made conservatism so popular, he forced Democrats to abandon the "liberal" label. Reagan was able to change the way Americans view government, because if he understood nothing else, he understood the importance of speechmaking to the twentieth-century president.

Nixon also recognized the power of speechmaking. But unlike Reagan, he had consistently played the leading role in the policymaking articulated in his speeches. Still, the way he eschewed writing collaborators, preferring image makers, differed markedly from the practice of his predecessors. Yet every subsequent president has followed suit to a greater or lesser degree with increasingly deleterious results.

Both presidents and their staffs created the prototype for image-age presidential speeches. Nixon's fate in particular indicates that packaging alone will not carry the day, but henceforth professional political commentators, advertising and television producers, and public relations experts will be permanent members of White House staffs. In such environments, what presidents say is calculated for its effect on their image, an ideal public persona, which is a construct determined by what pollsters say the public admires at any given moment. Presidents' public words no longer aim primarily at reflecting objective reality. Their end is virtual reality—the public presentation of an orchestrated perception.

4

THE MESSAGE IN
THE BOTTLE

Gerald Rudolph Ford   1974–1977
James Earl Carter   1977–1981
George Herbert Walker Bush   1989–1993

T HE presidents between Nixon and Reagan and Reagan's immediate successor, bore striking similarities in their approach to speechwriting. Gerald Ford, Jimmy Carter, and George Bush attached less importance to formal speechmaking than did their predecessors, but like Nixon and Reagan, they kept their writers at a distance and allowed them little involvement in policy. This separation of function and responsibility from authority led to patched-together speeches and seemingly haphazard policy.

Notwithstanding the muddied message making that their speechwriting structure engendered, the three presidents officially out-talked each and every predecessor. Gerald Ford is on record as having delivered 1,200 speeches in his two and a half years as president, which, taking into account presumably speechless weekends, works out to two public speeches a day, five days a week, during the almost thirty months that Ford occupied the Oval Office. This number does not include veto messages, proclamations, bill-signing statements, executive orders, news conferences, and the like. Jimmy Carter spoke even more frequently, so much so in fact that *Time* magazine's Hugh Sidey believed that the presidency had become diminished by his penchant to talk so frequently in public.

According to Reagan speechwriter John Podhoretz, George Bush spoke almost as much in four years as the very loquacious Ronald Reagan did in eight. And yet not one of the three uttered a word that is memorable unless one reckons Ford's "Our long national nightmare is over," Carter's "My name is Jimmy Carter and I'm still running for president," or Bush's "Read my lips: no new taxes." These statements, however, were uttered on or before the first day of their presidencies. Each of the three was liked and respected by the American people, but they were perceived as lacking a coherent message—their vision, sense of direction, agenda for the country. For all the public knew, these presidents might as well have stuffed their messages into bottles and set them adrift at sea.

GERALD Rudolph Ford took the oath of office in the East Room moments after the only president in the nation's history to resign from office lifted off in the presidential helicopter from the lawn of the White House. Ford was the only U.S. president to take office without having been elected either as president or vice president. Nixon, not the people, had chosen him as vice president after Spiro Agnew had been forced to resign to avoid indictment for accepting bribes. Acutely aware of his unusual position, Ford made the point in a few remarks after his swearing in that he had been "nominated and confirmed" by representatives of "both parties, elected by the people and acting under the Constitution in their name." To say that the nation breathed a collective sigh of relief that the "Constitution works;

our great republic is a government of laws and not of men" is to understate the surge of goodwill that flowed toward Ford on that historic day.

Speechwriter Robert Hartmann wrote these first of Ford's presidential words, just as he had written Ford's words as vice president and as minority leader of the House from 1965 until 1973. The new president appointed his longtime aide to be counselor to the president with Cabinet status. Since Hartmann continued to be in charge of Ford's speeches, it appeared that the president had repudiated Nixon's separation of writers from policy people. But in practice the same bifurcation persisted.

In the early days of the Ford administration, Hartmann drafted presidential statements as he had done in the past. But gradually he did less and less writing, concentrating on a liaison with the Republican National Committee, and farmed out speeches to the Writing and Research Department in the Old Executive Office Building. Speechwriting, headed by Paul Theis and later by Robert Orben, had six writers and thirty-five researchers and secretaries. When an assigned writer had finished a draft, he showed it to the department head, then circulated it among the staff, and finally wrote another draft or drafts incorporating suggested changes. The penultimate draft went to Hartmann, who revised or approved it and gave it to the president.

Before long, the president and his inner circle, especially staff coordinator Donald Rumsfeld, grew dissatisfied with the quality of the speeches. Hartmann found his access to the Oval Office curtailed, first by Chief of Staff General Alexander Haig, then by Rumsfeld, and finally by Richard Cheney, who had stepped into Rumsfeld's job when Rumsfeld moved to Defense. In retaliation, Hartmann boycotted senior staff meetings where policy matters were discussed. His speeches, not surprisingly, were "weak in complex areas of substance," according to Press Secretary Ron Nessen. Since Hartmann had chosen not to stay abreast of policy nuance, he could hardly help his writ-

ers, who as a matter of course were not asked to attend West
Wing policy meetings.

In a day-by-day diary kept during his two years of speechwriting for Ford, John Casserly's refrain is a complaint about
the writers' difficulties in trying to discern what exactly to
write. "Where was Hartmann while I wrote draft after draft
of the speech?" he recorded on December 10, 1974. "If he is
the president's chief of speechwriting, why didn't he sit in on
at least some of the policy discussions so he could clearly
understand differences?" Again on February 10, 1975, Casserly
wrote, "Those concerned with issues and policy, . . . such as the
speechwriting staff, receive no coordination of direction from
Rumsfeld. Since Hartmann does not attend most policy
meetings—and Rumsfeld is most aware of this—he knows it is
all the more imperative that someone offer the speechwriters
the latest guidance. Yet Rumsfeld does nothing. This is partly
because of his rivalry with Hartmann." Even on the occasions
when the writers met with Ford and Hartmann in the Oval
Office to discuss a specific speech, they got not guidance. "On
the surface, the meeting appeared to be one of substance. In
reality, the most critical decisions—what really went on in the
speeches—were made by the writers, not Hartmann or the
president, the two who would or could give but offered little
direction or real vision."

The *New Yorker* writer and novelist John Hersey spent a
week in March 1975 observing the Ford speechwriting process
at close hand, just as he had done in the Truman White House.
"I am still profoundly disturbed by what seemed to me the aim-
lessness of the speechwriting session," he wrote after sitting in
the Oval Office with the president, the writers, and Hartmann.
The usual speechwriting procedure, according to Theis, who
served primarily as department editor, included getting the
weekly schedule of speeches, making specific writing assign-
ments, circulating memos to key people, and coming up with a
list of options on how the president could handle the speech.

Then Hartmann, Theis, and on occasion the assigned writer met with the president, who made suggestions on subject matter and style but never on specific policy. To Hersey, this method of composition contrasted greatly with the process he had observed during the Truman administration. "I keep thinking . . . of a speechwriting session of Harry Truman's at which most of the principal advisers, including Dean Acheson, were present, and during which policy was really and carefully shaped through its articulation."

What developed in the Ford White House was a system of rival speech drafts. Rumsfeld and his inner circle started rewriting Hartmann's drafts. When Richard Cheney replaced Rumsfeld, he assured Hartmann that he would put a stop to "wildcat" speechwriting and short-circuiting the established procedure. Yet he hired David Gergen, whom Hartmann had fired, to provide alternative drafts. At least Cheney had asked Hartmann if he had any objection to his bringing Gergen back to the White House. "I have nothing against Gergen," Hartmann not very forthrightly replied. "Well the president told me I'd have to check with you," Cheney said. "But I assure you Gergen will have absolutely nothing to do with speeches."

After Gergen came on board, according to writer Patrick Butler, "the president spent an unusually large amount of time reviewing the details of these speeches. Usually there would be a draft from Gergen and another out of our shop. The president would review the drafts and take what he wanted. He seemed to find some way to take something from both drafts."

This competition between the president's counsel and staff coordinator, in which the two men jockeyed for influence with the president, caused the speechwriters intolerable stress, and often erupted in ongoing firings and rehirings. Hartmann, for example, discharged Butler at least three times; Cheney always rehired him. "I came to the White House when I was 25, and I had never imagined anything like the political warfare that was going on around me," Butler said. His final firing occurred on his twenty-seventh birthday on Air Force One on the way to Pittsburgh for a speech he had not written a word of. When Hartmann finished the editing, he gave it to Butler to carry to the president's airborne work box. Cheney stopped Butler to ask for the speech, since Gergen had already written the one the president would give, he said. The chief counsel spotted them talking, jumped out of his seat, and marched up to Butler. "Who do you think you're working for?" Hartmann demanded. "You," the writer answered. "Well not anymore," Hartmann barked as he strode back to his seat.

No two speeches better point up how chaotic the speechwriting process had become than the 1975 and 1976 State of the Union Addresses. The 1975 SOTU consisted of two parts: an FDR-like fireside chat that Ford delivered from the Lincoln Library on the ground floor of the White House on January 13, and the traditional SOTU before Congress on January 15.

The fireside chat consisted of a series of complex proposals for energy conservation and antirecession measures, and while not inspiring, the matter-of-fact speech was one of Ford's most successful, primarily because he had practiced using the Tele-PrompTer during the week before the speech. When Hartmann's final draft had gone on the prompter for rehearsal, Press Secretary Ron Nessen and Rumsfeld objected to its length and triteness. They persuaded Ford to let them edit it. During rehearsal they substituted new words, then phrases, next sentences, finally whole paragraphs. After three hours of the rewriting, Hartmann's draft had changed beyond recognition.

As soon as they had fixed the January 13 speech, they started in on the one for January 15. The day before delivery, Rumsfeld and his deputy, Cheney; Alan Greenspan, chairman of the Council of Economic Advisers; William Seidman, director of the White House economic policy board; Frank Zarb, energy administrator; and Nessen sat around a conference table in Rumsfeld's office for eight hours feverishly writing, rewriting, scissoring, pasting, and editing a speech draft to replace the one

Hartmann had submitted. At 9:00 P.M. everyone connected with the original and alternative speeches met with Ford. The president placed the alternative drafts in front of him. "The meeting degenerated into haggling," Nessen wrote. "Unfortunately the two factions couldn't seem to agree," the president said. "As a result I had to be the editor and I didn't approve the final version until nearly 4 A.M. It was a long, disagreeable night and a waste of my time, but it did teach me a lesson. In the future, I told Hartmann, important speeches had to be submitted to me well in advance of the scheduled delivery date." The speech was delivered at 1:00 P.M. the next day, and other than its opening, it was, as most SOTUs are, eminently forgettable.

> Twenty-six years ago, a freshman congressman, a young fellow with lots of idealism who was out to change the world, stood before Sam Rayburn in the well of the House and solemnly swore to the same oath that all of you took yesterday—an unforgettable experience, and I congratulate you all.
> Two days later, that same freshman stood at the back of this great chamber—over there someplace—as President Truman, all charged up by his single-handed election victory, reported as the Constitution requires on the state of the Union.
> When the bipartisan applause stopped, President Truman said, "I am happy to report to this 81st Congress that the state of the Union is good. . . ."
> Today, that freshman member from Michigan stands where Mr. Truman stood, and I must say to you that the state of the Union is not good.

As it turned out, Ford had not learned the right lesson. The speechwriting problems in this White House had little to do with last-minute drafting and everything to do with a lack of firmness on the president's part. This speech "exposed a serious weakness in the Ford White House organization," Ron Nessen said. "More distressingly it exposed Ford's unwillingness to get tough with his staff, to demand a better speechwriting operation and less infighting." Because nothing changed, the SOTU preparation process ran no more smoothly in 1976 than in 1975. "So long as words were my responsibility," Hartmann determined, "I resolved to get assurance from the president before going into the 1976 speechmaking marathon that I had the necessary authority to do the job." Accordingly, Ford announced in January that Hartmann was in charge of the 1976 SOTU, though, Hartman said, "hardly as emphatically as I'd hoped."

Hartmann and eight senior White House staffers closeted themselves in a hideaway in Williamsburg, Virginia, for two days of serious speech drafting. "It became clear," Hartmann noted, "that new sedition was brewing. Half the participants made it obvious that they were not there to draft a good speech but to prevent mine from being drafted."

Disappointed and disgruntled, the group returned to Washington, where Hartmann and one of his writers worked alone. The finished speech got to Ford twenty minutes before deadline on Thursday January 15, four days before the president would deliver the address. On Friday Greenspan, Cheney, and Gergen, who had drafted his own speech, confronted Ford and implored him to drop the laundry list of promises that Hartmann had developed and to make a philosophic statement to give the administration a clearer direction. Instead, the president dictated a third draft to his secretary, consisting of what he liked best in Hartmann's and Gergen's drafts. Friday morning he summoned Hartmann, who skimmed through Ford's version, pleased that his draft had pretty much survived. Ford told him to "go through theirs once more and see if I missed anything good that can be incorporated into ours. But I'm satisfied this is about 99% done, and I don't want a lot more changes. We'll have a final meeting Saturday afternoon."

Everyone who had had a hand in the writing assembled in the Cabinet Room on Saturday January 17 at 3:00 P.M. When Hartmann arrived and found all the Cheney people in attendance, he asked to have his own people present too. Ford agreed, so Hartmann sent for writers Milton Friedman, Robert Orben, and Patrick Butler. A three-hour attack on the draft began. Only Hartmann, the president, and possibly Cheney knew that the president himself had drafted the version that was being eviscerated. At 6:00 P.M. the president uncharacteristically exploded. With his left hand he struck the heavy conference table so hard it shook. "God damn it," he said. "I've had enough, and it's time to finish this thing." He ordered everyone to stay until an acceptable speech was ready, directed Hartman to have a final draft ready by noon Sunday, and left for the family quarters.

Kathy Wooten of Speechwriting had typed most of the SOTU drafts. Present at the Saturday meeting, she carried news of the president's rare temper tantrum to her fellow workers. "He thought they had done all their fighting at Williamsburg when they were there," she reported the president as saying. "Why were they coming to him less than three days before the speech, fighting about major points . . . when they should be discussing the fine points?" The wrangling continued right up to the day of delivery. "Most of the people in the West Wing who have seen it don't like it. They've been changing it. And the speech is tonight. It's crazy, crazy."

The *New York Times* called the speech pedestrian: "It was difficult to find a new or inspiring thought in the president's message." The speechwriters pronounced it the worst SOTU in recent memory. The internal strife made all the newspapers, since both sides in the dispute leaked their version of events.

Conceding concern about Ford's easygoing style—he is "too nice a guy"—Hartmann really blamed Nixon holdovers for the president's "serious administrative difficulties." A Ford loyalist through and through, he believed the Praetorians, as he called members of the Nixon staff who had remained in the Ford administration, were decidedly disloyal. If he was right, Ford had missed the perfect opportunity to clean house without rancor or ill will. The considerable goodwill that he had accrued in the first month in office abruptly dissipated on that September 8, 1974, when he announced "a full, free, and absolute pardon unto Richard Nixon." Many people suspected that a deal had been worked out with Nixon before his resignation, seriously damaging Ford's reputation for honesty and fairness. Had he fired all of Nixon's remaining aides at the same time, he might have enhanced his credibility. But since Ford did not share Hartmann's view concerning the Nixon people and suspected him of "stirring the pot," he saw no need to fire them.

It probably would have surprised Hartmann that his speech rival, too, thought Ford should have cleaned house. Gergen told an interviewer that Ford would have probably fared better managerially if he had retained Nixon's highly centralized style—whereby all work filtered through a chief of staff before reaching the chief—and fired the Nixon holdovers. Ford preferred the more collegial spokes-of-the-wheel style of management, even to the detail of titles. Chief of staff became staff coordinator under this president, for example, and Nixon's former staffers pervaded the West Wing and the Old Executive Office Building.

The infighting between the Praetorians and the Ford men continued. Even so, it is odd that Hartmann did not better organize his own speech process. He understood perfectly well that writing is thinking. A presidential speech, he said on more than one occasion, "is not merely a formal announcement of matters that have been internally debated and decided. The drafting of the document is the debate and the text the president finally accepts is the decision. That makes the writer more than a good wordsmith. . . . It puts him at the vortex of every top-level policy storm." But his writers were nowhere near the vortex of policy, and, owing to his refusal to attend inner-circle staff meetings, neither was he much of the time.

Ford writers sometimes became catalysts for policy by default. As Nixon, Ford, and Reagan writer Aram Bakshian explained, "The word will come down that the president wants to talk about a particular policy area. But the policy may not be ready yet and the apparatus may not be ready to move yet, with the result that you are very often reduced to saying, 'Well, let's give them at least five things we're doing about this.' So you end up with this itemized list of new initiatives which will sometimes take on a life of their own that they wouldn't have had otherwise."

A good example of such inadvertent policymaking is Ford's Commencement Address at Ohio State University on August 30, 1974. Ford told Hartmann that he wanted to talk about setting up a collaboration between the world of work and the academic world. "Kids in college keep complaining that their education is irrelevant," he said. "At the bottom of their gripes they mean that what they're required to master on the campus has little or nothing to do with getting a job." Hartmann passed the president's instructions to the Speechwriting Office, which produced the speech. At noon on the thirtieth, Ford stood in Columbus before the graduating class and proclaimed there will be "new ways to bring the world of work and the institutions of education closer together. There will be grants for state and local initiatives," he promised. According to Paul H. O'Neill, the deputy director of the Office of Management and Budget, before the president had gotten back to Washington, the media began "ringing the telephone off the wall at the OMB and the White House, wanting to know the details of this 'cooperative education program.'" Since O'Neill was the resident expert in human resources and community development programs, his telephone was the busiest. "What did he mean by that?" "How much money is available?" O'Neill had no idea, never having heard of a business–academic partnership such as the one the president described.

"I went banging around in the Executive Office Building trying to find out where this had come from," he said. Did the White House domestic policy staff know? They did not. Could the Council of Economic Advisers tell him? It was news to them. Finally O'Neill discovered that the promises got started in Speechwriting. A wordsmith even admitted that "we made it up."

"How and why are speechwriters given so much latitude?" Casserly asked, and immediately answered his own question. "We are simply told to write a speech for this conference or that annual meeting. Some speeches are obvious—the economy or energy. But even then, we must choose our own thrust for the speech, what to stress and what not to. We desperately need more and clearer direction." They did indeed, but they never got it, not from Hartmann, not from Rumsfeld or Cheney, and not in their meetings with Ford.

In the self-imposed absence of Hartmann, the head writer or the assigned writer should have been welcomed at appropriate West Wing staff meetings. Had a writer participated in the decision-making process, it is possible a central theme might have emerged from Ford's voracious speechmaking. "Ford made so many speeches," Theis said, "his message got diffused." His speeches lacked coherence, largely from a "lack of anything to say," explained speechwriter John Coyne. The other writers concurred.

Ford will be remembered not for his clear vision of the United States. But his cloudy message notwithstanding, he will be remembered as an open president who asked questions and listened to all viewpoints, as a people-person who knew government inside out, as a man of sound judgment who was never divisive or confrontational, and as a president of integrity. Despite having inherited the constitutional crisis triggered by the Watergate scandal, the waning days of the Vietnam War, very high interest rates, and inflation coupled with a recession, he restored faith in the Oval Office. But like Nixon, he used writers who were wordsmiths instead of senior aides. Unlike Nixon, he extended little control over the speechwriting process or the product. Had he handled the rhetorical presidency more astutely, he might have been granted a second term.

IN a statement applicable to all modern presidents and those who write for them, James Earl Carter's speechwriter Hendrik Hertzberg wrote: "The speechwriter's very existence is an affront to the politician, because it intimates that the politician is too lazy or too stupid to decide for himself what he is going to say. A retinue of secretaries and bodyguards and advance men and special assistants adds to a politician's glory, because those people are an outward sign of the politician's power and importance. . . . [But] the politician does not seem bigger or grander because he has a speechwriter."

Of all recent presidents, Jimmy Carter appears to have been the most uncomfortable with the idea of using speechwriters. Never having had one until his presidential campaign, and then not until after the Iowa caucuses, he had difficulty with his writers. Robert Shrum quit after one week. Patrick Anderson, who stuck it out until the inauguration, left disillusioned. Years later, Anderson wrote a book about his experience, in which he described how the candidate warned "the audience [whenever] he was going to read something his staff had prepared. Deep in his heart," Anderson explained, "he probably thought Kennedyesque rhetoric was frivolous and possibly sinful."

Hertzberg said that "anything that smacked of calculation" Carter mistrusted. Shortly after Gerald Rafshoon joined the White House staff on July 1, 1978, as communications assistant to the president, he decided to dramatize Carter's feat in having eliminated 5,000 regulations of the Occupational Safety and Health Administration. He assembled a great stack of paper on the table in the Cabinet Room and called in the press. But Carter undercut the drama by his literal explanation: "We've gotten rid of 5,000 OSHA regulations. This stack of paper here is just a prop prepared by my staff. It isn't actually the regulations, it is just a stack of paper the same size as these regulations. It's supposed to symbolize the number of regulations."

Not surprisingly, Carter rarely worked directly with the people who wrote his speeches. He kept his writers at such a distance, in fact, that they were all but invisible to him. James Fallows, for two and a half years the chief speechwriter, sent memo after memo to Rafshoon seeking guidance from the president. "In all but the most unusual cases, we end up working in the dark, without any clear instructions about what he wants his speech to say." One of Fallows's writers, Caryl Connor, made the point that "ghostwriting is an esoteric art, requiring psychological transference as well as subject matter expertise. I can't get into the head of Jimmy Carter because I've never met Jimmy Carter. The isolation of writers in this White House—never sitting in on policy discussions, no conference with the president—is like writing in a vacuum."

Hertzberg complained that "there was always somebody who had access to Carter about speeches, but it was almost never the person who actually wrote the speech. . . . We had too many layers between us and the president." Carter "was surrounded by non-writers," writer Achsah Nesmith complained. "I think that's an essential difference from Kennedy and Roosevelt who had close to them, even when they weren't writing, people who understood the business of writing and why it was so important to have access. When we would be writing a speech about a decision and we would want to find out what Carter had rejected because that's just as important . . . in the structure of the speech. . . . That was considered something that we had no business knowing. Why would you want to know that," the nonwriters repeatedly asked. Writer Gordon Stewart was not so sure even access would help. Carter terminated meetings, Stewart observed, "by closing his briefing materials, standing up and saying 'Thank-you,' and leaving. People would look at each other and they would have no idea" of what the president thought about a particular issue. Like Richard Nixon, Jimmy Carter listened to counsel, kept his views to himself, and came to a decision by himself.

Hertzberg believed access to the president was essential. Based on his experience in writing Carter's speech for the dedication ceremonies of the Kennedy Library on October 20, 1979—"one of the few that was done the way speechwriting ought to be done." In this case the solitary decision maker worked collaboratively with Hertzberg. The writer began by sending the president a long memo outlining his ideas. Next he scheduled a meeting with the president. Among other points, he asked Carter how he had heard about Kennedy's assassination, and this story became one of the "more powerful parts of that speech," Hertzberg later said.

> On that November day, almost 16 years ago, a terrible moment was frozen in the lives of many of us here. I remember that I climbed down from the seat of a tractor, unhooked a farm trailer, and walked into my warehouse to weigh a load of grain. I was told by a group of farmers that the President had been shot. I went outside, knelt on the steps, and began to pray. In a few minutes, I learned that he had not lived. It was a grievous personal loss—my President. I wept openly for the first time in more than 10 years—for the first time since my own father died.
>
> People wept in Boston and in Paris and in Atlanta and in Warsaw, in San Francisco and in New Delhi. More than anyone had realized before that day, the spirit of this young American president had taken hold of the hearts and the imaginations of countless millions of people all over the world.

Hertzberg wrote a draft and sent it "through all the heavy thinkers around the White House for their comments." He incorporated their ideas and words into an annotated draft "with footnotes and brackets which explained arguments for saying something or not saying it and who was on what side." Carter chose what he liked, and once again Hertzberg met with the president for another session. Hertzberg then wrote the final draft.

The speech is a standout for eloquence and content; it is one of the best in the large corpus of the president's public papers. Carter was going up there to the lion's den to take on "not just Ted Kennedy," as Hertzberg put it, "but the whole universe of Kennedys in this shrine to honor Kennedy, and it was important to him." Its composition depended on the close collaboration of speaker and writer.

Unfortunately, such cooperative writing between the president and writer was "really quite unusual," Hertzberg said. More typical of the writers' experience was their drafting of the Panama Canal Speech. "We've been asked to get up a speech on the canal treaties," one of the writers told a *Washington Post* reporter late in 1977. "We've given them many drafts. But nothing has happened. Is one of them going to be given or not? And when?" When the reporter mentioned that he had just come from speaking to Chief of Staff Hamilton Jordan about Panama, another writer asked, "You actually spoke to him? Then you know more than we do." Yet the transfer to Panama of control over the canal was the centerpiece of Carter's Latin American policy.

During 1977, Carter had spoken frequently about the canal but never to the country on national television. The two Panama Canal treaties were signed in September 1977, one providing for joint U.S.–Panamanian control in the year 2000. Carter had set his speechwriting staff in motion six weeks before the signing of the final negotiations. By August 22, speechwriters Jerry Doolittle, Joe Aragon, and Landon Butler had generated sets of questions and answers to coordinate the president's positions on the issue for his press conference the next day. Fallows wrote a fireside chat for Carter that basically answered all of the New Right's objections. But it was not delivered. This is the speech the writers groused about to the *Post* reporter.

Not until January 25, 1978, was the fireside chat revised by Fallows, with input from the president and Press Secretary Jody Powell. It was to be short, ten to fifteen minutes, but Carter's proposed outline had listed twenty-eight major and minor points. In discussion, the three men managed to think of thirteen additional points. This left Fallows in an impossible situation: There was no time for an introduction or a conclusion, and only fifteen seconds for each point. Of necessity, the speech grew to twenty-three minutes. When Carter delivered it on February 1, he presented only "the facts," but his insistence on disseminating facts in speeches—often with every maybe, but, if, perhaps, in this circumstance included—left listeners bored. This was quite a contrast to the tactics of the New Right, led by Congressman Philip Crane and former governor of California Ronald Reagan, which succeeded in whipping up opposition by dramatizing the controversy. In the end, the treaties were ratified by the Senate but at great political cost to Carter and political gain to the Right and Ronald Reagan.

Carter's compulsive listing of facts shows up in speech after speech. His third energy address on April 5, 1979, is a typical example. Hertzberg, who had managed to gain some access when he was lead writer, sat in on three of the numerous energy meetings. The first of his three, on March 29, included the president and the administration's energy experts. Each attendee had considered a memo that had been prepared beforehand with the details of existing policy and possible remedies for the present energy crisis, caused by the nation's dependence on oil from an increasingly unstable Middle East, especially Iran. From these details, the president and his advisers were to forge a decision. What struck Hertzberg as startling about the meeting was what it revealed about Carter's decision-making style. The president told everyone that "he just took the decision memo off alone up at Camp David, and checked things off 'almost arbitrarily.' What an extraordinary admission!" Hertzberg wrote in his diary. And then Hertzberg described what happened when the participants started discussing a proposal to lengthen the time during which the amount of lead in gasoline had to be gradually eliminated.

Schlesinger [secretary of energy] was disparaging an EPA as-
sertion about the health damage of lead in the atmosphere,
saying it was cooked up in a hurry, based on subjective interpretation of unreliable statistics, ignored other variables, etc.
Kitty Schirmer [domestic policy staff member], bless her,
jumped in to say, "That's simply wrong, Jim," and to say that
the EPA study was indeed reliable, was not cooked up in a
hurry but had been in the works for a long time, etc. Carter
jumped in to say, "I think you're both right." The disagreement just sort of disappeared. It was never resolved. . . . It just
got kind of quashed. This quality of Carter's obviously has
what lawyers call a chilling effect on disagreements in meetings and on the expression of strong views in general.

Immediately after the meeting Hertzberg talked to Gerald
Rafshoon, whose department oversaw speechwriting, about the
content of the speech and then drew up an outline, which he
sent to the president. Carter made a few changes and returned
it to Hertzberg, who wrote a first draft, working all through
one night and the weekend. Copies went to the president Sunday night. By Monday morning the president had sent it back
to Rafshoon complaining that it "was one of the worst speeches
I've ever seen. No one will listen except the Mobil p.r. man.
List what we want to say. . . . Then say it plainly and bluntly."
Rafshoon told Hertzberg to rewrite. At 2:30 P.M. Rafshoon sent
the president the rewritten draft and assembled twenty to thirty
energy experts in domestic adviser Stuart Eizenstat's office, but
not Hertzberg, to go over the amended draft word for word.
Using their confused edits, Hertzberg rewrote the speech again.
Carter made final edits.

On April 5, 1979, Carter delivered his third energy address
to the nation. In this speech he proposed additional conservation measures like a phased-in decontrol of oil prices and a
windfall-profits tax on oil companies with the tax to go to an
energy security fund for low-income families, public transportation, and development of additional energy supplies, all sensi-

ble and necessary proposals. But with his penchant for lists—"I just turn 30 or 35 different items in my mind [listing] the points I want to make, just like an engineer," the president admitted—Carter did not stop there. He added dozens of companion measures to conserve energy, including picayune measures like asking citizens to drive fifteen miles less a week and to use woodburning stoves. Overlong and repetitious, the speech was flat, even after Rosalyn Carter had persuaded her husband to cut much of the technical language.

"At best," as the president himself said, "there was a cool reception to these ideas." Thirty million Americans heard the speech, a considerable decrease from his first speech to the nation, which had attracted eighty million listeners. Had Hertzberg had more central control in the sense of serving as the conduit at every point for the president and the energy people, the likely result would have been a more orderly, coherent message. As it happened, Congress and the people more or less ignored it.

"A model for how a speechwriter should behave if he wants to be a player in policy," Hertzberg explained, was Gordon Stewart, who went so far as to insist on being made deputy chief speechwriter. "I wanted the title," he said, "because it made it a little easier to go into the tent with some of these policy people and use a little bit of clout, and try to learn their subject matter." When Stewart had mastered "allocation charts" in energy matters and knew "entitlements as well as they did, they'd finally listen." He had "literally crashed every party," Hertzberg said. Today Stewart remembers that it was the April 5 speech that had impelled him to start forcing his way into meetings in order to get involved in the policy process.

Forcing one's way "in" notwithstanding, the writers still had to deal with Carter's pronounced proclivity toward cataloging every detail, even those that fit his subject only peripherally. After his retirement from *Time* magazine, Hedley Donovan served as speech adviser to the president, and while he marveled at Carter's quickness in soaking up masses of material, the more technical the better, he noted that his boss often put sets of facts together that did not fit together. He apparently made little effort to interpret the meaning of the facts he had gathered. Fallows, too, complained that Carter cut out explanatory portions of a draft and added meat by listing facts with no concern about their order or hierarchy. Just before giving a speech in Houston that defended his energy policy, he sent two lists to the writers and told them to restructure the supposedly finalized speech. The first enumerated ten proposals for "what we will do," including develop a "defense capability second to none," fight inflation, balance budget, cut taxes, reform welfare and civil service, impose a "Turkey arms embargo," and a few others that had at best a borderline relationship with his energy policy. Donovan also noted Carter's habit of placing ideas that were in conflict together in a single speech. He regularly fused contradictions and tried to reconcile opposites rhetorically. Carter's address on Soviet-U.S. relations at the U.S. Naval Academy on June 7, 1978, is a good example.

Major differences between the conciliatory secretary of state Cyrus Vance and the hard-line national security adviser Zbigniew Brzezinski had elicited much comment in the press in the months preceding the address. Vance had urged the president to give a speech to set the record straight on precisely how the administration meant to deal with the Kremlin leaders. In a May 10 memo Fallows asked the president what subject he had in mind for the upcoming Naval Academy speech and suggested the role of the military in light of its flagging morale as a result of the U.S. defeat in Vietnam. "No. See Zbig: my opening statement to the JCS [Joint Chiefs of Staff] yesterday at lunch," Carter responded. "Strength of U.S.—regional alliances— MIL/POL/Econ interrelated also above theme [i.e., Fallows's idea] can be included. List many individual ideas and items and then see me."

Fallows had already instructed his writers to solicit advice for the address from various outside experts like George Kennan and George Ball, and from the inside inner circle, including Vance and Brzezinski. He submitted a list to the president that comprised the best of these comments, a quotation from a speech Woodrow Wilson had delivered at Annapolis, comments from military experts, and an outline. Carter retired to Camp David on the first weekend in June. He wrote out by hand a list of points he wanted to make, his outline for the speech, and the speech itself on thirty-six pages of a yellow legal pad, which can now be examined in his presidential library in Atlanta. When Carter had finished, he called for a Sunday evening meeting of his senior foreign policy advisers. Each got a copy of the not-yet-typed speech. He asked them to look it over carefully and incorporate changes they thought necessary, and he left. No speechwriter was present for the editing.

Two days later, the day before Carter went to Annapolis, the same group met again with the addition of the president, Press Secretary Jody Powell, and communications head Gerald Rafshoon, but again no speechwriter. Granted, first Powell and later Rafshoon were responsible for the Speechwriting Office, but neither wrote speeches. Rafshoon, the writers contended, was not even verbal. They doubted he ever read the speeches they submitted to him as their intermediary to the president. Rafshoon's expertise was the visual, the image, television.

At both meetings a consensus developed about the content of the speech. Not until the end of the process did the speechwriters get the speech in order to make stylistic improvements. They also shortened the rambling comparison of the Soviet and U.S. navies. Carter looked at it once more, got it typed, and left for Annapolis.

The speech as delivered was basically the one he had composed at Camp David with certain emphases added by Vance and Brzezinski. Its thrust can be summed up in one of its closing lines: "The Soviets can choose either confrontation or cooperation. The United States is adequately prepared to meet either choice."

Reaction to the speech was mixed, but many commentators felt the president had still not clarified U.S. policy. In fact Rafshoon in a briefing for a press conference two days later proposed possible questions Carter would face from reporters.

A couple of days after your speech at Annapolis you received a letter from members of the House International Relations Committee asking for an explanation of U.S. policy toward the Soviet Union and asking you to send Secretary of State Vance or whoever could best articulate U.S. policy to explain it to them. Isn't the letter an indication that your speech failed to clarify U.S. policy? How will you respond to the committee and to others who remain confused about exactly where your administration is headed in this area?

Which way do you see U.S.-Soviet relationship going, and what are you doing to ensure that it moves in the direction of cooperation, not confrontation?

Don't you have an increasing problem with coordinating the more dovish State Department with the hawkish NSC? Do you lean more heavily on the advice of Dr. Brzezinski or Secretary Vance? Who's ahead?

Neither was ahead with the president. He listened to both advisers. Hertzberg speculated that perhaps the gap between their views was a mechanism for Carter for making foreign policy. He was in charge and would not "be shackled by one or the other," Hertzberg suggested. "Unlike other presidents," historian Robert Strong wrote, "he was unwilling to present himself or his policies in simplified terms," even presumably when too much detail sacrificed clarity in his speeches. The writers, who edited the final version, scrawled on a worksheet, "trying to reconcile too many views." Greg Schneiders, Rafshoon's assistant in matters of public perception, concurred.

In a memo to his boss he wrote, "I think it will reinforce a sense of confusion, internal conflict, and inconsistency."

Vance agreed with the writers. In his memoir, *Hard Choices,* he made his displeasure with the speech abundantly clear.

> I sent him a draft of a speech that emphasized the complex need for lowering political tensions on a reciprocal basis. Brzezinski also gave him a more confrontational draft. Carter drew from both, splitting the difference between the two poles of advice he was receiving. The end result was a stitched-together speech. Instead of combating the growing perception of an administration rent by internal divisions, the image of an inconsistent and uncertain government was underlined.

After Fallows left the White House to become *Atlantic Monthly*'s Washington editor in early 1979, he wrote a lengthy two-part article for the magazine, using the Annapolis speech as an illustration of what Hertzberg would call Jimmy Carter's "instinct for harmony, for immediately forcing conflicts out of existence." As Hertzberg recorded in his diary about another big speech, Carter's "immediate response to a disagreement is not to sharpen it, so as to make it the occasion for illuminating debate, but to smooth it over as soon as it rears its head." Because Fallows's articles had appeared in April and May 1979, while Carter was still president, White House insiders cried foul. It was a betrayal of the man he had worked for, they claimed. "We all have to make a living" was Carter's only public response. Hertzberg, who replaced Fallows as head speechwriter, called the articles "excellent. No kiss and tell stuff; just very persuasive descriptions of what's wrong with the way Carter goes about being president." Fallows accurately identified the president's persistent failure "to project a vision larger than the problem he is tackling at the moment," which resulted in an inability to "explain what he is doing." Hertzberg's diary entry expresses the "hope that the inner circle will respond to [Fallows's articles] constructively, but I doubt that they will."

Indicating that the inner circle had not taken Fallows's remarks constructively, a similar sense of confusion prevailed after Carter's most famous speech, Energy and National Goals (the so-called Malaise Speech), delivered on July 15, 1979. By the summer of 1979, inflation had climbed into double-digit figures. Gasoline shortages caused long lines at service stations, and prices for gasoline had greatly increased; Carter's approval rating had dropped to 26 percent. Stuart Eizenstat urged the president to talk to the nation.

In order to get a draft ready for Carter to take to Camp David, where he was spending the midweek Fourth of July holiday, Gordon Stewart worked through the weekend, including all night Sunday, but as hard as he tried, he could not come up with something that pleased him. Before leaving Washington for the Hamptons and his own Independence Day break, he dispatched the draft to the president with a note in which he practically begged him not to deliver the speech on July 5 as scheduled. "This is the best I can do going down the old road. I don't think there's any point to it. There's nothing you have not said in your previous three energy speeches." Carter apparently agreed, because on the Fourth he abruptly canceled the next day's speech with no public explanation. Instead he summoned more than 100 leaders from all walks of life to Camp David to confer with him about what to do. During the final week of meetings, Hertzberg and Stewart went up to the mountain retreat to write the speech, which by this time had been scheduled for July 15.

Although the writers were not present at the meetings, they got secondhand reports from pollster Pat Caddell. "We were seeing and hearing some of the weirdest things I've ever encountered," Hertzberg told an interviewer. They heard about the fights that raged between those who felt the speech should be a strong energy speech and nothing else and those who felt the real trouble was a crisis of confidence in the country, an idea Caddell had been pushing since the beginning of the administration. Carter, true to nature, decided to do both, without worrying about how to reconcile the two points of view and give them some kind of coherence. During one of Hertzberg's and Stewart's all-night sessions, a sort of synthesis was effected. "I don't know when it happened," Stewart said. "There was a way in which . . . these two things [could] be put together in a causal relationship with each other. The idea of one being a solution to the other popped up, . . . but that gave us [part] of the speech and then the president gave us the rest when he did the opening."

The speech began with nineteen quotations from the 100-plus Camp David conferees that added up to a mea culpa on the president's part. He accepted part of the blame for the crisis in confidence. Then he proceeded to the general crisis in self-confidence and trust that he perceived in the nation, saying he looked to the people to solve the crisis. The crisis-in-confidence portion of the speech took four-fifths of the thirty-two minutes of delivery time. Ostensibly an energy speech, only the last fifth addressed energy. In it, Carter listed six *new* points to go along with his previously enunciated points and said he would spell out details the next day. The alleged synthesis rested on seeing energy as a way to start solving the country's problems. In other words, the president seemed to be saying that the way to regain national confidence was to solve the energy problem.

The crisis-in-confidence part of the speech and the energy crisis should have been two separate speeches. Despite the illogic of combining them, the July 15 energy speech was a resounding success with the public. Carter gave the promised details of his energy plan in Kansas City and in Detroit the next day, and both speeches were well received. Carter's polls showed a rise of nearly a dozen points. Then suddenly, on Tuesday afternoon, July 17, immediately after the stock exchange closed for the day, Jody Powell announced to the press that *all* the Cabinet officers had offered the president their asked-for resignations, and immediately following that, eighteen of Carter's senior White House assistants also "offered" to resign. No explanation was given for what Hertzberg had called a political Jonestown, not even to the two lead writers. The Sunday speech was forgotten, and Carter's public-approval rating dropped lower than it had been before the speech. The Cabinet purge had been Carter's idea, but his timing was atrocious. "I was dumbfounded," Stewart said. Had he fired his energy secretary, for instance, symbolically that would have made sense to the country.

Speeches that list disparate items and combine irreconcilable ideas without a unifying theme have little chance to win over the public for the simple reason it cannot understand what the policies are. The speechwriters tried to forge a unifying theme in the sense of defining "Carterism," what the administration stood for, but with twenty-five speeches a week to turn out in a department a third the size of Ford's, they had too little time. Still, they tried to figure out a way to bring Carter's various programs together under one rubric like New Deal or New Frontier, to give coherence to Carter's message. There had been fitful attempts to introduce slogans, but Carter did not like slogans. Even so, he had spoken of a "new spirit" in his Inaugural Address, but it went nowhere. "Every reforming president of this century has adopted a brief, evocative phrase summarizing his program or approach," Hertzberg had written in a memo to Fallows. In nine single-spaced pages he argued that the idea of a "beloved community" summed up the administration's theme and encapsulated its noblest impulses, and was true to President Carter's own personality, background, and beliefs. It never caught on. Two years later "new foundation" did, but only for a short time.

The 1979 State of the Union, the New Foundation Speech, is one in which the writers, in this case Hertzberg, succeeded in ordering a series of hierarchies that could create a relationship among Carter's programs. From the beginning ("Tonight I want to examine in a broad sense the state of our American Union—how we are building a new foundation for a peaceful and prosperous world"), to the eleven additional mentions of "new foundation," there was no mistaking the administration's chosen theme. This administration is "laying a new foundation for dealing with problems, domestic and foreign, in the 1980s and beyond," Rafshoon announced, lest anyone miss the thrust.

Asked to give his ideas about this theme, Theodore Sorensen had suggested "new pathways" instead of new foundation, a term that begged for ridicule, sounding as it did "like Macy's bra and girdle sale." But ridicule, Hertzberg had insisted, was a sure sign a slogan was a success. Predictably, political cartoons appeared the next day in the nation's newspapers; Johnny Carson's monologues on the *Tonight Show* were full of new foundations; the comic strip Doonesbury featured it; and a few commentators made fun of it. William Safire, who had learned of the new theme from Hertzberg the day before the speech, praised it. But the popularizing of new foundation stopped dead in its tracks when the president held his first press conference after the speech. Asked if new foundation was his idea of the theme of the administration, Carter answered negatively, adding it was just something in his speech. Writer Christopher Matthews said it was another case in which the president "would be willing," if the press and the public picked it up and used it, "but he didn't want to have his fingerprints on it. He didn't want to say, 'here I am saying what the theme of my administration is.' "

Carter was blamed for the energy crisis, recession, high interest rates, and inflation, but he did not create these problems and they were probably beyond his or any other president's control. At the same time, he got little credit for the Camp David agreements, his human rights policy in foreign affairs, the Panama Canal treaties, the normalization of relations with

China, and his recognition of the constraints imposed by a maturing welfare state. His rhetorical miscues fostered the belief that he was not in control of his presidency. Part of the problem was that he did not communicate clear priorities.

Preachy, disjointed, poorly delivered—he had flatly refused a voice coach—Carter talked himself out of the White House in one term just as surely as he had talked himself in. He may have aspired to be a teaching president, but his efforts to educate the American public fell short, mainly because he did not maintain a collaboration with his writers. Had he given at least one of his highly talented writers continual access and the mandate to act as a Sorensen or a McPherson, he likely would have constructed more convincing, focused speeches and, perhaps, policies to match.

—

ALTHOUGH George Herbert Walker Bush had been elected as Reagan's heir, he lacked his predecessor's driving vision. "The fox knows many things, but the hedgehog knows one big thing," the British philosopher Isaiah Berlin wrote long ago. Clearly Reagan knew the one big thing about the twentieth-century presidency, namely, that speeches are its heart and soul. By his own admission, George Bush was a fox, seeing speeches as only one piece among many—press conferences, trips, presidential appearances, personal diplomacy, written statements, and the like—to create a mosaic of a presidency. In that mosaic, speechmaking was a low priority. As a result, Bush never articulated a vision of the future direction of the country.

No recent president, not even Ford or Carter, had so poor a working relationship with his speechwriters as Bush. Very early in the administration, and acting on Chief of Staff John Sununu's orders, David Demarest, the communications director whose office was responsible for speechwriting, cut the writers' pay, moved them to less grand offices than those speechwriters from other administrations had been accustomed to, turned to outside writers like Peggy Noonan, Nixon writer Raymond Price, media consultant Roger Ailes, and former Ford writer Craig Smith, and worst of all, stripped them of White House Mess privileges. "Mess privileges were, next to access to the president, the *ne plus ultra* of White House status," said Reagan's budget director David Stockman. Like an executive dining room, the White House Mess "was a collegial thing," Carter writer Chris Matthews said. "Lunch was the one time of day when you actually met everyone else. Everybody who worked in policy would come together at that one round table and eat lunch and that's how you really got your collegial feel of the place." It was also how increasingly isolated speechwriters learned what policy matters were being discussed.

The demoralized Bush writers asked Demarest what their downgrading meant. "There certainly wasn't any attempt to look at the writers per se and downgrade them," he replied disingenuously, and then gratuitously added an insult. "Only 'commissioned officers'—assistants, deputy assistants, and special assistants—are given Mess privileges and speechwriters no longer hold these titles because of budget constraints." Quite naturally, the writers interpreted their situation as a symbolic rebuke to the power of rhetoric. "In terms of political pecking order," Peggy Noonan observed of the Bush writers, "they're just above the people who clean up after Millie." As if Demarest, who had hired the five writers from other executive branch departments, had not made the writers' status abundantly clear, he announced that "speeches are a less important form of communication for Bush than they were for Reagan or for many other presidents."

According to political journalist Sidney Blumenthal, Bush had no regard for Reagan's speechmaking skill, and even considered it a form of "legerdemain." He took pains to distance himself from Reagan's stagecraft. Speechwriter Andrew Ferguson said Bush "cut anything from his speeches that put him in his predecessor's shadow." Safire claimed that Bush was "fearful of comparison with Reagan's speechifying and instead shows off his ad-libbing advantage over his predecessor—perversely boasting of his inadequate speech delivery." Like Carter, Bush disdained rehearsal or coaching, despite his nonstop public talking. Unlike Reagan, Bush liked reporters, frequently appearing unexpectedly in the White House Briefing Room to hold unannounced and informal press conferences.

Mismanagement of the Speechwriting Office made rhetorical matters worse. The turnover of writers and even head writers was rapid. When Samuel Skinner replaced Sununu as chief of staff, he moved head writer Tony Snow to media affairs and put in Communications Director Demarest, not a writer, as head of the department. Then he turned the Speechwriting Office over to Press Secretary Marlin Fitzwater, a man who shared Bush's view about the unimportance of formal speeches from the Oval Office. Finally, in the summer of 1992, in the middle of a presidential campaign, Skinner hired a new communications director who also doubled as head speechwriter.

Steven Provost had come to the White House from his position as spokesman for Kentucky Fried Chicken. "This is absolutely ludicrous," an insider told a reporter. "I am sure the guy is fine, maybe great in what he does, but this is a presidential campaign. This is a crisis. You don't go out and get a guy who's never laid eyes on the president or tried to maneuver through the horrible White House bureaucracy to be your chief speechwriter and communications director. It is totally ridiculous." Right or not for the position, Provost soon showed himself to be in charge. Less than a month on the job, he fired four of the five writers. Before too long, Provost was out. After Bush persuaded Secretary of State James Baker to resign from that post and to replace Skinner as chief of staff, Baker installed his deputy, Robert Zoellnick, over Provost in writing and Margaret Tutwiler as head of communications.

In a department as unsettled as this one, the drafting process necessarily suffered. Typically, a speech started with the writers who turned out a draft. Then Richard Darman, who as budget director wielded real power in the administration, rewrote it. "We'd be sold on an idea," speechwriter Mark Davis said, "and write an energized draft. Fitzwater would promote it, Darman would gut it, and it would be a mess. This became the pattern for every speech on domestic issues." If it was a foreign affairs speech, National Security Adviser Brent Scowcroft had it re-written, after which an ad hoc committee worked on it. When the president got it, he "took out the red meat," the writers complained. In the end, they tried to edit the drafts into some kind of coherence. "And then you ask why it doesn't sing," a disgruntled writer said of the final product.

Bush's speeches were mediocre at best. Their shapelessness symptomized the president's policy drift. He seemed unable to figure out what he wanted his administration to accomplish and repeatedly acknowledged his difficulty with the "vision-thing." When Snow had been hired early in 1991, alliteration-addicted Safire advised him that "the rhetorical trick is divining the drift and declaiming the direction." The president blamed his writers for not having "initiatives to present to the public." But it was the president who never forged an agenda.

He hopscotched from one issue to another—drugs one day, the deficit the next, education the third day. Because he ap-peared to stand for nothing, he offended those who cared deeply about something, especially the Reaganites. One of Reagan's former writers called Bush's a " 'split the difference' presidency." The Bush writers were far more conservative than the man they wrote for. "We'd send him stuff that was more right wing than he wanted to say," according to Ferguson. "Bush would say—well, I don't want to say this, but then I don't know what I want to say."

It is not surprising that Bush would have had trouble telling the writers what to say. Before 1980 Bush had characterized Reagan's economics as voodoo and his pro-life stands as rigid, but for the eight years of his vice presidency, he had been meticulously loyal to the president—at some cost to what were perceived to be his more centrist leanings. In fact, he did not enter politics as a centrist. During his first campaign, the 1964 U.S. Senate race in Texas, Bush had run as a Goldwater conservative, against civil rights laws, against the welfare state, against the Nuclear Test Ban Treaty, against union shops, and the like. After he lost, he told a postelection symposium run by *National Review* that he "should repackage [his] philosophy." Whatever his actual views were, as president he was determined to be his own man. How to convey his independence of his predecessor in his speeches without appearing disloyal was the never-solved rhetorical problem that faced Bush and his writers.

This was a president whose word of choice was "prudent." As another Reagan writer, John Podhoretz, observed, someone who is obsessed with prudence is less interested in what is happening than in how it will be perceived. Bush courted popularity by skirting controversy. Budget deficits and health care languished as issues because they could not be confronted without proposing changes that would discomfit too many voters. Small wonder the speeches never improved.

A Bush insider said the speeches "have no weight. They have no sense of history. They rarely reach out to America. They are not documents that historians will look at to capture the hopes and fears and dreams of the Bush era." Nothing illustrates the accuracy of that complaint better than Bush's response to the breaching of the Berlin Wall, a truly momentous event. What was needed was an inspirational message to match the crumbling of Communist control of eastern Europe and the triumph of freedom. What was needed was an eloquent reaffirmation of the course of freedom by the leader of the free world and president of the world's oldest democracy. What did Bush say? That the historic development "certainly conforms with the Helsinki Final Act" and "clearly is a good development in terms of human rights." It is inconceivable that either Teddy Roosevelt or Ronald Reagan or just about any president in between would have ignored a political situation so rich with rhetorical potential.

A far more politically damaging evasion of the bully pulpit occurred when Bush broke his no-new-taxes pledge. In the light of ballooning deficits, he had a strong case, but he failed to explain it to the American people. Despite the much-publicized campaign pledge, he reversed himself on June 26, 1990, but he did not do so via a televised address from the Oval Office. Instead, he employed a written communication in which he said that there was a need for "tax revenue increases." On June 29 he explained his new position by claiming it was necessary to keep budget talks with Congress alive. Not until October 2 did he speak to the nation, in a speech "pretty much written by Darman," Davis says. It was a disaster, because instead of "making it seem as if this is the price we've got to pay to get other things done, Bush made it sound like his own idea." By this time many Americans and nearly all Republicans had expressed their outrage at having been betrayed. Bewildered, Bush wondered how Reagan had gotten away with raising taxes in 1982, 1983, 1984, 1986, and 1987 without the uproar that had accompanied his action. What he failed to understand was that Reagan's heavy reliance on selling his policies in major addresses and the consistency of his rhetoric made all the difference. Bush had flip-flopped on this issue several times publicly before capitulating. The bully pulpit, after all, is a president's unparalleled opportunity to shape and inform the public debate. By the time Bush took to the airwaves, the debate had been raging for months.

Bush seemed unable to explain anything. Even his justification for Desert Storm was muddled. To get Americans cranked up for the operation, he had to make Iraqi leader Saddam Hussein into a major threat. This was not an easy task for a number of reasons. During the Iran-Iraq war, the United States had assisted Iraq by selling it arms. In addition, Iraq had been taken off the list of terrorist nations (even though terrorism continued unabated), and in November 1984 full diplomatic relations were restored between Washington and Baghdad. In fact, right up to the day he invaded Kuwait on August 1, 1990, Hussein had been looked on by the United States as a valuable commercial customer and balancing force in the Middle East. Assistant Secretary of State John Kelly had testified before Congress in support of more loans to Hussein just three days before the invasion. This was the man whom Bush by the end of the month began calling the political heir of Adolf Hitler.

On August 8, 1990, seven days after the Iraqi invasion, the president addressed the American people to announce the deployment of armed forces to Saudi Arabia "to assist the Saudi Arabian Government in the defense of its homeland." Bush implied, but did not say explicitly until his press conference after the speech, that "King Fahd requested such support." In fact Bush, who excelled at one-on-one persuasion, had to twist the king's arm. He insisted that an Iraqi invasion of Saudi Arabian oil fields, less than 200 miles from the Kuwaiti border, was imminent. Few people believed this—not the Saudi royal family, nor Defense Secretary Cheney, nor Generals Colin Powell and Norman Schwarzkopf—but Bush succeeded in making the defense of Saudi Arabia "the fig leaf for American intervention," as Jean Edward Smith wrote in his book *George Bush's War*.

But then Bush went on in his address to the nation to add other justifications. Additionally, the troops would effect the immediate withdrawal of Iraqi forces from Kuwait, preserve the stability of the Gulf region, protect Americans in the region, and preserve the flow of oil. The mission was "wholly defensive," he concluded. On September 11, when he addressed a joint session of Congress, he reiterated these goals and added more. The fifth objective, he said, was "a new world order, . . . an era in which the nations of the world . . . can prosper and live in harmony. . . . This is the vision that I shared with President Gorbachev in Helsinki. He and other leaders from Europe, the Gulf, and around the world understand that how we manage this crisis today could shape the future for generations to come." Then he turned to the future when the troops come home. "Our role then: to deter future aggression. . . . And something else: to curb the proliferation of chemical, biological, ballistic missile and, above all, nuclear technologies."

Then Bush switched to domestic issues, primarily the budget, which he connected to the Persian Gulf situation tenuously at best. "Americans must never again enter any crisis, economic or military, with an excessive dependence on foreign oil and an excessive burden of federal debt." In adding a new mission in the Persian Gulf, the president offered specific tax cuts, breaks, and initiatives, all of which would make the budget deficit worse.

Rationalizations for the troops, and later for war, continued for the next six months in a succession of speeches. At first Bush had maintained that the United States could not idly stand by and allow "naked aggression" against a friendly nation. Later he flatly stated that "our way of life, our own freedom . . . will suffer if control of the world's oil reserves falls into the hands of Saddam Hussein." Cries of "no blood for oil" put an end to that notion, so Bush returned to the new world order idea.

He tended to shift emphasis among various justifications that were at times contradictory. After comparing Hussein to Hitler and invoking the threat posed by his nuclear weapons, Bush promised that Hussein only had to withdraw from Kuwait for the United States to bring its troops home. Moreover, he insisted that the United States would not reward Hussein's aggression, yet in a speech before the UN in October, Bush promised favorable settlement of Iraq's claims against Kuwait if Hussein would withdraw. On March 2, 1991, in an address to the U.S. armed forces in the Gulf, when he gave thanks for their stellar performance in liberating Kuwait in 100 hours, he announced that "the specter of Vietnam has been buried forever in the desert sands of the Arabian Peninsula." Commentators speculated on whether this had been the reason the United States had been there in the first place.

"There had been a lot of groping while seeking a justification that the American people would buy," speechwriter Mark Davis said. Bush, after all, could not rely on the Soviet threat as an ideological call to arms as his predecessors had done. He had to rely on rhetoric to pump up public support. But his advisers were split as to why the United States' presence in the Gulf was necessary. Budget director Darman said a Gulf engagement was necessary to keep the price of gasoline down and to protect the nation's economy. The NSC argued geopolitically that if Saddam Hussein were to corner the international oil market, as control of Kuwait would make possible, the world's economic balance would be upset. The speechwriters were more preoccupied with the nuclear threat.

On his part, Bush steadily and almost unilaterally, acting even over the reluctance of the military high command, escalated U.S. goals in the Persian Gulf. In August, the aim was to defend Saudi Arabia; by September, to liberate Kuwait; in October, to avenge Iraqi war crimes; in November, to prepare for an alleged Iraqi invasion of the Saudi Arabian desert (he doubled the American troops in the area to over a half a million); and in December, to destroy Iraqi chemical and nuclear weapons.

Never one to give much attention to domestic policy speeches, Bush took part in the preparation of every Gulf War address. According to Mark Davis, the principal writer for the important speech before Congress on September 11 on the "new world order," Bush kept in touch with the writers through a regular flow of phone calls and memos. He personally put together a most extraordinary coalition of countries in the Arab League, Western Europe, the Soviet Union, and nearly every other UN country. When he flatly rejected a continued policy of economic sanctions and dismissed Baghdad's overtures for settlement, it became abundantly clear that for whatever reason, Bush wanted this war. In retrospect, however, it appears that the rhetorical confusion of goals gave rise to the eventual postwar disillusionment that had developed by early 1992, a presidential election year.

The overworked and mostly ignored speechwriters were suddenly in the spotlight during 1992. Administration pollster and soon-to-be campaign manager Robert Teeter told them that Bush's reelection depended on them. Every speech the president made in 1992 was billed as the one that would define George Bush—who he was and what he stood for. This seemed odd to the writers. Why would a man considered to be the ultimate insider, a member of the Washington establishment for the past quarter of a century, almost twelve of those years in the White House itself, need definition? "This is the one, the one that's really going to turn it around," became Teeter's rallying cry before each speech assignment. The speech hype began with the first major speech of 1992, the State of the Union.

Chief speechwriter Tony Snow got the assignment. Administration "spin doctors" told the press that the January 28 speech was the blueprint for the future. Snow, Teeter, Skinner, and Darman huddled over what had been billed as a thematic speech. No one else took part in the process until the president saw it five days before delivery. He disliked it. Peggy Noonan, author of "No new taxes; read my lips," was summoned from New York. She flew to Washington on Friday, worked all night, and met with Bush, Teeter, and Skinner to discuss her draft on Saturday. Changes were suggested that Noonan incorporated into a new draft. Next Scowcroft was consulted. Noonan added his suggestions to a third "new" draft. Sunday afternoon she met again with the president, Teeter, Darman, and Skinner, and together they struggled over language and ideas until they ran out of time.

The president delivered a disappointing speech that defined him no more than the hundreds that had preceded it. It opened with a celebration of Operation Desert Storm. Next, on the basis of the success of the Patriot missile during the war, Bush called for a renewal of funding for the Strategic Defense Initiative. But according to information provided by the Israeli military and a U.S. Defense Department official, Patriots hit fewer than 20 percent of the incoming Scuds that the Iraqis directed at Israel. The remainder of the speech was the usual SOTU laundry list of requests.

George Will summed up the public response best in his critique of the speech in the next day's *Washington Post*.

> His rhetoric rarely rises to seriousness because it is just so much obligatory noise, necessary for presidential events but not otherwise important. . . . How about aid to give educational choice beyond public schools for inner-city parents of poor children? He's for that. But not enough to fight for it, or to raise a ruckus when the Senate last week defeated it on an essentially party line vote. . . . The deficit? Tuesday night he denounced it while proposing tax cuts and other charges that will expand it. Abortion? Once every January, on the anniversary of the 1973 Supreme Court decision, he waxes ardent on the subject. But there is no follow-through. Civil rights? He is for them, too. But he is opposed to quota bills like the one he opposed until he endorsed it. Free trade? He's for it. "Fair Trade" meaning managed trade—affirmative action for U.S. industry—with quotas and guaranteed incomes? He's for that, too. Backward reels the mind.

At the end of June, a desperate Teeter met with the writers. He presented each with a computer-made chart that was meant to coordinate the themes of the campaign. On the left side of the chart were two boxes that listed Bush's accomplishments ("foreign and domestic, tremendous benefits for all Americans, some disappointments") and domestic problems ("must solve these problems if we are ever to fulfill our promises *[sic]* as a country. Describe problems using examples that connect"). On the right side of the chart, six boxes listed arguments for the president's stands on major issues. The crucial box, in the center of the chart, to which all other boxes were to be connected, had three words: "Theme/Slogan/Name." "What I want from you," Teeter told the writers, "is to help me fill this empty box."

That no one succeeded in filling the empty box is history. Ultimately, the administration was defined as an administration without definition. To wage a successful campaign, a message is essential. Bush had no message.

Early in his administration, the president had had one of his rare meetings with the speechwriters. They gathered in the Roosevelt Room in the White House. After a few minutes of trying to get to know each other, Mark Davis asked Bush, "Who's your personal hero?" The president thought a moment and then gestured to the portrait of Teddy Roosevelt above the fireplace mantel—odd choice from a man who would abdicate the bully pulpit.

——

FORD, Carter, and Bush followed Nixon's practice of using professional wordsmiths to write speeches instead of the president collaborating on speeches with senior aides. But for the most part, despite their multitude of speeches, they did not rely on public speaking as a personal public relations tool to the extent that Nixon had, nor did they present to their writers a strong political viewpoint like that in Reagan's "A Time for Choosing," to be revamped to suit every occasion.

Since the creation of separate speechwriting departments, presidents started speaking in public more and more. Presidents Ford, Carter, and Bush took this trend to new heights, giving the impression that they believed speaking was synonymous with governing. Just as putting too much money in circulation causes inflation and diminishes the value of the currency, too much presidential talk cheapens the value of presidential rhetoric. They could have benefited from Roosevelt's example: He used words wisely by using them sparingly. Although most people supposed that Roosevelt took to the microphone every couple of weeks, the record shows that he delivered only twenty-seven of his famous fireside chats during more than twelve years in the White House. Eisenhower, too, would have looked askance at the sheer quantity of present-day speechmaking. Whenever Ike was asked to make a speech, he responded with irritation. "What is it that needs to be said? I'm not going out there to listen to my tongue clatter."

No such restraints touched Ford, Carter, or Bush, to their ultimate detriment, for their very garrulity undermined any possibility of conveying a sense of priority among their numerous stated policies. Had they and their senior policymaking aides collaborated more often with at least one of the writers, chances are they might have established priorities or, at least, coherence.

As the speechwriting process got progressively more removed from these three presidents, their speeches became less effective. When infighting broke out between policymakers and writers, Ford did not forge a consensus, as Truman, Eisenhower, and Kennedy had done—he didn't even sort out the squabbles. Carter's meetings with his writers usually ended in frustration: The writers got little response from him, and he found it hard to trust their literary instincts over his own penchant for lists and excessive details. In the Bush White House, speechwriters were all but banished and the bully pulpit reduced to a series of off-the-cuff remarks. The confused messages of these three presidents illustrates better than any of the others that the separation of the people who help a president devise policy from the people who put that policy into words is an inherently flawed practice.

5

STRIKE UP THEIR BAND

William Jefferson Clinton   1993–

H AVING never had a speechwriter until his first presidential campaign, William Jefferson Clinton quite naturally played an active role in writing his own speeches. Yet despite a plethora of political consultants and public relations mavens, more than any president before him, he lost control of his message at the beginning of his presidency. Television reporters told his story over his mute gestures; radio talk-show hosts pummeled his policies.

Early in his administration, Clinton told *Washington Post* columnist David Broder that because the nation is "awash with news," he must work harder than previous presidents at being communicator in chief. To Clinton, working harder seems to have meant talking more; he gave 600 speeches in his first presidential year alone.

Perpetual speechgiving was only one symptom of a badly managed White House. Not only did Clinton have an inexperienced staff—the Democrats had been out of executive power for twelve years—but he himself was chronically disorganized and always in overdrive. "The whole place runs on Clinton standard time," a speechwriter opined, which translated into regular fourteen-hour days. Worse, there was no central locus of authority except the president and the first lady, Hillary Rodham Clinton.

So harried was the inadequately staffed speechwriting department that head writer David Kusnet gladly relinquished foreign policy speechwriting to the National Security Council in the early days of the administration. This responsibility fell to Anthony Lake, national security adviser; Samuel (Sandy) Berger, his deputy; and Jeremy Rosner, senior director for legislative affairs. Rosner, who did most of the writing, hired Eric Liu, a speechwriter for Secretary of State Warren Christopher, to assist him. Never before in the history of the White House had the domestic- and foreign-policy areas of speechwriting been separated, and the president by no means treated them equally. Probably because Clinton at first did not feel as comfortable with foreign affairs as he did with domestic issues, he regularly consulted with those in charge of the former, making for intellectually coherent speeches in this area. By contrast, the domestic writing operation suffered from the speechwriters' complete lack of access to the Oval Office.

Mark Gearan, as director of communications, had charge of the writing shop, yet he rarely kept the writers informed. Kusnet, an exceptional writer, never managed to develop a close relationship with the president, so he and the writers often had to second-guess Clinton's wishes for a particular speech, even why the speech had been scheduled. They managed to stay up-to-date on developing policy details only because the writers shared writing chores of major speeches with policy people like Bruce Reed and Gene Sperling, who spent much of their time developing the fine points of legislation, and with communications aides Michael Waldman and Robert Boorstin. Still, since no writer had been authorized to take charge, a lot of wasted effort resulted.

The speechwriters' continuous cry for more time, staff, and direction went largely unheeded. Clinton had promised to cut White House staff by 25 percent, and the Speechwriting Department was no exception to the retrenchment. To make matters worse, there was little connection between the president's Scheduling Office and Speechwriting, making it impossible to develop an orderly process for producing speeches or even the outlines, which Clinton preferred over finished texts. He is, after all, an extraordinarily articulate man, able to speak on a subject for an hour or more without a note, in perfectly parsed sentences and paragraphs. Part teacher, part preacher, as well as domestic policy expert, Clinton "had thought through the nation's essential problems more thoroughly than any of his recent predecessors," political journalist Elizabeth Drew observed, and more than any president in recent memory, he speaks for himself.

When Donald Baer was hired away from *U.S. News & World Report* in late spring of 1994, he asked Clinton what he wanted from the speechwriters. "I don't know," the president replied. "Until a couple of years ago, I did all my own writing." His acceptance speech at the Democratic convention, even if most of the words were his own, is probably the first major speech on which he ever collaborated with others. He still "does his own thing in speeches," Rosner says today. "He's a jazz improviser who riffs all over the place." Other writers also have used the jazz metaphor to describe Clinton's tendency to "go off text." "He has a native desire to voice things his own way, to freely delineate his own ideas," echoes David Dreyer. This former deputy to George Stephanopoulos, when Stephanopoulos was director of the Communications Department, occasionally doubled as speechwriter. Dreyer says that "Clinton just wants material with which to improvise."

"[This] is a man with knowledge of the basic texts of American oratory," Kusnet says. Clinton can quote from memory long passages of speeches by Jefferson, Lincoln, FDR, and JFK.

He knows Shakespeare and the Bible, which is how he knows the right rhythms and cadences for any audience he addresses. This is especially the case with black audiences in the South.

Using three pages of points that writer Carolyn Curiel had developed, Clinton gave a speech on November 13, 1993, from the same Memphis pulpit where Martin Luther King, Jr., had preached the night before his assassination. Speaking in Dr. King's very rhythms and cadences, the president exhorted the 5,000 black ministers and leaders at the Temple Church of God in Christ, and by extension all citizens, to look squarely at how far the country had come in the struggle for racial equality and at the great distance it still must travel. He described in chilling detail the violence and drug trafficking that ravage cities in which children, afraid of random killing, plan their own funerals. He warned that the victories of the civil rights movement were being undermined by a "great crisis of the spirit that is gripping America today," that while Martin Luther King would take pride in the election of black Americans to political office and in the growing black middle class, were he to speak today, in all probability he would express utter dismay. Clinton even imagined the words King might have used:

> I did not live and die to see the American family destroyed. I did not live and die to see 13-year-old boys get automatic weapons and gun down 9-year-olds just for the kick of it. I did not live and die to see young people destroy their lives with drugs and then build fortunes destroying the lives of others. That is not what I came here to do. I fought for freedom, he would say, but not for the freedom of people to kill each other with reckless abandon, not for the freedom of children to have children and the fathers to walk away from them . . . as if they don't amount to anything.

The underlying cause of this social decay is unemployment, Clinton continued. "I do not believe we can repair the basic fabric of society until people who are willing to work have work. Work organizes life." Every institution needs to help. Government alone cannot nurture a child, and government alone cannot rebuild whole communities, Clinton said. Each American has an obligation to help turn the country's permissiveness and violence around, he concluded.

This speech was presidential suasion on a grand scale and in the finest tradition of moral leadership. Rising above party and ideology, the president summoned Americans to their highest ideals and to their personal and collective responsibilities, even as he reminded them of certain home truths. The speech, in short, illustrated the symbolic and inspirational side of the bully pulpit. Yet after an early flurry of favorable comments in the national press, the president's words seemed to disappear from the national consciousness. Their fate was partly the result of the president's excessive verbiage and partly of his fascination with the details of governing.

From the first days of the administration, the first lady kept reminding her husband that the presidency was about more than getting things done, something Clinton kept losing sight of in his efforts to win legislative victories. A typical "policy wonk," he often got lost in the minutiae of whatever policy was under consideration. During the difficult period of putting a first budget together, Mrs. Clinton had called her husband a "mechanic-in-chief," put in the position of tinkering instead of being the president who exercised a moral voice and vision. The economic plan was not about numbers, she kept reminding him; it was a values document.

Although the February 17, 1993, speech to promote his economic plan had been his first before a joint session of Congress, Clinton could not leave the details alone. When he appeared in the White House family theater for an announced single TelePrompTer run-through, the principal writers of the "final" draft, Kusnet, Dreyer, and Waldman, watched in horror as the president trimmed language and agonized over spending cuts, all the while scrawling comments over, under, and in the margins of the text right up to a half hour before delivery time. The men from the Army Signal Corps who operate the Tele-PrompTer had never seen anything like it. "We never received anything but a finished draft from Bush. We put it in, and he read it." With Clinton, they had to race the actual final draft to Capitol Hill for insertion in the House TelePrompTer minutes before the speech.

Clinton's rhetorical brinkmanship was repeated for his next appearance before a joint session. On the night of September 22, 1993, the president delivered his health care proposals to a packed House. Yet less than an hour earlier Clinton was still rewriting. He showed up in the family theater for a final rehearsal on the TelePrompTer, still scribbling new ideas all over the text. He kept it up until there was barely time to get to the Capitol. Rosner and Dreyer, who had been brought into the writing process because the president did not like what the speechwriters had produced, readily admitted that the president's changes improved the speech. They had written, for example, "Tonight those of us in this room, and those of you in your homes, have come together." Clinton's edit produced, "Tonight we come together." They wrote that the American story had started 350 years ago. The president drafted, "Our forefathers enshrined the American Dream: life, liberty, and the pursuit of happiness. Every generation of Americans has worked to strengthen that legacy." But Clinton's scramble to get the words right led to a near disaster during delivery.

At 9:10 P.M. he stood at the rostrum, acknowledged the ovations, and glanced at the prompter. The displayed speech was the text on the economy he had delivered on February 17. Taken aback, he opened the binder on the rostrum that contained the typed version of the health speech, but he had forgotten his glasses. The last-minute redrafting had left no time for a big-type version of the speech to be prepared. The president turned and whispered to Vice President Al Gore, standing behind him. Gore vigorously gestured to Stephanopoulos, who happened to be nearby. The communications chief ran to find Dreyer, who had transferred a copy of the final draft onto the hard drive of his laptop computer in the limousine en route to the Capitol. Dreyer raced to the TelePrompTer and told the operator to wipe the diskette clean, even though the health-care speech was on the disk following the economic speech that the operator had forgotten to erase. Dreyer then transferred the text from his laptop onto the cleaned diskette and gave it back to the operator. All the while Clinton was speaking. Seven minutes into his unexpected extemporaneous delivery, the text caught up with him. At the time, no one in Congress had any idea of what had happened, so smoothly had the president handled the situation. Because he had taken part in the composition of the speech from inception until delivery, he knew all thirty-four pages of the typed version cold and probably could have made the whole speech without the prompter. Clinton seemed to have become the apotheosis of speechwriter as president.

Treasury Secretary Lloyd Bentsen blamed near misses like this on Clinton's doing too much at one time. In a private meeting in the Oval Office he had told Clinton that he "had too many issues out there, and the public is losing focus on what you're trying to do." In addition to the important health care speech, Clinton had made four other important speeches: one at the signing of the historic Israeli-Palestine Peace Accord; another on the North American Free Trade Agreement (NAFTA), attended by Presidents Ford, Carter, and Bush; a third at Johns Hopkins University; and a fourth before the General Assembly at the UN—all delivered in less than a month. No wonder Bentsen was concerned.

Although Clinton promised the treasury secretary and his wife that he would slow down, he charged on anyway, dealing with one policy problem after another. He cut the federal budget, and successfully campaigned for a family medical leave bill, an expansion of the earned-income tax credit for the working poor, an Americorps (a program of national service for college tuition credit), NAFTA, the General Agreement on Tariffs and Trade, the Brady bill (which requires a waiting period for the purchase of handguns), a crime bill, and an assault weapons ban that, for the first time, outlaws the sale and distribution of nineteen kinds of assault weapons.

"So much was being done," Kusnet says, "little was noticed." What did make the nightly news were stories about Clinton's temporizing on foreign policy and his failures in the campaign for universal health care. Yet in persuading Congress to pass 88 percent of the measures he sent to Capitol Hill, he compiled a record surpassed only by Eisenhower. Although Clinton was frustrated by the lack of recognition for his legislative accomplishments, he most likely would have pushed on anyway had the Republican takeover of Congress in the election of 1994 not stopped him dead in his tracks.

His first public reaction to the Republican rout came the day after the election. At a press conference he gave reporters his initial assessment of what had gone wrong. "If you ask me for one of the mistakes I think that I have made since I have been here, I have spent so much time trying to pass bills through Congress that I haven't spent as much time as I was able to when I was running for president making sure people understood, were in on and felt part of, the process by which we make decisions."

Echoing this confession, while at the same time not appearing to understand his own serious lack of discipline that had infected White House management, especially speechwriting, he blamed his troubles solely on his absorption in legislation. "I totally neglected how to get the public informed. I have to get more involved in crafting my message, in getting across my core concerns." The soul-searching continued in his 1995 State of the Union Address. He apologized not once, but twice, for not having better connected with the public. Trying to unify his agenda under one umbrella, thereby enunciating an overall vision, he reintroduced the campaign term "new covenant," using it nine times in a flabby, eighty-two-minute laundry list of past successes and future hopes.

The hopes quickly faded as Clinton faced an increasingly hostile Congress that took aim at his favorite programs and succeeded in putting him on the defensive. House Democrats longed for another Truman, but Clinton, who is conciliatory by nature, would not lambaste his opponents, despite their personal attacks on him. Unsure of what to do and badly shaken by events, the president turned to political consultant Dick Morris for help in shaping his message. A man who also works for Republicans, Morris had known Clinton since 1978 and, according to the president, was the one who resuscitated his political career after his 1980 gubernatorial defeat. Before long, Morris displaced strategists James Carville and Paul Begala, and Morris's pollster Doug Shoen supplanted Stan Greenberg. Under Morris's tutelage, the president played rhetorical possum. Not until House Republicans celebrated their first 100 days did he speak out. In Dallas on April 7, 1995, before the American Society of Newspaper Editors, Clinton outlined what he was for and what he was against in the Republican Contract with America. Speaking once more of his "new covenant," he showed that he had found his line in the sand. "My test is: Does an idea expand middle-class incomes and opportunities? Does it promote values like family, work, responsibility, and community? Does it strengthen the hand of America's working families in a global economy? If it does, I'll be for it, no matter who proposes it. And if it doesn't, I will oppose it."

After stops in Texas and California, Clinton returned to Washington and accidentally diverted attention from his stellar performance in Dallas. On April 18, taking advantage of a congressional recess, he held a prime-time televised press conference to detail the specifics of issues he had raised in the ASNE speech. But when a reporter asked if he was afraid of his voice not being heard, and that he had become irrelevant, he injudiciously replied, "The Constitution gives me relevance. . . . The president is relevant here." Mocking accounts of the president's self-proclaimed relevance dominated news stories that night and the next morning; they drowned out the positive accounts of his forceful reemergence from the White House. But not for long.

The next morning at 10:00 A.M., the White House got word that the federal building in Oklahoma City, housing more than 500 workers, had been blown up. Press Secretary Michael McCurry gave Clinton the news just before the president welcomed Turkish prime minister Tansu Ciller to the Oval Office. At noon the president met with top aides in Chief of Staff Leon Panetta's office to assess the situation. At 4:30 they reconvened in the Situation Room in the basement of the West Wing. At 5:00 Clinton reworked the statement his speechwriters had prepared for him to make to the nation. He read through it a few times and then asked everyone to leave. Alone with his thoughts, he sat there for a few moments, and then at 5:30 he began to speak to the country.

He listed steps the Justice Department was taking to find the "evil cowards" responsible for the explosion and to protect Oklahoma City and the country from further attacks on federal property. He warned citizens not to jump to conclusions about who might be guilty—Senators Philip Gramm and Robert Dole had already advocated retaliation against whatever foreign government had perpetrated the act. The president asked Americans to pray "for the people who have lost their lives, . . . for the families and friends of the dead and wounded, and for the people of Oklahoma City."

After Timothy McVeigh's apprehension on April 21, when it became known that he was probably connected with the Michigan militia, the nation began learning about the growing popularity of paramilitary groups across the country that trained men in the use of weapons and perpetrated paranoia about the federal government. In lieu of his regular Saturday morning radio address, the president and the first lady met with twenty-six children of federal employees in the Oval Office. There, before television cameras, they stood in as parents to the nation's children by listening and responding to the children's concerns about the tragedy. On Sunday they flew to Oklahoma City for a memorial service.

Like the Memphis speech in 1993, Clinton's eulogy for the bombing victims was moving and powerful. It was Clinton at his preacherly best. Near the conclusion of his brief remarks he introduced a topic he would elaborate upon in the coming weeks.

> To all my fellow Americans beyond this hall, I say, one thing we owe those who have sacrificed is the duty to purge ourselves of the dark forces which give rise to this evil. They are forces that threaten our common peace, our freedom, our way of life. . . . When there is talk of hatred, let us stand up and talk against it. In the face of death, let us honor life. As St. Paul admonished us, let us not be overcome by evil, but overcome evil with good.

The nation listened to the president as they had not listened to him since his inaugural speech. In his ceremonial role as chief of state, he was expected to speak of tragedy and console a grieving nation. In honoring Oklahoma City's dead, he consoled the survivors and provided solace and hope for all Americans in the process.

During the next three weeks, the president spoke out against armed bigotry. Allowing that those citizens who spread paranoia were acting within their constitutional rights, he urged Americans who did not agree with them to exercise their own right to speak against them. In one speech the president quoted a few words of the hate mongering that was a ubiquitous drumbeat on the nation's radios. In another ringing condemnation of the preachings of militias during a commencement speech on May 5 at Michigan State University, not far from the farm in Dexter, Michigan, where investigators believed Timothy Mc-

Veigh had conspired to make bombs, he addressed the militiamen directly: "If you appropriate our sacred symbols for paranoid purposes and compare yourselves to Colonial militias who fought for the democracy you now rail against, you are wrong. How dare you suggest that we in the freest nation on earth live in tyranny? How dare you call yourselves patriots and heroes?" Echoing his own 1992 campaign oratory, he said, "The real American heroes today are the citizens who get up every morning and have the courage to work hard and play by the rules." And he warned the graduates that the technologies of instant worldwide communication and the openness of democratic societies made them vulnerable to the forces of organized destruction and evil. "The great security challenge for your future in the twenty-first century will be to determine how to beat back the dangers while keeping the benefits of this new time."

The president had worked hard to get the words just right, telling a *Detroit Free Press* reporter he had stayed up most of the night agonizing over their proper tone. Despite distortions of what he had said from the mainstream press and from political opponents who accused him of scapegoating and of trying to stifle criticism of the government, he dominated the national response to the bombing tragedy. Once again he had fulfilled one of the major duties of a president, which is to speak out in public about a clear danger to the nation's peace and to take steps to meet the danger. He did the latter by urging civil discourse and by proposing new antiterrorism measures. After Clinton's response to this crisis, no one spoke of his relevance or irrelevance again. He had clearly established his national voice, as he would again and again in the future.

At no time would this voice be more forceful than when Clinton responded to the deaths of thirty-three Americans in an air crash on April 3, 1996. The casualties included Commerce Secretary Ronald Brown and other members of a mission to Croatia, who were on their way home. From the moment he had hurried to an auditorium in the Commerce Department to console the agency's employees to his appearance a week later in the Gothic grandeur of the National Cathedral for Brown's memorial, both his actions and his words were presidential. At Hangar 70-6 at Dover Air Force base in Delaware, where he had gone to meet the plane bearing the thirty-three flag-draped coffins, he paid tribute to the victims.

> These 33 lives show us the best of America. They are a stern rebuke to the cynicism that is all too familiar today. . . . Nearly 5,000 miles from home, they went to help people build their own homes and roads, to turn on the lights in cities darkened by war, to restore the everyday interchange of people working and living together with something to look forward to and a dream to raise their own children by. . . . I say to all of you, to every American, they were all patriots; whether soldiers or civil servants or committed citizens, they were patriots.

President Reagan had set the recent standard for ceremonial and eulogistic performance in speeches like the one he delivered at Pointe du Hoc in 1984, which memorialized D-Day on its forty-year anniversary, and the Challenger Speech in 1986, delivered after the space shuttle blew up minutes after launch. Since spring 1995, however, when President Clinton comforted the nation after the Oklahoma City bombing, he has shown himself to be the undisputed contemporary master of consolation and inspiration. Oddly enough, Clinton paid less attention to Reagan's skillful handling of national symbols than to Reagan's successful control-the-agenda strategy, and yet controlling the agenda was precisely what Clinton seemed unable to do. No matter how often he talked or how well-crafted his speeches, others defined his message.

As early as June 1981, when Clinton spoke at the North Carolina Institute of Political Leadership, he showed he had already adopted Reagan as a speechmaking role model. Although

Reagan had been in office only five months, Clinton recognized his extraordinary knack for getting his message across. Ten and a half years later, he got his own chance to experiment with Reagan's methods of controlling the message. Right after his own election, Clinton's transition team procured the Initial Action Plan that speechwriter Gergen and pollsters Wirthlin and Beale had drawn up for Reagan's day-to-day schedule during his first 100 days in office. The success of this plan depended on political consultants and pollsters, which Clinton uses to an extent that goes way beyond Reagan, and on managers to set a schedule for the chief executive to follow. Only once or twice did Ronald Reagan deviate from the script written by others. But scripted speaking is the very opposite of Clinton's improvisational style. Moreover, his multifaceted agenda was not at all like Reagan's primary policy of cutting government and expanding the military. Clinton's obsession with every nuance of procedure contrasted sharply with Reagan's noninterest in policy. The exceedingly informed Clinton sometimes got lost in his facts, whereas the underinformed Reagan could be utterly clear about simple goals. For all these reasons, Clinton's emulation of Reagan's control-the-agenda strategy did not work for this activist president. It took two national tragedies and the midterm congressional election to bring him to his rhetorical senses. But he staged a stunning comeback.

Jettisoning his unrealistic tactics, he appropriated Reagan's values turf. Just as Reagan had clothed his conservative doctrine in the rhetorical manner of Franklin Roosevelt—inspirational, optimistic, generous, high-minded—so too did Clinton begin taking back Roosevelt's style from Reagan. With the help of his professional image-makers he learned to wrap his agenda in values rhetoric. He also relied on a better-organized speechwriting operation to assist him in remaking his rhetoric.

Donald Baer had been brought to the administration in 1994 precisely to try to establish some kind of orderly process in speechwriting. Less than a year later he became the new director of communications, moving from a commodious, high-ceilinged suite in the Old Executive Office Building to a windowless box in the basement of the West Wing, which provided quarters closer to the president. He also became a regular attendee of Clinton's weekly meeting of his message-packaging brain trust. No major decision was made that had not first been vetted by the two dozen regulars of the Wednesday night sessions. Although the new job required more than writing, he still devoted a third of his time to it. He brought in Michael Waldman to head the department, thereby giving the writers a still more intimate connection with the subtleties of domestic policymaking. The writers now had more access to Clinton and better understood his specific goals; consequently, they wrote speeches more in tune with the president. Al From, one of the founders and current director of the Democratic Leadership Council, Bruce Reed, another new Democrat, and others kept Clinton on the straight-and-narrow centrist path, although always under the watchful eyes of liberals like Panetta, his deputy Harold Ickes, and Special Assistant Stephanopoulos. Armed with flawless rhetorical packaging, a fully confident Clinton returned to the political game.

On June 13, in an uncharacteristic short, tight television address, the president translated budget arcana into values, thus spelling out "the fundamental differences between Democrats and Republicans about how to balance the budget." On July 6 at Georgetown University he called on the nation's political leaders for "more conversation and less combat" to help Americans find "common ground as Republicans and Democrats debate the proper role of government." On July 10 in Nashville at a conference on the family and the media that had been organized by Vice President Gore, he endorsed the V-chip, a relatively simple and inexpensive device to enable parents to block violent television programs from their home television sets. To stave off a Republican effort to get a constitutional amendment permitting school prayer in the schools, the president spoke to students and parents at James Madison High School in Washington, D.C., on July 12. In his remarks he showed what could be done to foster prayer in the schools without amending or violating the Constitution. On July 19 Clinton spoke on the most divisive and controversial issue of all: affirmative action.

Because Republicans had taken so vociferous a stand against all affirmative action and because roughly three-quarters of the nation agreed with them, Clinton had to make his own position on the issue clear. As early as March he had ordered a review of all affirmative-action programs and put Christopher Edley, Jr., associate director for economics and government, in charge. "We've got to do this right if we want to move the debate," Clinton told Edley.

When Edley's team had finished their fact-finding effort, the inner circle held a series of meetings in the Oval Office and in the Cabinet Room to discuss the thorny and complex issues the study had raised. Taking much longer than anticipated, and clearly worried about the nearly universal unpopularity of affirmative action, Clinton and his policy people were unexpectedly helped in June when the Supreme Court handed down a decision in the Adarand case that applied strict new standards to existing affirmative-action programs but implicitly approved the overall concept. Not until mid-July was the wide-ranging and in-depth examination of affirmative action complete, enabling the principal writers, Donald Baer and Carolyn Curiel, to start drafting. A strong draft had emerged by the afternoon before the scheduled speech. The president worked on it until 3:00 A.M., adding more biography and economics, urging civility about the issue, and adjusting tone and metaphor.

In a reaffirmation of the goals and results of affirmative action, President Clinton told his audience at the National Archives, "mend it, but don't end it" in a forty-five-minute talk. He reminded everyone that the poll tax and segregated schools and washrooms were facts of life in his Arkansas youth and that improvements did "not happen as some sort of random, evolutionary drift" but because of hard work, legal challenges, and personal courage. Any program should be eliminated or reformed, he continued, if it creates quotas or preferences for unqualified people or produces discrimination (including reverse discrimination) or continues after its purpose has been achieved. But he concluded that "affirmative action has been good for America." The speech was a political tour de force. He had managed to keep both traditionally liberal and centrist Democratic Leadership Council Democrats happy, and at the same time, not unduly offend his opponents. More important, he came across to the public as principled, a trait he badly needed to convey.

"As the president demonstrated in affirmative action, just the use of the bully pulpit can change the debate," said Charles Kamasaki, a vice president of a Hispanic advocacy group. "We were in a free fall on affirmative action until the time the president made his speech. And almost since that time, from a policy perspective, the Republicans have been on the defensive."

Clinton made his most sweeping and soaring values speech on October 16, 1995, the day of the Million Man March on Washington, D.C. He had planned to speak about racial reconciliation since the O. J. Simpson verdict. Disturbed by the depth of racial divisions in the land, he decided to make it on this particular day after a tactical debate within his inner circle. Baer did the initial work on the speech, typing out seventeen topic sentences that became its essential structure. He also came up with one of the speech's core lines that alluded to Louis Farrakhan without actually naming him. "One million men are right to be standing up for personal responsibility, but one million men do not make right one man's message of malice and division." Then Baer assigned the speech to writers David Shipley and Terry Edmonds, the first black presidential speechwriter.

The two writers started drafting on the Friday before the Monday speech. After consulting with the president in the Oval Office on Saturday, they did a second draft. On Sunday, they left with Clinton for a policy event in Connecticut, working on another draft that they had ready for the president by the time Air Force One took off for Austin, Texas, the site of the speech. When the plane touched down at 8:00 P.M., Clinton called Shipley and Edmonds to the presidential compartment and went over his changes with them. He then left the plane for dinner. When Clinton got to the hotel at 11:00 P.M., the writers had a new draft ready. The three men worked until 3:00 A.M. Up at 7:00, Clinton made still more changes. "There's not a word in that speech untouched by the president," Shipley says today. "Our text was a little bit of yeast for him." Edmonds agrees that it was "a good team effort, an ideal collaborative process," adding that for him, as the only black in Speechwriting, it was a "defining speech."

In the forty-minute address, Clinton summoned up solemn images of national unity. "Long before we were so diverse," he said, "our nation's motto was 'e pluribus unum'—out of many, we are one." Now, he continued, "whether we like it or not, we are one nation, one family, indivisible, and for us, divorce or separation are not options." Indicting both blacks and whites for racism, he said that "recognizing one another's real grievances is only a first step. We must take responsibility for ourselves, our conduct, our attitudes. America, we must clean our house of racism." Finally, in a tone more fatherly than fiery, he warned that "the single biggest social problem in our society may be the absence of fathers from their children's homes. Building a family is the hardest job a man can do," Clinton said, "but it's also the most important."

After the fact, the president's aides referred to the addresses since June as "common ground" speeches. In them Clinton enunciated two themes—new covenant and common ground. Neither was new; he had been speaking about them since his 1992 campaign. What *was* new was that after his speeches on the Oklahoma City bombing he learned to subsume legislative details under family and community values. Ironically, it was

Republicans who gave him the opportunity. Their takeover of Congress and the open dismissal of his leadership forced him to make the kind of speeches that let him be presidential.

Shaping public understanding of issues, not in terms of programs or dollars but in terms of inspiration and moral imperatives, is why the president still won the budget battle, even though he gave way in budget matters to House Republicans, even consenting to their seven-year limit to balance the budget. By developing a strong voice on social issues when the Republicans pushed to cut back on education, to roll back decades of environmental regulations, and to curtail Medicare and Medicaid spending, he positioned himself as the protector of social progress. At the same time his message resonated, people were having second thoughts about the Contract with America. Republicans lost political control of the budget issue when they gave Clinton an ultimatum: Choose their budget, or the governmental will shut down. Having already succeeded in dramatically shifting the political landscape in less than a year, Clinton held his ground.

Twice in his 1996 State of the Union, he said, "The era of big government is over," and portrayed himself as a reasonable man who shared many of the Republican goals but who thought they went too far and were too harsh. This Democratic president, who was trying to position himself in an uncertain time—which saw the partial undoing of an era initiated by Franklin Roosevelt and extended for six decades by other Democrats in the White House and on Capitol Hill—said he would cut back programs but in a more compassionate way than Republicans. In short, he offered his own vision of limited government to compete with the Republican version. Poll numbers indicated that the public responded favorably. So angered and frustrated were congressional freshman Republicans by the president's preempting of their own ground to use for his contrary purposes, their leaders worried that they would stage a spectacle of revolt that would further distance voters from their message. Taking no chances, they scheduled a pre-SOTU lecture on decorum for the Republican freshmen.

Budget negotiations continued until April 1996. On April 25 in the White House Briefing Room, the president had the last word on the 1995–96 struggle. "The budget reflects our values by preserving our commitments to education, to the preservation of the environment, and to health care. . . . We have shown that we can work together and that when we do we can get results that are good for the American people. . . . But when the leadership in Congress insists on going it alone, one party alone, we get gridlock, stalemate, vetoes, government shutdowns."

By 1996 it appeared that President Clinton had achieved a remarkable turnaround in regaining control of the agenda through speechmaking reinvention. While a preoccupation with rhetorical packaging in itself is not harmful, it brings public relations professionals to the vortex of governing, and in that respect Clinton is like every other president since Nixon. He differs from them in establishing a closer link with his speechwriters and giving them greater access to policy debate. By bringing policy experts and other senior advisers into the speechwriting process, he has begun to reverse the long-held practice of keeping the wordsmiths separated from the inner circle. As a result, his speeches have revitalized his presidency and enabled him to win a second term, an achievement realized by only two other Democrats—FDR and Woodrow Wilson—in this century.

EPILOGUE

T HE story of the twentieth-century presidency divides neatly into two halves: prior to 1968, presidents spoke the words *they* wrote, either alone or with their closest aides; from 1969 until the present, presidential words often were drafted by writers whose access to the presidents and their policy advisers was curtailed, to varying degrees. Once the product of careful deliberation, presidential speeches have become the products of ad hoc thinking, carefully pretested on focus groups and designed to be as substance-free as possible so as not to offend. Images are carefully constructed for their appeal, not for their content; hence, tough issues are rarely discussed in the speeches and certainly not on television, an essentially image-driven medium.

Many people would argue that TV is to blame for the high number of generic, somewhat content-free speeches contemporary presidents have given, but in fact television merely exacerbates the damage incurred by presidents who do not see that by participating in the writing of their speeches, they would be making more effective policy. For policy is, after all, or should be, carefully shaped through articulation. Presidents, however, have become so "audience-driven," communications scholar

Roderick Hart wrote, "they unconsciously use polling data to substantiate the essential wisdom of the positions they champion. The old notion of leadership . . . seems to be out of date." A president now may appear to lead millions when in reality he is tamely echoing their every shifting mood.

In their rush to be reelected, presidents are too much in touch with the public and too likely to listen to it without paying attention to consequences. Polls merely register what people think they think without having thought much, if at all, about the issue being polled. Yet the president as popular leader is dependent on polls to help define his image. Every White House since Nixon has been dominated by people professionally involved in creating public images: pollsters, political consultants, campaign strategists, advertising experts, trained publicists. Their image game consists basically in perceiving and calculating the direction in which the electorate is moving and then rushing the president to the head of the crowd via his public speaking. Great conflicts between nations and important domestic issues are influenced and even decided by public opinion.

Recent chiefs of state with their spin doctors create psuedo events and photo ops to market virtual-reality versions of themselves to the public, based on what polls tell them the public wants or expects. Old precepts like truth and knowledge are displaced by new ones of opinion, perception, and credibility. David Gergen, who served Presidents Nixon, Ford, Reagan, and Clinton in various speech and communication capacities, admitted that image making "has nothing to do with anything that is real. Eventually it becomes selling the sizzle without the steak." Presidential relegation of speechwriting to wordsmiths who are not essentially involved in decision making, combined with reliance on polls, undermines the role of the president as educator and often creates a disconnection between words and actions. The greatest loss from the evolution of the rhetorical presidency has been a decrease in the integrity of the word. Yet government is about ideas and their manifestations as words. Words count. The Constitution and the nation's laws, words carefully written down, are the bedrock of personal rights and liberties. When words are devalued, the political system is at risk.

To stem the gradual debasement of the national voice, a president needs to be less willing to follow public opinion and more assertive in leading it. In a democracy leaders *must* be responsive to public opinion, but using polls to decide which way to veer is not leadership; it is followership. With the brave new world of interactivity made possible through the communications superhighway, it is critical that presidents not be as readily swayed by this emerging electronic plebiscite as they have been by polls. Otherwise, the representational government the Founders so carefully crafted to ensure deliberateness of governmental decision making will be jeopardized. As it is, deliberation between the executive and legislative branches has frequently been displaced by rhetoric designed to enhance image, especially when very popular presidents cow members of Congress into supporting programs against their better judgments.

The Founding Fathers set up representational institutions to protect the national government from direct decisions by an ill-informed and shortsighted populace. The idea of the president as a popular leader is precisely what they sought to avoid. Given the size and diversity of the United States today, it is conceivable they could have been persuaded of the need for Wilson's version of the president as "the only national voice," but not as it has evolved. The Founders would likely have denounced modern image-driven presidential speechifying. And so should every other American. The displacement of the language of ideas with the language of images has spawned a considerable number of cynics. Surely it is not wholly coincidental that as the number of presidential speeches has risen, voter participation has fallen correspondingly. The ratio could be reversed, but only if presidents matched their fewer spoken words with more directly congruent deeds.

Franklin Roosevelt, like his cousin Theodore, regarded politics as an honorable profession. "Politics, after all," he once said, "is only an instrument through which to achieve government," and what was government, he often said, but "the art of formulating a policy, and using political technique to attain so much of that policy as will receive general support by persuading, leading, . . . teaching, always teaching because the greatest duty of a statesman is to educate." For twelve tumultuous years FDR convinced a majority of his countrymen to trust his leadership by putting into practice his policies for dealing with a devastating depression and a world war. Anyone anywhere is free to measure his achievement: What he said was what he did. No citizen could ask for more of a politician.

N O T E S

p. 1 "The most important factor." Theodore Roosevelt, *An Autobiography,* quoted in Arthur Schlesinger, Jr., *The Imperial Presidency,* Boston: Houghton Mifflin, 1973, p. 83.

p. 2 "Roosevelt had the knack of doing things." Elmer Cornwell, Jr., *Presidential Leadership of Public Opinion* (Bloomington: Indiana University Press, 1965), p. 15.

p. 3 "Stressing the need to make his pronouncements." Jeffrey Tulis, *The Rhetorical Presidency* (Princeton: Princeton University Press, 1987), p. 80. Although their point is very different from my own, I am indebted to James Ceaser, Glen Thurow, J. Tulis, and Joseph Bessette for their article "The Rise of the Rhetorical Presidency," *Presidential Studies Quarterly* (Spring 1981): 158–171 for the term "rhetorical presidency," which is what the twentieth-century presidency has become.

p. 4 "Only because the president has the nation behind him." Woodrow Wilson, *Constitutional Government* (New York: Columbia University Press, 1908), pp. 65, 68.

p. 4 Wilson "let it be known." *New York Times,* April 8, 1913, p. 1.

p. 5 Congress started "delving into old records." *Congressional Record,* 63rd Cong., 1st sess., 1913, part 1, p. 75.

p. 5 "The town is agog." Woodrow Wilson to Mary Hulbert, April 8,

1913, *The Papers of Woodrow Wilson*, ed. Arthur Link, vol. 27 (Princeton: Princeton University Press, 1978), p. 273.

p. 5   Presidential message as "speech from the throne." *Congressional Record*, p. 58.

p. 5   A question of "highest privilege." Ibid.

p. 6   "Gentlemen of the Congress." Wilson, *The Papers of Woodrow Wilson*, vol. 27, pp. 269, 270.

p. 7   "Going to the Hill." Ibid, p. 109.

p. 7   The country "was vastly interested." Ray Stannard Baker, *Woodrow Wilson: Life and Letters* (New York: Charles Scribner's, 1931), p. 109.

p. 7   "Is the national legislature to be held *in terrorem?*" *Financial World*, April 12, 1913, p. 3.

p. 7   "Cannot afford to take a chance." *World*, April 10, 1913.

p. 7   Wilson's "new bossism." A. Maurice Low, "The New Bossism," *Harper's Weekly*, April 19, 1913.

p. 7   Common sense of a president's taking charge of tariff matters. *American Review of Reviews*, 47 (May 1913): 515.

p. 7   Wilson's brevity, focus. *Outlook*, 105 (September–December 1913): 771.

p. 7   Wilson's "dignity" and "impressiveness." *Chicago Tribune*, April 9, 1913. Quoted in Baker, *Woodrow Wilson*, p. 110.

p. 8   Loquaciousness of Ford, Carter, Reagan. Bradley Patterson, Jr., *The Ring of Power* (New York: Basic Books, 1988), p. 191.

p. 9   Judson Welliver was "attached to White House organization." *Who's Who in America*, vol. 15 (Chicago: Marquis, 1928–29), p. 2181.

William Safire, former speechwriter for Richard Nixon, has established a Judson Welliver Society, which meets biennially at his home outside of Washington, D.C. The society's membership is composed of former presidential speechwriters.

1. POINT-TO-POINT NAVIGATION

The following abbreviations are used here:
FDRL: Franklin Delano Roosevelt Library, Hyde Park, New York

PP&A: The Public Papers and Addresses of Franklin D. Roosevelt
    Vols. 1–5 (New York: Random House, 1938).
    Vols. 6–9 (New York: Macmillan, 1941).
    Vols. 10–13 (New York: Harper and Brothers, 1950).
PPF: President's Personal File, FDRL

p. 11   Essence of presidency is teaching. In 1932 during his presidential campaign in a speech before the San Francisco Commonwealth Club.

p. 12   "It's a terrible thing to look over your shoulder." Quoted in Samuel Rosenman, *Working with Roosevelt* (New York: Harper and Brothers, 1952), p. 107.

p. 12   FDR's mail. Before Roosevelt took office, one man was enough to handle presidential mail. FDR required a staff of fifty to answer the 8,000 letters that came into the White House each day, plus a deluge after certain speeches. After the First Inaugural, for example, 450,000 letters arrived at 1600 Pennsylvania Avenue.

p. 12   Roosevelt didn't "change his mind." Quoted in Elmer Cornwell, Jr., *Presidential Leadership of Public Opinion* (Bloomington: Indiana University Press), 1965, p. 248.

p. 12   Cantril's poll. Hadley Cantril, *Public Opinion: 1935–1946* (Princeton, N.J.: Princeton University Press, 1951), p. 966.

p. 13   "Roosevelt knew that all those words would constitute [his legacy]." Robert Sherwood, *Roosevelt and Hopkins, An Intimate History* (New York: Harper and Brothers, 1948), p. 212.

p. 13   Writing process in FDR's White House. This material comes from different parts of two books—Samuel Rosenman's *Working with Roosevelt* and Sherwood's *Roosevelt and Hopkins*—from the president's introduction to *PP&A*, vol. 10, pp. vii–xii, and from Barnet Baskerville, *The People's Voice, The Orator in American Society,* Lexington: The University of Kentucky Press, 1979, pp. 175, 176.

p. 14   Hopkins's role as speechwriter. Illness forced Hopkins to retire earlier than Rosenman and Sherwood on most speechwriting nights.

p. 15   "New Deal." Raymond Moley says he (Moley) thought up the words "New Deal." See his *After Seven Years* (New York: Harper and Brothers, 1939), p. 123.

p. 16   "I am like a cat." Quoted in Doris Kearns Goodwin, *No Ordinary Time* (New York: Simon and Schuster, 1994), p. 608.

p. 18 "The real perils of the international situation." FDR to Harrison Conant, October 2, 1937, PPF 4896, FDRL.

p. 18 FDR assured Morgenthau. From Morgenthau's diary, quoted in Robert Dallek, *FDR and American Policy, 1932–1945* (New York: Oxford University Press, 1979), p. 147.

p. 18 "He insisted on leaving it vague." Rosenman, *Working with Roosevelt,* p. 172.

p. 19 "Present reign of terror" and following quotes from FDR's speech of October 5, 1937. *PP&A, 1937,* vol. 6, pp. 406–11.

p. 19 "I thought . . . there would be . . . criticism." October 19, 1937, Box 82, PPF 222.

p. 19 "As time goes on." Ibid.

p. 20 "I want our great democracy." *PP&A, 1937,* vol. 6, pp. 429–38.

p. 21 FDR complains about "Republican propaganda." PPF 153, FDRL.

p. 21 "Much of the trouble . . . has sprung from . . . inaction." *PP&A, 1938,* vol. 7, pp. 1–4.

p. 21 "Democracy has disappeared." Ibid., pp. 230–48.

p. 21 "There can be no peace." Ibid., pp. 563–66.

p. 22 "Aggressive acts . . . undermine all of us." *PP&A, 1939,* vol. 8, pp. 1–12.

p. 22 Meeting with Foreign Affairs Committee. See appendix to Ralph Towne, Jr., "Roosevelt and the Coming of World War II: An Analysis of the War Issues Treated by FDR in Selected Speeches" (Ph.D. dissertation, Michigan State University, 1961).

p. 23 "Every effort of your government will be directed"; "Even a neutral cannot be asked." *PP&A, 1939,* vol. 8, pp. 460–64.

p. 23 United States should stay out of war. A gallup poll held at the time revealed that of those who favored aid to Britain, 88 percent were against U.S. entry into the war.

p. 23 Roosevelt's fear of isolationists' "large funds" and connections with "handful of [filibustering] U.S. Senators." *PP&A, 1940,* vol. 9, p. xxvii.

p. 24 "Vast difference." Ibid., pp. 1–10.

p. 24 "One eye on the war cables." Rosenman, *Working with Roosevelt,* p. 195.

p. 25 "These are ominous days" and following quotes from FDR's speech of May 16, 1940. *PP&A, 1940,* vol. 9, pp. 198–204.

p. 26 "The hand that held the dagger." Ibid., pp. 259–264.

p. 27 "Farmers and businessmen" and following quotes from FDR's speech of September 11, 1940. Ibid., pp. 407–16.

p. 28 "For almost seven years" and following quotes from FDR's Madison Square Garden speech of Oct. 28, 1940. Ibid., pp. 494–510.

p. 29 Martin, Barton, and Fish. Rosenman, *Working with Roosevelt,* p. 240.

p. 30 "Any particular news" and following quotes from FDR's press conference of December 17, 1940. *PP&A, 1940,* vol. 9, pp. 604–15.

p. 32 "By the brilliant but simple trick." Arthur Schlesinger, Jr., *The Coming of the New Deal* (New York: Houghton Mifflin, 1957), p. 566.

p. 32 "Arsenal of democracy." The term was first attributed to Jean Monnet, an influential French businessman and member of the famous cognac family, and picked up and used again by William Knudsen, former president of General Motors but at the time head of the just-created Office of Production Management.

p. 32 "I tried to convey to the great mass of American people" and following quotes from FDR's radio speech of December 29, 1940. *PP&A, 1940,* vol. 9, pp. 633-44.

p. 33 Joseph Grew comment: *Soldier of Freedom, Roosevelt 1940–1945* by James MacGregor Burns (New York: Harcourt Brace Jovanovich, 1970), p. 29.

p. 34 "You say you have been a pacifist." FDR to Mrs. Ogden Mills Reid, May 31, 1940, PPF, FDRL.

p. 34 "The terrible responsibility of bringing a divided nation into war." Arthur Schlesinger, Jr., *The Imperial Presidency* (New York: Houghton Mifflin, 1973), p. 109.

p. 35 50 percent of Americans were willing to consider aid to Britain; 60 percent after Arsenal of Democracy Speech. *Public Opinion Quarterly,* 1940, p. 326.

p. 35   Lend-Lease figures from Doris Kearns Goodwin, *No Ordinary Time* (New York: Simon and Schuster, 1994), p. 602.

p. 35   FDR was "in the midst of a long process of education." Quoted in James MacGregor Burns, *Roosevelt, the Lion and the Fox* (New York: Harcourt Brace, 1956), p. 135.

p. 35   "A nation has to be educated." Quoted in Cornwell, *Presidential Leadership of Public Opinion,* p. 118.

p. 35   "More than any other president." Quoted in Barnet Baskerville, *The People's Voice* (Lexington: University Press of Kentucky, 1979), p. 175.

2. HOLDING THE LINE

The following abbreviations are used here:
FDRL: Franklin Delano Roosevelt Library, Hyde Park, New York
HSTL: Harry S. Truman Library, Independence, Missouri
DDEL: Dwight David Eisenhower Library, Abilene, Kansas
JFKL: John Fitzgerald Kennedy Library, Boston, Massachusetts
LBJL: Lyndon Baines Johnson Library, Austin, Texas
PPP: Public Papers of the Presidents of the United States
Note: Not until Lyndon Johnson did the presidents have more than one volume of public papers (*PPP*) published per year. With Johnson's and subsequent presidencies, volumes were referred to as Book I and Book II (if there was more than one volume).

p. 36   "You could stand on this Tuesday." William Leuchtenburg, *In the Shadow of FDR* (Ithaca, N.Y.: Cornell University Press, 1983), p. ix.

p. 38   Vice President Truman was never in the Map Room. Ibid., p. 6.

p. 38   "Here was a man." Clifford oral history, March 23, 1971, p. 4, HSTL.

p. 38   "Somebody had to work on the speeches." Ibid., p. 10.

p. 39   "From Stettin in the Baltic to Trieste." March 5, 1946.

p. 39   Truman was not ready to abandon era of wartime cooperation with Soviet Union. Robert Ferrell, *Truman* (New York: Viking, 1984), p. 176.

p. 40   "The Russians are trying"; "I want to be ready." Clark Clifford with Richard Holbrooke, *Counsel to the President* (New York: Random House, 1991), p. 110.

p. 40   "An integrated policy and coherent strategy," Ibid., p. 124.

p. 41   Clifford says in his memoirs, *Counsel to the President,* that the report was 26,000 words long (p. 125). In others' memoirs, the figure is 100,000. In any case, it was lengthy.

p. 42   Truman was willing to "lay it on line." Ibid., p. 132.

p. 42   "It's funny how a pending speech will clear the air on policy." Quoted in John Hersey, *Aspects of the Presidency* (New York: Ticknor and Fields, 1980), p. 76.

p. 43   State's draft sounded like an "investment prospectus." Harry S. Truman, *Memoirs: Years of Trial and Hope* (Garden City, N.Y.: Doubleday, 1956), p. 105.

p. 43   "The most significant speech"; Memo from George Elsey to Clark Clifford, March 7, 1947, George Elsey Papers, Box 17, HSTL.

p. 43   "Hardly a line (. . .) wasn't criss-crossed by (. . .) corrections." Elsey Papers, John Jay Iselin, Folder, "The Truman Doctrine: A Study in the Relationship between Crisis and Policymaking" (Ph.D. dissertation, Harvard University, 1964), chap. 11, p. 219.

p. 44   When Truman "had made a decision, he moved fast." Dean Acheson, *Present at the Creation* (New York: Norton, 1969), p. 221.

p. 44   "I believe that it must be the policy of the United States." *PPP,* January 1–December 31, 1947 (Washington, D.C.: Government Printing Office, 1963), pp. 176–80.

p. 45   "Right in the middle." Elsey oral interview, HSTL.

p. 45   Speechwriting process reminded Clifford of his experiences as trial lawyer. Edward Rogge, "The Speechmaking of HST" (Ph.D. dissertation, University of Missouri, 1958), p. 523.

p. 45   "Where the moving and shaking [goes] on." Clark Clifford Oral History, March 23–July 26, 1971, p. 9, HSTL.

p. 46   "A key figure in [his] creative idea department." Sherman Adams, *Firsthand Report* (New York: Harper and Brothers, 1961), p. 42.

p. 46   "Often providing them with imagery and telling phrases." Stephen Ambrose, *Eisenhower, Soldier and President* (New York: Simon and Schuster, 1990), p. 324.

p. 47 "We don't want to scare the country to death." Quoted in John Lear, "Ike and the Peaceful Atom," *Reporter,* January 12, 1956, p. 11.

p. 47 The Candor Speech "shows every appearance of being loused up." Quoted in Martin Medhurst, "Eisenhower's Atoms for Peace," *Communication Monographs* vol. 54 (June 1987): 207.

p. 48 Eisenhower "search[ed] the impasse to action." Dwight D. Eisenhower, *A Mandate for Change* (Garden City, N.Y.: Doubleday, 1963), p. 252.

p. 48 Operation Wheaties. Eisenhower attributed the name also to the regular early-morning breakfast meetings of Jackson and Strauss at the Metropolitan Club.

p. 48 Speech process "was getting off the rails." Jackson to Cutler, October 20, 1953, C. D. Jackson Papers, Box 56, Time, Inc. Files, Log 1952, DDEL.

p. 48 Candor section as "too truculent and heavy." White House Central Files, Box 12, Candor and UN Speech Folder (6), DDEL.

p. 49 "The project is firmly on the rails." Jackson to Hughes, November 6, 1953, ibid.

p. 49 "Red lights blinking"; "reprise in Foster's office." C. D. Jackson Papers, Box 56, Time, Inc. Files, Log 1952, November 25 and 27, DDEL.

p. 49 "Two agonizingly awful hours." Ibid., November 30.

p. 49 "Danger of frittering away." November 30, ibid.

p. 50 "Perfect world audience." Jackson to Merlo Pusey, February 5, 1955, C. D. Jackson Papers, Box 24, Time, Inc. Files, Atoms for Peace (1), DDEL.

p. 51 "Foster's client having made up his mind." C. D. Jackson Papers, Box 56, DDEL.

p. 52 "The governments principally involved." *PPP,* January 20–December 31, 1953, (Washington, D.C.: Government Printing Office, 1960), pp. 813–22.

p. 54 "Whether anyone who had abandoned the Cuban invading forces." Quoted in Kenneth W. Thompson, "Contrasting Views of the Kennedy Administration," *Miller Center Journal* (spring 1994): 137, 138.

p. 55 "I have to show [Khrushchev]." Quoted in Donald Kagan, *On the Origins of War and the Preservation of Peace* (Garden City, N.Y.: Doubleday, 1995), p. 466.

p. 55   "I think [Khrushchev] thought." Quoted in ibid., p. 475.

p. 56   "100 per cent reliable." Quoted in Arthur Schlesinger, Jr., *Robert Kennedy and His Times* (New York: Houghton Mifflin, 1978), p. 506.

p. 56   "We're probably going to have to bomb them." Quoted in Richard Reeves, *President Kennedy: Profile of Power* (New York: Simon and Schuster, 1993), p. 370.

p. 57   Kennedy and Sorensen deserved credit for success. Theodore Sorensen–Carl Kaysen oral interview, April 6, 1964, p. 67, JFKL. Kaysen had been a member of the White House staff.

p. 57   Membership of ex comm, in addition to Robert Kennedy and Ted Sorensen. From the State Department: Dean Rusk, secretary of state; George Ball, undersecretary; Alexis Johnson, deputy undersecretary; Edward Martin, assistant secretary for Latin American affairs; Paul Nitze, assistant secretary; and Llewellyn Thompson, Soviet specialist. From the Defense Department: Robert McNamara, secretary of defense; and Roswell Gilpatric, deputy secretary. Plus: Douglas Dillon, secretary of the treasury; John McCone, CIA director, Maxwell Taylor, chairman of the Joint Chiefs of Staff; and McGeorge Bundy, national security adviser.

p. 57   A clear sense of an emerging policy. Sorensen-Kaysen oral interview.

p. 57   Secrecy was of the utmost importance. Reeves, *President Kennedy,* p. 382. JFK made this comment to Bundy and Thompson.

p. 57   "Each of us changed his mind." Theodore Sorensen, *Kennedy* (New York: Harper and Row, 1965), p. 680.

p. 58   "It can be argued that in the fall of 1962." Michael Beschloss, *The Crisis Years: Kennedy and Khrushchev, 1960–1963* (New York: HarperCollins, 1991), p. 438.

p. 59   A surprise attack looked too much like Pearl Harbor. Dean Acheson thought RFK's argument sophomoric.

p. 59   "We took a vote." Quoted in Reeves, *President Kennedy,* p. 383.

p. 59   The number of sorties had risen to 800! Ibid., p. 384.

p. 60   "As the concrete answers were provided." Theodore Sorensen, *Kennedy* (New York: Harper & Row Publishers, 1965), p. 692.

p. 60 "By answering those questions." Sorensen-Kaysen oral interview, p. 53.

p. 60 "This is a choice between limited and unlimited action." Sorensen-Kaysen interview, p. 54.

p. 61 Deployment of military forces. William Manchester, *The Glory and the Dream* (New York: Bantam, 1975), p. 964.

p. 62 "That statement was false" and following quotes from JFK's speech of October 22, 1962. *PPP,* January 1–December 31, 1962 (Washington D.C.: Government Printing Office, 1963), pp. 806–9.

p. 63 "Relief from the pressures of the Cold War." Schlesinger, *Robert Kennedy and His Times,* p. 530.

p. 63 JFK "plays a damn good hand of poker." Quoted in Beschloss, *The Crisis Years,* p. 543.

p. 63 Hydrogen warheads. Richard Rhodes, "The General and World War III," *New Yorker,* June 19, 1995, p. 59.

p. 63 A major speech is "where policy is made." Quoted in Schlesinger, *A Thousand Days: John F. Kennedy in the White House* (Boston: Houghton Mifflin, 1965), p. 689.

p. 63 "The answer in the Cuban missile crisis." Quoted in Dom Bonafede, "Report/Speech Writers Play Strategic Role in Conveying, Shaping Nixon's Policies," *National Journal,* February 19, 1972, p. 315.

p. 64 "It was as if the lead end of a reel of unseen film." Theodore White, *The Making of the President, 1968* (New York: Atheneum, 1969), p. 108.

p. 64 "The end begins to come in view." Quoted in Clark Clifford and Richard Holbrooke, "Serving the President: The Vietnam Years," part 1, *New Yorker,* May 6, 1991, p. 75.

p. 64 Public support of Johnson's handling of the war at 26 percent Doris Kearns, *Lyndon Johnson and the American Dream* (New York: Harper and Row, 1976), p. 336.

p. 65 "We shall not give up." Harry McPherson oral interview, March 24, 1969, p. 8, LBJL.

p. 65 Clifford's swearing in. He called upon his former Truman administration speechwriting assistant, George Elsey, to take a leave from the company where he had been working and serve as his special assistant.

Eighteen years after their first government experience together, the two men once again were deeply immersed in the nation's foreign policy.

p. 66   "The main field of battle." Clifford and Holbrooke, "Serving the President: The Vietnam Years," part 2, *New Yorker,* May 13, 1991, p. 66.

p. 66   "When you've spent as much time." McPherson oral interview, pp. 10, 11.

p. 67   "Old boy." Quoted in Harry McPherson, *A Political Education* (Boston: Little, Brown, 1972), p. 431.

p. 67   "One of my most deeply trusted associates." Clifford and Holbrooke, "Serving the President," part 2, p. 79.

p. 67   "The guts of the Vietnam decision." McPherson oral interview, pp. 2, 3.

p. 67   "A major step to the insiders." Speech Drafts Collection, Box 273, March 28 Draft, Folder, LBJL.

p. 68   "Well we could stop the bombing." Clifford and Holbrooke, "Serving the President," part 2, p. 68.

p. 68   "Serious political and military risks." As quoted in memo: "Decision to Halt the Bombing," W.W. Rostow to LBJ, March 19, 1970, LBJL.

p. 68   "Get on your horses"; "So during March we prepared a plan." W.W. Rostow oral interview, March 21, 1969, p. 88, AC 74-242, LBJL.

p. 68   "It is quite clear." Quoted in Walter Cronkite's CBS News Special: "LBJ, the Decision to Halt the Bombing," February 6, 1970, transcript, p. 12. During the interview, Cronkite commented on the discrepancy between the secretary's two positions, "It does seem puzzling that Secretary Rusk said on March fourth let's try a bombing pause and one week later go to the Senate and say it can't possibly lead to anything."

p. 68   Rusk's proposal as a public relations ploy. Clifford oral history, July 14, 1969, tape 3, pp. 24, 25, LBJL. Rusk said both in his oral interview and in his memoirs that "Mr. Clifford's views hadn't reached the point at that time as they apparently later became—that we should have begun turning back military action." Clifford did not, Rusk said, change his "reputation of being a hawk" until after his stint at Defense and certainly not by the time of the March 31 speech. Records at the LBJL do not sustain this view.

p. 69   "You have got to stop bombing." Rusk oral interview, March 24, 1969, p. 16, LBJL.

p. 69   "If it doesn't work." McPherson oral interview, March 24, 1969.

p. 70   "We can no longer do the job." Quoted in McGeorge Bundy summary memo, March 26, 1968, LBJL.

p. 70   "We were not seeking a military victory." Quoted in Clifford and Holbrooke, "Serving the President," part 2, p. 78.

p. 71   "The best [meeting] I ever went to." McPherson oral interview, p. 16.

p. 71   "This speech (. . .) is wrong." Quoted by McPherson in ibid., p. 17.

p. 71   "Dean Rusk is a curious man." JFK's close advisers said essentially the same thing about Rusk. RFK went so far as to think the man must have had a breakdown during the missile crisis, so unforthcoming with his views was he. (See Robert F. Kennedy, *Thirteen Days* [New York: NAL Dutton, 1969].) The theory that Rusk had a breakdown is not sustainable by the evidence.

p. 71   Rostow called the White House. Lyndon Baines Johnson, *The Vantage Point* (New York: Holt, Rinehart, and Winston, 1971), p. 420.

p. 72   "Tuck our tails." Quoted in *New York Times,* March 7, 1969, p. 14.

p. 72   "Hunkering down." Ibid.

p. 72   "The speech was uppermost in [his] mind"; "I think that (. . .) he was using the drafts (. . .) to make up his mind." Larry Temple oral history, June 26, 1970, pp. 1, 2, 3, 4, LBJL.

p. 73   "Tonight, I have ordered." *PPP,* January 1–June 30, 1968, Book I (Washington D.C.: Government Printing Office, 1970), pp. 469–76.

p. 73   Rehearsal of LBJ's speech of March 31, 1968. Videotape of rehearsal at LBJL.

p. 73   "One of the things I've learned in government." McPherson oral interview, tape 1, pp. 1, 2.

p. 74   "I may have one of my own." Quoted in the *New York Times,* March 7, 1969.

p. 74 "You can't separate words from policy." Quoted in Charles Maguire oral interview, July 8, 1969, pp. 16, 17, LBJL.

3. THE VIRTUAL PRESIDENCY

—

The following abbreviations are used here:
RNPA: Richard Nixon Presidential Archives, College Park, Maryland
PPP: Public Papers of the President (cf. previous chap.)

p. 76 "In the modern presidency, concern for image." Richard Nixon, *The Memoirs of Richard Nixon* (New York: Grosset and Dunlap, 1978), p. 354.

p. 76 "Nixon spent half his working time." John Ehrlichman, *Witness to Power* (New York: Simon and Schuster, 1982), p. 266.

p. 77 "Taft infinitely more effective than Teddy Roosevelt." Nixon's memo of February 2, 1970, quoted in H. R. Haldeman, *The Haldeman Diaries, Inside the Nixon White House* (New York: G. P. Putnam's Sons, 1994), p. 125.

p. 77 "Ike had been distant." Ibid.

p. 77 "JFK did nothing but appeared great." Ibid.

p. 77 "Teddy Roosevelt and JFK both well-born charmers." Nixon's memo of May 19, 1970, quoted in ibid., p. 168.

p. 77 "Kennedy was colder." Nixon's memo of May 16, 1971, quoted in ibid., p. 287.

p. 77 "Kennedy blew practically everything." Nixon's memo of February 28, 1973, quoted in ibid., p. 582.

p. 77 "We have to be clear on this point." Quoted in Joe McGinnis, *The Selling of the President* (New York: Trident Press, 1969), pp. 193, 194, 195.

Kathleen Hall Jamieson, one of the nation's most distinguished scholars of presidential speech, made the point in *Packaging the Presidency* (New York: Oxford University Press, 1984) that Joe McGinnis's book *The Selling of the President* "tended to create the impression that what its author had found in the Nixon campaign was new to American politics or unique to the campaign he had examined. Neither was the case." No problem there: Presidential image making is as old as the Republic. FDR claimed that he and Orson Wells were the best actors in the land, to give one instance. What was new in the Nixon story was his obsession with image over everything else.

Professor Jamieson went on to deny that Nixon's admen sold a wholly new image of the man to the public. She based one of her arguments on a portion of the Raymond Price memo quoted by me. One sentence of the lengthy memo that I did not quote is the following: "I know the whole business of contrived imagemongering is repugnant to RN, with its implication of slick gimmicks and phony merchandising." All one has to do is read some of the evidence of Nixon's senior aides like Kissinger, Ehrlichman, Haldeman, or Nixon biographer Stephen Ambrose to be thoroughly convinced of the disingenuousness of Price's statement.

p. 78   "Create a more friendly image of the P." Haldeman, *Diaries,* May 18, 1969, p. 58.

p. 78   "We've totally failed." Ibid., December 3, 1970, p. 214.

p. 78   "The problem with government." Quoted in Michael Kelly, "The Game: How Image Became the Sacred Faith of Washington," *New York Times Magazine,* October 31, 1993, p. 68.

p. 79   "He insisted that he be given one hundred words." Quoted in Hedrick Smith, *The Power Game, How Washington Works* (New York: Random House, 1988), pp. 405, 406.

p. 80   "He was the supreme prime time president." Arthur Schlesinger, Jr., *The Imperial Presidency* (New York: Houghton Mifflin, 1973), p. 226.

p. 80   "Assault books." Pat Buchanan's memo to John Mitchell of June 8, 1972: "Attached is the Assault Book which Bob Haldeman requested . . . on which Ken Khacigian and I have been working this past week. In addition to that, we sent along some ideas on assault strategy. At present there are only two copies of the memo and the book that are extant. We are holding the attack material very tight . . . for obvious reasons." RNPA.

p. 81   "I left [at] the end of 1970." Author's interview with Keogh, June 1996.

p. 81   "Reviewed Price's first real draft." Haldeman, *Diaries,* p. 118.

p. 81   "On January 12, 1971, I had a series of Sunday phone calls." Ehrlichman, *Witness to Power,* p. 268.

p. 82   Haldeman was "an honest doorkeeper." Author's interview with Price, April 1996.

p. 82   " 'House philosopher.' " Raymond Price, *With Nixon* (New York: Viking, 1977), p. 98.

p. 82   "Each major speech takes a week at least." Quoted in James David Barber, *The Presidential Character, Predicting Presidential Performance in the White House* (Englewood Cliffs, N.J.: Prentice-Hall, 1972), p. 374.

p. 83   "Thinking a speech through." Richard Nixon, *In the Arena* (New York: Simon and Schuster, 1990), p. 150.

p. 83   "It has always been my view." Nixon's memo of April 8, 1972, RNPA.

p. 83   "So much of it as will receive general support by teaching." FDR in a 1932 campaign speech before the San Francisco Commonwealth Club.

p. 83   "[Nixon's] most significant [speech] on foreign policy." Nixon, *In the Arena*, p. 150.

p. 83   "Old" policies in effect. In a press conference in Guam on July 25, 1969, Nixon said that nations threatened by communism must take primary responsibility for their own defense. "We must avoid that kind of policy that will make countries in Asia so dependent on us that we are dragged into conflicts such as the one we have in Vietnam." Senate Majority Leader Mike Mansfield dubbed the remarks the Nixon Doctrine.

p. 83   Withdrawal of U.S. troops. If a withdrawal was announced, Hanoi would have no incentive to negotiate, so an announcement was self-defeating.

p. 84   "And so tonight . . . I ask for your support" and following quotes from Nixon's speech of November 3, 1969. *PPP*, 1971, pp. 401–9.

p. 84   "Silent majority." Nixon had publicly used similar phrases before like "silent center," "new majority," "quiet Americans," "quiet majority." Vice President Spiro Agnew had used "silent majority" before the November 3 speech. (Haldeman, *Diaries*, p. 103)

p. 84   "He wanted to draw the battle lines." William Safire, *Before the Fall* (Garden City, N.Y.: Doubleday, 1975), p. 172.

p. 85   Emerging Republican majority. Kevin Phillips, *The Emerging Republican Majority* (Garden City, N.Y.: Anchor Books, 1970).

p. 85   "Colson organized a supposedly spontaneous support." Stephen

Ambrose, *Nixon: The Triumph of a Politician, 1962–1972* (New York: Simon and Schuster, 1989), p. 311.

p. 85   "Who might be speaking on this subject." Nixon to Haldeman, November 12, 1969, RNPA.

p. 85   "Strike forces." Nixon to Haldeman, November 24, 1969, RNPA.

p. 85   "Released" favorable remarks. Nixon to Haldeman, October 26, 1969, RNPA.

p. 85   Second barrage of wires. Butterfield to Nixon, October 12, 1969, RNPA.

p. 85   "Obsessed with the cosmetics of public relations." *National Journal,* June 23, 1973, p. 909.

p. 86   "The substance [of] the November 3 speech," Nixon to Haldeman, November 12, 1969, RNPA.

p. 86   "The President has curious work habits." Quoted in Ehrlichman, *Witness to Power,* p. 266.

p. 86   "Incredible hours alone"; "no one except Theodore Roosevelt and Woodrow Wilson." Nixon to Haldeman, November 24, 1969, RNPA. Over and over again, Nixon made this point in memos.

p. 86   Nixon's "strong predilection for secretive and isolated decision-making." Henry Kissinger, *The White House Years* (Boston: Little Brown, 1979), p. 306.

p. 86   "Surprise will increase the size of the audience." Nixon, *In the Arena,* p. 215.

p. 87   "Channels of communication." Schlesinger, *The Imperial Presidency,* p. 272.

p. 87   "When I objected to the torrent of interviews." *Safire, Before the Fall,* p. 274.

p. 87   "His own complex antennae kept [LBJ] in . . . touch with reality." Schlesinger, *The Imperial Presidency,* p. 187.

p. 87   Surprise at announcement of withdrawal of 150,000 troops from Vietnam. Rogers had been informed shortly before the announcement; Laird had expected Nixon to do something in the neighborhood of 40,000.

p. 88   "Secret plan to end the war." Quoted in Stephen Ambrose, *Rise to Globalism*, 2d ed. (New York: Penguin, 1980), p. 309.

p. 89   Nixon wanted CIA "to develop and implement a plan." Kissinger, *The White House Years*, p. 465.

p. 89   Recommendations to Nixon, Ibid., p. 490.

p. 89   "So he could concentrate on [the] Cambodia decision." Haldeman, *Diaries*, p. 153.

p. 89   "This was not the time." Safire, *Before the Fall*, p. 183.

p. 89   "But in the days before announcing this most fateful decision." Kissinger, *The White House Years*, p. 503.

p. 89   "You can't ram [your resolution] down their throats." Ibid., p. 497.

p. 90   Nixon "was shocked and disappointed." Nixon, *Memoirs*, p. 457.

p. 90   "My most controversial foreign-policy decision." Nixon, *In the Arena*, p. 333.

p. 90   Cambodia had been a "neutral nation" and following quotes from Nixon's speech of April 30, 1971. *PPP*, pp. 405–10.

p. 90   B-52s had conducted 3,620 secret raids. William Manchester, *The Glory and the Dream* (New York: Bantam, 1974), p. 1210.

p. 92   "It was the old man's speech." Quoted in Barber, *The Presidential Character*, p. 434.

p. 92   Buchanan's changed speechwriting role. Author's interviews with Price and Keogh, June 1996.

p. 93   "Nixon gets very little firsthand." Barber, *The Presidential Character*, p. 439.

p. 93   "Game plan to sell the making of a decision." Safire, *Before the Fall*, p. 188.

p. 93   "Only the president has all the facts." Ibid., p. 186.

p. 93   "PR game plan." Ibid., p. 188.

p. 93   "Don't worry about divisiveness." Nixon, *Memoirs*, p. 190.

p. 94   Senate committee castigates Nixon. On May 11, the Senate Foreign Relations Committee adopted two amendments and a resolution requiring Nixon to get American troops out of Cambodia by June 30.

p. 94 "The operation had been a complete success." Nixon, *Memoirs,* p. 467.

p. 95 "To affirm the word passionately." Hughes to Eisenhower, December 2, 1958, DDEL.

p. 97 Reagan's Knute Rockne Speech of March 9, 1988. Book I (Washington, D.C.: Government Printing Office, 1990), pp. 305–11.

p. 98 "Pre-advance." Author's interview with Gilder, June 1996.

p. 98 "Standing here before a mural of your revolution." *PPP,* 1988, Book I (Washington, D.C.: Government Printing Office, 1990), pp. 683–92.

p. 99 "We wanted to control what people saw." Quoted in Kelly, "The Game," p. 71.

p. 99 "We would go through the president's schedule day by day." Quoted in ibid.

p. 99 Reagan was the most photographed president. Every month 4,000–6,000 photographs of him were released by the White House.

p. 99 "As opposed to Kissinger." Quoted in Mark Rozell, "Presidential Imagemakers on the Limits of Spin Control," *Presidential Studies Quarterly* (Winter 1995): 83.

p. 100 Reagan treated like "supreme anchorman." Quoted in Michael Schaller, *Reckoning with Reagan* (New York: Oxford University Press, 1994), p. 57.

p. 100 Reagan required a "very strong stage manager." Quoted in ibid.

p. 100 "I can't think of a single meeting." Quoted in Hedrick Smith, *The Power Game* (New York: Simon and Schuster, 1991), p. 402.

p. 101 Reagan's State of the Union Address, February 4, 1986. *PPP, 1986,* Book I (Washington, D.C.: Government Printing Office, 1988), pp. 125–130.

p. 101 "Reach for the stars" and following quotes by Wirthlin and Noonan. Peggy Noonan, *What I Saw at the Revolution* (New York: Random House, 1990), pp. 283, 284.

p. 102 "After careful consultation with my advisers." *PPP, 1983,* Book I (Washington, D.C.: Government Printing Office, 1984), pp. 437–443.

p. 102   Robert McFarlane and SDI. MacFarlane looked on SDI as a bargaining tool with the Soviets. As he saw it, the United States would launch a huge ballistic missile defense research program. The Soviets would object because, as Richard Nixon realized in 1972, it would look "like a prelude to an offensive strategy threatening nuclear deterrent." The United States would then offer to scrap the program in return for Soviet agreement to reduce its ICBM force so a defensive system would not be needed. McFarlane, however, never told Reagan about his idea and according to Lou Cannon, did not realize until too late how strongly Reagan was committed to SDI as an end in itself.

p. 102   "We didn't tell anyone." Quoted in Lou Cannon, *President Reagan: The Role of a Lifetime,* p. 331.

p. 102   Speechwriter clueless about SDI. Author's interview with Bakshian, May 1996.

p. 103   "We don't have the technology to do this." George Shultz, *Turmoil and Triumph* (New York: Charles Scribner's Sons, 1993), p. 250.

p. 103   "It's too sweeping." Ibid., p. 251.

p. 103   "If a new defensive system could not be penetrated." Quoted in ibid., p. 251, 252.

p. 103   "The idea and the rhetoric don't fit together." Ibid., p. 254.

p. 103   Reagan's belief in American ingenuity. Author's interview with Parvin, May 1996.

p. 104   "Space shield"/"concept." Quoted in Schaller, *Reckoning with Reagan,* p. 131.

p. 104   "He didn't know or care." Quoted in Mark Hertsgaard, *On Bended Knee: The Press and the Reagan Presidency* (New York: Farrar, Straus, Giroux, 1988), p. 346.

p. 104   Star Wars. After the expenditure of tens of billions of dollars researching laser and kinetic-energy weapons, Reagan's Strategic Defense Initiative was scaled both to a more realistic research program focused on plausible technologies like ground-based interceptors and spaced-based sensors that can monitor the launch and flight of an intercontinental ballistic missile.

p. 104   Reagan's speechwriters. Over eight years, fourteen writers served Ronald Reagan. They are: Bently Elliott, Tony Dolan, Kenneth Khachigian, Aram Bakshian—all directors of the department; Peggy Noonan, Peter Robinson, Landon Parvin, John Podhoretz, Josh Gilder,

Clark Judge, Mari Maseng, Mark Klugman, Dana Rohrabacher, Allan Meyer.

p. 105   "I believed in the things." Author's interview with Dolan, May 1996.

p. 105   "The conscience of the presidency." Quoted in William K. Muir, Jr., *Ronald Reagan's Bully Pulpit* (San Francisco: Institute for Contemporary Studies Press), 1992, p. 35.

p. 105   Elliott spent "three weeks reading all [Reagan's] speeches." Quoted in ibid., p. 25.

p. 105   "Reagan was easy to write for." Author's interview with Parvin, May 1996.

p. 105   "Ronald Reagan had a superior gift." Author's interview with Elliott, June 1996.

p. 106   "[Poland] magnificently unreconciled to repression." *PPI, 1982,* Book I (Washington, D.C.: Government Printing Office, 1983), pp. 742–48.

p. 107   "Dave is a consensus person." Author's interview with Elliott, June 1996.

p. 107   "In the end all substance and tactics came down to the drafting of words." Quoted in Francis X. Clines, "Reagan's Master of Compromise," *New York Times Magazine,* February 16, 1986, pp. 35, 37.

p. 108   "It would come back tapioca." Noonan, *What I Saw at the Revolution,* p. 77.

p. 108   "A bureaucrat from state." Ibid., p. 72.

p. 108   [She] "would use the 'hand-grenade' technique." Ibid., p. 77.

p. 108   "I can't write well without hearing the person." Ibid., p. 64.

p. 109   "As long as his A-team was in charge." Author's interview with Bakshian, April 1996.

p. 109   "The TV speech was scheduled for Thursday evening." David Stockman, *The Triumph of Politics* (New York: Harper and Row, 1986), pp. 324, 325.

p. 110   "No one . . . taught people more emphatically." *New York Times Magazine,* August 11, 1996, p. 32.

p. 110   "President Reagan's reliance on speechwriters." Kathleen Hall

Jamieson, *Eloquence in an Electronic Age: The Transformation of Political Speaking* (New York: Oxford University Press, 1988), pp. 220, 221.

p. 110   "Ultimately the guy behind [Iran-Contra]." Shultz, *Turmoil and Triumph,* p. 811.

p. 111   "The only way to contain damage." Ibid., p. 786.

p. 111   "I was amazed." Ibid., p. 787.

p. 111   "Iran is playing us for suckers." Ibid., p. 814.

p. 111   "Our policy of not making concessions." Quoted in ibid., p. 815.

p. 111   Charges were "utterly false." *PPP, 1986,* Book II (Washington, D.C.: Government Printing Office, 1989), pp. 1546–48.

p. 111   Speech crafted largely from information about Oliver North. Author's interviews with Dolan and Parvin.

p. 111   "Carping, angry, defensive." Cannon, *President Reagan,* p. 684.

p. 111   "The president's speech convinced me." Shultz, *Turmoil and Triumph,* p. 819.

p. 112   "We're going to continue on this path." Quoted in ibid., pp. 830, 831.

p. 112   McFarlane's memo "was not . . . accurate account." Tower Report, p. D–S, quoted in Cannon, *President Reagan,* p. 687.

p. 112   "If actions . . . were taken without my authorization." Ibid., pp. 1594–95.

p. 113   "Conclusion portrayed the president." Schaller, *Reckoning with Reagan,* p. 166.

p. 113   Choice of Landon Parvin as writer of Reagan's speech of March 4, 1987. Author's interview with Parvin.

p. 113   "A few months ago I told the American people" and following quotes from Reagan's speech of March 4, 1987. *PPP, 1987,* Book I (Washington, D.C.: Government Printing Office, 1989), pp. 208–11.

p. 113   "I didn't do it." Quoted in Kurt Ritter, "Ronald Reagan," *U.S. Presidents as Orators,* ed. Halford Ryan (Westport, CT: Greenwood Press, 1995), p. 327.

p. 113   Cannon's account of how Reagan was persuaded to make a semi-apology. Cannon, *President Reagan,* p. 734.

p. 114   "Once he had something fixed in his mind." Frank Carlucci, "The Reagan Presidency," *Miller Center Journal* (spring 1995): p. 45.

p. 114   Reagan tended "to remember only the evidence." Richard Darman, *Who's in Control, Polar Politics and the Sensible Center* (N.Y.: Simon and Schuster, 1996), pp. 39, 40.

p. 114   Reagan understood that governing is not "about meetings." Author's interview with Dolan, May 1996.

4. THE MESSAGE IN THE BOTTLE
—

The following abbreviations are used here:
GRFL: Gerald Rudolph Ford Library, Ann Arbor, Michigan
JCL: Jimmy Carter Library, Atlanta, Georgia
PPP: Public Papers of the Presidents of the United States

p. 116   Ford's frequency of speaking. Robert Hartmann's memo of December 8, 1976, GRFL. The cumulative word count as of December 21, 1976, was 2,738,563.

p. 117   Hugh Sidey associated a diminished presidency with Carter's penchant for too frequently addressing the public. Roderick Hart, *The Sound of Leadership* (Chicago: University of Chicago Press, 1987), p. 3.

p. 117   Ford was "nominated and confirmed [by representatives of] both parties." August 9, 1974, *PPP, 1974* (Washington, D.C.: Government Printing Office, 1975), pp. 103–4.

p. 118   The position of staff coordinator. Eager not to repeat anything resembling the Nixon-Haldeman system, Ford initiated a "lesser" chief of staff called a staff coordinator. Al Haig had been Nixon's last chief of staff, so with Ford he retained his title.

p. 118   Robert Hartmann's speeches were "weak in complex areas of substance." Ron Nessen, *It Sure Looks Different from the Inside* (Chicago: Playboy Press, 1975), p. 84.

p. 119   "Where was Hartmann?" and following quotes Casserly diary. John Casserly, *The Ford White House, A Diary of a Speechwriter* (Boulder: Colorado Associated University Press, 1977), p. 18.

p. 119   "I am still profoundly disturbed"; "I keep thinking (. . .) of a speechwriting session of Harry Truman's." John Hersey, *The President* (New York: Knopf, 1975), pp. 29, 30.

p. 119   The usual Ford speechwriting procedure. Author's interview with Theis, June 1996.

p. 120   "I have nothing against Gergen." Robert Hartmann, *Palace Politics: An Inside Account of the Ford Years* (New York: McGraw-Hill), p. 341.

p. 120   "The president spent an unusually large amount of time." William Syers's interview with Pat Butler, June 27, 1985, William Syers, Collection, Box 1, Pat Butler Folder, GRFL.

p. 120   "I came to the White House when I was 25." Author's interview with Butler, June 1996.

p. 121   Ford's fireside chat of January 13, 1975. *PPP, 1975,* Book I (Washington, D.C.: Government Printing Office, 1977), pp. 30–35.

p. 122   "The meeting degenerated into haggling." Nessen, *It Sure Looks Different From the Inside,* p. 84.

p. 122   "Unfortunately the two factions couldn't seem to agree." Gerald Ford, *A Time to Heal, Autobiography of Gerald R. Ford* (New York: Harper and Row and the Readers Digest Association, 1979), p. 233.

p. 122   "Twenty-six years ago, a freshman congressman (. . .) stood before Sam Rayburn." January 15, 1975, *PPP, 1975,* vol. 1, pp. 36–46.

p. 122   Ford's 1975 SOTU Address "exposed a serious weakness." Nessen, *It Sure Looks Different From the Inside,* p. 85.

p. 123   "So long as words were my responsibility." Hartmann, *Palace Politics,* p. 383.

p. 123   "Hardly as emphatically as I'd hoped." Ibid., p. 390.

p. 123   "It became clear that new sedition was brewing." Ibid., p. 391.

p. 123   The Gergen draft of the 1976 SOTU Address. A. James Reichley's interview with Gergen, February 21, 1978, GRFL.

p. 123   "Go through theirs once more." Quoted in Hartmann, *Palace Politics,* p. 391.

p. 123   Meeting of January 17, 1976, in Cabinet Room. Accounts by Hartmann and Butler, author's interviews with each.

p. 124   "He thought they had done all their fighting at Williamsburg." Quoted in Casserly, *The Ford White House,* p. 287.

p. 124   "Most of the people in the West Wing (. . .) don't like it." Ibid., p. 288.

p. 124   Ford's SOTU Address of January 19, 1976. *PPP, 1976–77* Book I (Washington, D.C.: Government Printing Office, 1979), pp. 31–42.

p. 124   "It was difficult to find a new or inspiring thought." *New York Times,* January 20, 1976.

p. 124   [Ford] is "too nice a guy." William Syers interview of Hartmann, May 3, 1985, pp. 2, 3, GRFL.

p. 125   Ford announces "a full, free, and absolute pardon unto Richard Nixon." *PPP, 1974* (Washington, D.C.: Government Printing Office, 1975), pp. 103–4.

p. 125   Hartmann suspected of "stirring the pot." Ford, *A Time to Heal,* p. 185.

p. 125   Ford's management style. Reichley's interview with Gergen.

p. 125   A presidential speech "is not merely a formal announcement." Hartmann, *Palace Politics,* pp. 384, 385.

p. 125   "The word will come down." Quoted in William Gage Chapel, "Speechwriting in the Nixon Administration," *Journal of Communications* (spring 1976): 67, 68.

p. 126   "Kids in college keep complaining." Quoted in Hartmann, *Palace Politics,* pp. 218, 219.

p. 126   "New ways to bring the world of work and the institutions of education closer together." Ford's speech of August 30, 1974. *PPP, 1974, 1975,* pp. 68–74.

p. 126   Media began "ringing the telephone." Paul O'Neill, "President Ford and the Budget," *The Ford Presidency,* ed. Kenneth W. Thompson (Lanham, Md.: University Press of America and the Miller Center, University of Virginia, 1988), p. 115.

p. 126   "What did he mean by that?" Bradley Patterson, Jr., *The Ring of Power, The White House Staff and Its Expanding Role in Government* (New York: Basic Books, 1988), p. 196.

p. 126   "I went banging around in the Executive Office Building." O'Neill, "President Ford and the Budget," p. 115.

p. 127   "We made it up." Quoted in Patterson, p. 196.

p. 127   "How and why are speechwriters given so much latitude?" Casserly, *The Ford White House,* p. 58.

p. 127　"Ford made so many speeches." Author's interview with Theis, June 1996.

p. 127　Ford's "lack of anything to say." John Coyne, Jr., *Fall in and Cheer* (Garden City, N.Y.: Doubleday, 1979), p. 97.

p. 128　"The speechwriters very existence is an affront." Hendrik Hertzberg, "Jimmy Carter 1977–1981," *Character Above All,* ed. Robert A. Wilson (New York: Simon and Schuster, 1995), p. 172.

p. 128　Candidate Carter warned "the audience." Patrick Anderson, *Electing Jimmy Carter, The Campaign of 1976* (Baton Rouge: Louisiana State University Press, 1994), p. 34.

p. 128　Carter's mistrust of "anything that smacked of calculation." Carter Presidency Project, Speechwriters Session, Miller Center of Public Affairs, University of Virginia, December 3, 4, 1981, p. 11. (Hereafter cited as Miller Center.)

p. 129　"(. . .) we [writers] end up working in the dark." Fallows to Rafshoon, June 8, 1978, JCL.

p. 129　"There was always somebody who had access to Carter about speeches." Miller Center, pp. 11 and 28.

p. 129　"[Carter] was surrounded by non-writers." Ibid., pp. 113 and 116.

p. 130　"One of the few [speeches] that was done the way speechwriting ought to be done." Ibid., p. 18.

p. 130　"On that November day (. . .) a terrible moment was frozen in the lives of many of us here." *PPP, 1979,* Book II (Washington, D.C.: Government Printing Office, 1980), pp. 1979–80.

p. 131　Carter to take on "not just Ted Kennedy." Miller Center, p. 18.

p. 131　"We've been asked to get up a speech on the canal treaties." Quoted in Martin Scham, *Washington Post,* December 30, 1977, p. A2.

p. 131　Carter's Panama Canal Speech of February 1, 1978. *PPP, 1978,* Book I (Washington, D.C.: Government Printing Office, 1979), pp. 258–62.

p. 132　"He just took the decision memo off alone up at Camp David." Hendrik Hertzberg's unpublished diary, courtesy of Hertzberg.

p. 133　"One of the worst speeches I've ever seen." Carter's handwritten note on memo that Rafshoon sent to the president on April 1, 1979, and Rafshoon's exit memo, pp. 11, 12, JCL.

p. 133   Carter's energy speech of April 5, 1979. *PPP, 1979,* Book I (Washington, D.C.: Government Printing Office, 1980), pp. 609–14.

p. 134   "I just turn 30 or 35 items in my mind." Harvey Shapiro, "A Conversation with Jimmy Carter," *NYTBR,* June 19, 1977, p. 1.

p. 134   "At best, there was a cool reception to these ideas." Jimmy Carter, *Keeping Faith* (New York: Bantam, 1982), p. 111.

p. 134   "A model for how a speechwriter should behave." Author's interview with Hertzberg, April 1996.

p. 134   "I wanted the title." Miller Center, p. 128.

p. 134   Carter's April 5 speech impelled Stewart to force his way into meetings. Author's interview with Stewart, May 1996.

p. 135   Ten proposals for "what we will do." James Fallows, "The Passionless Presidency," *Atlantic Monthly,* May 1979, p. 42.

p. 135   Carter's memo of May 10, 1978. Speechwriting Chronological File, Box 26, JCL.

p. 136   "The Soviets can choose either confrontation or cooperation." Carter's speech of June 7, 1978, *PPP, 1978,* Book I, pp. 1052–57.

p. 137   "A couple of days after your speech at Annapolis." Rafshoon Collection, press conference briefing papers, n.d., JCL.

p. 137   Carter would not "be shackled by one or the other." Miller Center, p. 54.

p. 137   "Unlike other presidents, he was unwilling to present himself (. . .) in simplified terms." Robert Strong, "Anecdote and Evidence: Jimmy Carter's Annapolis Address on U.S.-Soviet relations," *Miller Center Journal* (spring 1994): 37–40.

p. 137   The writers . . . "trying to reconcile too many views." Speech file, Annapolis Speech, JCL.

p. 138   "I think it will reinforce a sense of confusion." Rafshoon Papers, June 5, 1978, JCL.

p. 138   "I sent him a draft of a speech." Cyrus Vance, *Hard Choices* (New York: Simon and Schuster, 1983), p. 101.

p. 138   Carter's "instinct for harmony." Hertzberg's unpublished diary.

p. 138   Carter's failure "to project a vision." Fallows, "The Passionless Presidency," p. 43.

p. 139   "This is the best I can do." Author's interview with Stewart.

p. 139   "We were seeing and hearing some of the weirdest things." Miller Center, p. 73.

p. 140   "I don't know when it happened." Quoted in ibid., p. 70.

p. 140   Carter's Malaise Speech of July 15, 1979. *PPP, 1979,* Book II, pp. 1235–40.

p. 141   "I was dumbfounded." Author's interview with Stewart.

p. 141   "Every reforming president has adopted a brief, evocative phrase." Hertzberg to Fallows, January 5, 1977, JCL.

p. 141   Carter's New Foundation Speech of January 23, 1979. *PPP, 1980,* Book I (Washington, D.C.: Government Printing Office, 1980), pp. 103–8.

p. 141   The administration is "laying a new foundation." Memo for the President, January 3, 1979, Rafshoon Papers, JCL.

p. 142   Sorensen's "new pathways" suggestion. Memo to Rafshoon, January 15, 1979, Greg Schneiders Notes, Box 33, 1979 SOTU, JCL.

p. 142   The president "would be willing." Miller Center, p. 23.

p. 143   "The fox knows many things." Attributed to the Greek poet Archilochus but made famous by Berlin's famous essay "The Hedgehog and the Fox."

p. 144   "Mess privileges were (. . .) the *ne plus ultra.*" David Stockman, *Triumph of Politics* (New York: Harper and Row, 1986), p. 101.

p. 143   Mess "was a collegial thing." Miller Center, p. 118.

p. 144   "There certainly wasn't any attempt to (. . .) downgrade them." Quoted in "Bush Writers Leave a Mess," *New York Times,* April 2, 1989, p. 9.

p. 144   "In terms of political pecking order." Ibid.

p. 144   "Speeches are a less important form of communication for Bush." Quoted in John Maltese, *Spin Control: The White House Office of Communication Management of Presidential News* (Chapel Hill: University of North Carolina Press, 1994), p. 214.

p. 144   Bush "cut anything that put him in his predecessor's shadow." Author's interview with Ferguson, May 1996.

p. 144   Bush was "fearful of comparison with Reagan's speechwriting." William Safire, "Bush Hires a Writer," *New York Times,* February 11, 1991.

p. 145   "This is absolutely ludicrous." Quoted in Anne Devoy, "Bush Communication Chief Named," *Washington Post,* July 9, 1992.

p. 146   "We'd be sold on an idea." Author's interview with Davis, June 1996.

p. 146   The president "took out the red meat." Ibid.

p. 146   "And then you ask why it doesn't sing," Ann Devoy, "Bush's Speech Writers," *The Washington Post,* January 31, 1990, The Federal Page.

p. 146   "The rhetorical trick is divining the drift." Quoted in Safire, "Bush Hires a Writer."

p. 146   Writers don't have "initiatives to present to the public." Andrew Rosenthal, "Bush's Son Rides into Town," *New York Times,* April 10, 1992, p. A27. Quote from George Bush, Jr.

p. 146   " 'Split the difference' presidency." Burt Solomon, "Being a Good Manager Is Not Enough," *National Journal,* May 27, 1981, p. 1316.

p. 146   "We'd send him stuff." Author's interview with Ferguson, May 1996.

p. 147   Bush said he "should repackage [his] philosophy." Quoted in Michael Duffy and Dan Goodgame, *Marching in Place, the Status Quo Presidency of George Bush* (New York: Simon and Schuster, 1992), p. 67.

p. 147   Bush's word of choice "prudent." John Podhoretz, *Hell of a Ride, Backstage at the White House Follies, 1989–1992* (New York: Simon and Schuster, 1994), p. 224.

p. 147   Bush's speeches "have no weight." Devoy, January 31, 1990.

p. 147   "Certainly conforms with Helsinki Final Act." *PPP, 1989,* Book II (Washington, D.C.: Government Printing Office, 1991), pp. 1488–90.

p. 148   Need for "tax revenue increases." Bush's written communication of June 26, 1990. *PPP, 1990,* vol. 2, pp. 1349–50.

p. 148   Bush's speech of October 2, 1990, was "pretty much written by Darman." Author's interview with Davis.

p. 148   Desert Storm. On August 2, 1990, Iraq invaded Kuwait. The Bush administration mounted Operation Desert Shield, consisting of diplomacy (putting together a coalition of nations) and economic embargo. When Hussein did not withdraw by the January 15 deadline imposed by the UN Security Council, Allied forces led by the United States launched Operation Desert Storm, an offensive military campaign that consisted of massive aerial bombardment of Baghdad, on January 17. When Hussein still defied Bush's ultimatum to withdraw unconditionally by February 23, the Allied forces launched a ground offensive on February 24, which routed Iraq in 100 hours.

p. 149   Bush's address to the nation of August 8, 1990. *PPP, 1990*, Book II (Washington, D.C.: Government Printing Office, 1991), pp. 1107–1109.

p. 149   Defense of Saudi Arabia was "the fig leaf for American intervention." Jean Edward Smith, *George Bush's War* (New York: Henry Holt, 1992).

p. 149   Bush's vision of "a new world order" and following quotes from his speech of September 11, 1990. *PPP, 1990*, Book II (Washington, D.C.: Government Printing Office, 1991), pp. 1218–22.

p. 150   Could not . . . allow "naked aggression." Remarks in Cabinet Room, August 2, 1990, *PPP, 1990*, Book II (Washington, D.C.: Government Printing Office, 1991), pp. 1083–85.

p. 150   "Our way of life . . . will suffer." Ibid., pp. 1138–39.

p. 151   "There had been a lot of groping." Author's interview with Davis.

p. 152   "No new taxes." From Bush's Convention Speech in New Orleans in August 1988.

p. 153   "His rhetoric rarely rises to seriousness." *Washington Post*, January 29, 1992.

p. 153   Bush's "foreign and domestic" accomplishments. John Podhoretz, *Hell of a Ride: Backstage at the White House Follies, 1989–1993* (New York: Simon and Schuster, 1994), p. 196.

p. 154   Theodore Roosevelt as Bush's personal hero. Davis says Bush later reconsidered this answer and said he saw himself as another Ike, meaning "above the fray." The Ike paradigm, says Davis, was his undoing.

5. STRIKE UP THEIR BAND

—

The following abbreviation is used here:
PPP: Public Papers of the President

p. 157   "The whole place runs on Clinton standard time." Author's interview with Rosner, April 1996.

p. 158   "[Clinton] had thought through the nation's essential problems." Elizabeth Drew, *On the Edge* (New York: Simon and Schuster, 1984), p. 80.

p. 158   "I don't know." Quoted in author's interviews with Baer, July 1994, April 1995, May 1996.

p. 158   "[Clinton] does his own thing in speeches." Author's interview with Rossner.

p. 158   "He has a native desire to voice things his way." Author's interview with Dreyer, April 1996.

p. 158   "[This] is a man with knowledge of the basic texts." Author's interview with Kusnet, July 1994.

p. 159   Points prepared for Clinton's speech of November 13, 1993. Author's interview with Curiel, April 1996.

p. 159   "[The] great crisis of the spirit that is gripping America today" and following quotes from Clinton's speech of November 13, 1993. *PPP, 1993,* vol. 2. (Washington, D.C.: Government Printing Office, 1994), pp. 1981–86.

p. 160   "Mechanic-in-chief." Quoted in Bob Woodward, *The Agenda* (New York: Simon and Schuster, 1994), p. 255.

p. 161   "We never received anything but a finished draft from Bush." Author's interview with Taylor Branch, March 1993.

p. 161   "Tonight we come together." Quoted in David Broder and Haynes Johnson, *The System* (New York: Simon and Schuster, 1996), p. 28.

p. 162   "[Clinton] had too many issues out there." Quoted in Drew, *On the Edge,* p. 166.

p. 163   "So much being done." Author's interview with Kusnet, July 1994.

p. 163   "If you ask me for one of the mistakes . . . I have made." *PPP, 1994,* Book II (Washington, D.C. Government Printing Office, 1995), pp. 2045–52.

p. 163   "I totally neglected how to get the public informed." Quoted in Elizabeth Drew, *Showdown* (New York: Simon and Schuster, 1996), p. 66.

p. 163   Clinton's 1995 State of the Union Address. *Weekly Compilation, Presidential Documents,* vol. 31, January–April 1995, *Federal Register* (Washington, D.C.), pp. 96–107.

p. 164   "My test is." Ibid., p. 569.

p. 164   "The Constitution gives me relevance." Ibid., p. 567.

p. 165   "For the people who have lost their lives. . . ." *PPP,* 1995, Book I (Washington, D.C.: Government Printing Office, 1996), p. 552.

p. 166   "To all my fellow Americans." Ibid., vol. 32, p. 689.

p. 167   "If you appropriate our sacred symbols" and following quotes from Clinton's speech at Michigan State University on May 5, 1995. Ibid., vol. 31, pp. 769–74.

p. 168   "These 33 lives show us the best of America." Ibid., vol. 32, pp. 626–30.

p. 168   As early as June 1981. See David Broder, *Washington Post,* 12/9/92, p. A23.

p. 170   "The fundamental differences between Democrats and Republicans." *Weekly Compilation, Presidential Documents,* vol. 31, April–June 1995, pp. 1051–52.

p. 170   Clinton calling on nation's political leaders for "more conversation, less combat." Ibid., pp. 1190–1200.

p. 171   "We've got to do this right." Quoted in Christopher Edley, "The Road to Clinton's Big Speech," *Washington Post,* July 23, 1995, pp. C1, C2.

p. 171   "Mend it, but don't end it" and following quotes from Clinton's speech of July 19, 1995. *PPP, 1995,* ibid., pp. 1255–64.

p. 172   "As the president demonstrated in affirmative action." Quoted in *New York Times,* October 20, 1996, p. 14.

p. 172 "One million men are right." Clinton's speech of October 16, 1995. Ibid., pp. 1847–53.

p. 172 Composition of Clinton's speech of October 16, 1995. Author's interviews with Baer, Edmonds, and Shipley, May 1996.

p. 174 "The era of big government is over." Clinton's 1996 State of the Union Address. *Weekly Compilation,* Presidential Documents, vol. 32, January–March 1996, pp. 90–98.

p. 175 "The budget reflects our values." Ibid., week ending April 26, p. 273.

p. 176 Presidents as "audience-driven." Roderick Hart, *The Sound of Leadership* (Chicago: University of Chicago Press), p. 200.

p. 177 Image making "has nothing to do with anything that is real." Michael Kelly, "David Gergen, Master of the Game," *New York Times Magazine,* October 31, 1993, p. 66.

p. 179 Government as "the art of formulating a policy." FDR in 1932 during his presidential campaign in a speech before the San Francisco Commonwealth Club.

p. 179 What he said was what he did. Many people erroneously believe that Roosevelt made budget balancing a major theme of his 1932 campaign. He did not. In Pittsburgh he did say he would reduce federal expenditures. When he opened his 1936 election with a speech in Pittsburgh, he asked Rosenman how he could get around his 1932 statement. "Deny you ever made it" is Rosenman's purported answer, and the two men had a good laugh.

INDEX

ABM Treaty, 103
Access to presidents, 53, 176
  Carter, 129
  Clinton, 157, 170
  Nixon, 81, 82, 96
  Reagan, 107
Acheson, Dean, 41–43, 44, 56, 59, 63, 70, 120
Adams, John, 5, 8–9
Adams, John Quincy, 8–9
Adams, Sherman, 46, 49
Affirmative action, 171–72
Agnew, Spiro, 92, 117
Aides, x, 96, 155
  Nixon, 87
  Reagan, 108, 109
  F. Roosevelt, 16
Ailes, Roger, 144
Air Force Tactical Bombing Command, 60–61
Ambrose, Stephen, 46, 85
America Firsters, 27
American Institute of Public Opinion polls, 12
American Review of Reviews, 7
American Society of Newspaper Editors, 46, 164

Americorps, 162–63
Anderson, Patrick, 128
Anti-Comintern Pact, 17
Antiwar movement, 83
Apollo XIII, 88
Aragon, Joe, 131
Atlantic Monthly, 138
Atomic Energy Agency, 52
Atomic Energy Commission, 46
Atoms for Peace, 45–47, 49–54
Atwater, Lee, 100
Axis powers, 17, 22–23, 25, 32
Azerbaijan, 39, 41

Baer, Donald, 158, 169–70, 171, 172
Baker, James, 96, 107, 109, 145
Baker, Ray Stannard, 7
Bakshian, Aram, 102, 109, 125–26
Ball, George, 57, 68, 70, 136
Bancroft, George, 8
Barton, Bruce, 29
Battle of Britain, 26
Bay of Pigs, 54, 55
Beale, Richard, 96, 169
Begala, Paul, 164
Belgium, 24
Bentsen, Lloyd, 162

Berger, Samuel (Sandy), 157
Berle, Adolf, 15
Berlin, Isaiah, 143
Berlin Wall, 147
Beschloss, Michael, 58
Blumenthal, Sidney, 144
Bohlen, Charles, 50
Boorstin, Robert, 157
Bradley, Omar, 70
Brady bill, 163
Brain trust
  Clinton, 170
  F. Roosevelt, 15–16
Brandt, Willy, 61
Broder, David, 156
Brown, Ron, 167–68
Brzezinski, Zbigniew, 135, 136, 137
Buchanan, Patrick, 81, 89, 91–92, 111
Bully pulpit, 1–2, 3
  Bush, 148, 154, 155
  Clinton, 160, 172
  Reagan, 104
  F. Roosevelt, 16–17, 34
Bundy, McGeorge, 56, 59, 60, 70
Bundy, William, 69, 71, 73
Busby, Horace, 73
Bush, George Herbert Walker, 105, 116,
  117, 143–55, 161, 162
  State of the Union Speech, 152–53
Bush administration, 97
Butler, Landon, 131
Butler, Patrick, 120–21, 124
Butterfield, Alexander, 85

Caddell, Pat, 139, 140
Cambodia, 88–95
Camp David, 87, 89, 132, 136, 139, 140
Camp David agreements, 142
Cannon, Lou, 111, 113–14
Cantril, Hadley, 12, 18
Carlucci, Frank, 114
Carroll, Wallace, 70–71
Carson, Johnny, 142
Carswell, G. Harrold, 88
Carter, James Earl, 8, 116, 117, 128–43,
  145, 154–55, 162
  Energy and National Goals speech
  (Malaise Speech), 139–41

New Foundation Speech, 141–42
Panama Canal Speech, 131–32
U.S. Naval Academy speech, 135–38
Carter, Rosalyn, 134
Carterism, 141
Carville, James, 164
Casey, William, 110
Casserly, John, 119, 127
Castro, Fidel, 54
Central Intelligence Agency, 40, 54, 56,
  63, 89
Cheney, Richard, 118, 120, 121, 123–24,
  127, 149
Chew, David, 107
Chicago Tribune, 7, 23
Chief(s) of staff, 93, 125
China, 17
Christian, George, 69, 73
Christopher, Warren, 157
Churchill, Winston, 14, 34, 37, 49–50
  Iron Curtain speech, 39, 40
Ciller, Tansu, 165
Civil War, 3
Clark, Bennett, 23
Clark, Champ, 5, 6
Clark, William, 102
Clifford, Clark, 37–39, 40, 41, 43, 44, 45,
  65, 66, 67, 68–69, 70, 71–72, 73, 74
Clinton, Hillary Rodham, 157
Clinton, William Jefferson, xi, 8, 156–75,
  177
  "common ground" speeches, 173–74
  State of the Union Address, 163–64,
  174–75
Cohen, Benjamin, 21–22, 24
Cold war, 43, 44, 53, 63
Collaboration, x, 9, 37, 96, 131, 143, 154,
  155, 173
Colson, Charles, 85
Commager, Henry Steele, 95
Commerce Department, 12
Committee to Defend America by Aiding
  the Allies, 27
Committee to Defend America First,
  26–27
Communism, 41, 65–66, 67, 107
Congress, 1, 2, 3, 42, 92, 110–11
  Clinton and, 164

House Ways and Means Committee, 4
  powers of, 3–4
  president and, 178
  Republican takeover, 163, 174
  F. Roosevelt and, 20, 21, 22, 23, 24,
    25, 28
  Senate Foreign Affairs Committee, 22
  Senate Foreign Relations Committee,
    88, 94
  Wilson's Inaugural Address before, 4–8
*Congressional Government in the United
  States* (Wilson), 3
Connor, Caryl, 129
Constitution, 1, 2, 3, 178
Constitutional Government (Wilson), 3
Contract with America, 164, 174
Coolidge, Calvin, 9
Corcoran, Thomas, 15–16, 21–22, 24
Coughlin, Charles, 23
Council of Economic Advisers, 126
Coyne, John, 127
Crane, Philip, 132
Cronkite, Walter, 76
Cuban missile crisis, 54–63, 66–67, 92
Curiel, Carolyn, 159, 171
Cutler, Robert, 48

Darman, Richard, 96, 97, 107, 108, 114,
  146, 148, 151, 152
Davis, Mark, 146, 148, 151, 154
Dean, Arthur, 70
Deaver, Michael, 96, 99, 104, 109
Decision making
  Carter, 129, 130, 132
  consensus-style, 63
  Ford, 127
  Nixon, 86
  Reagan, 109
  writers and, 75
Decision Making Information, Inc., 100
Defense buildup, 22, 25, 26, 28–29
Defense Department, 86, 93, 102
Demarest, David, 143–44, 145
Democracy, 25, 178
Democratic Leadership Council, 170, 172
Democratic party, 4
Desert Storm, 148–52, 153
Dillon, Douglas, 70

Dolan, Anthony, 105, 107, 114
Dole, Robert, 165
Donovan, Hedley, 134–35
Doolittle, Jerry, 131
Drafting process
  Bush speeches, 145–46
  effect on policy, 64–75
Drafts of speeches, 28, 120, 123, 131
  Carter, 131
  Eisenhower, 47, 50
  Ford, 120, 123
  F. Roosevelt, 14
Drew, Elizabeth, 158
Dreyer, David, 158, 160, 161, 162
Duberstein, Kenneth, 100
Dulles, Allen, 54
Dulles, John Foster, 46, 47, 48, 49, 50–
    51, 53

Eagleburger, Lawrence, 103
Edley, Christopher, Jr., 171
Edmonds, Terry, 172–73
Educator, president as, 177
  see also Teaching by president
Ehrlichman, John, 76, 81–82, 86
Eisenhower, Dwight David, ix, 36–37,
    45–54, 61, 66, 70, 74, 77, 80, 81,
    92, 95, 155, 163
  Atoms for Peace Speech, 45–47, 49–54
Eizenstat, Stuart, 133, 139
Elder Wise Men, 69–70, 73
Elliott, Bently, 101, 105–6, 108
Elsey, George, 38–39, 40, 41, 42, 45
England, 17, 21, 22, 23, 24, 26, 30, 32–33
Ethiopia, 17
Executive branch/power, 1, 178

Fahd, King, 149
Fair Deal, 37
Fallows, James, 129, 131–32, 135–36,
    138–39, 141
Farrakhan, Louis, 172
Ferguson, Andrew, 144, 146
Financial World, 7
Fireside chats
  Carter, 131–32
  Ford, 121

Fireside chats (*cont'd*)
  F. Roosevelt, 11, 17, 19–20, 25–26,
    104, 155
Fish, Hamilton, 23, 29
Fitzwater, Marlin, 145, 146
Focus groups, 100–101, 102, 104, 176
Ford, Gerald Rudolph, 8, 116, 117–27,
    143, 154–55, 162, 177
  Ohio State University Commence-
    ment Address, 126–27
  State of the Union Addresses, 121–24
Foreign policy
  Carter, 137, 142–43
  Clinton, 157, 163
  Eisenhower, 46, 54
  Nixon, 83, 90, 91–92
  F. Roosevelt, 20, 24, 27
  Truman, 39, 40–41, 44
Founding Fathers, 2–3, 9, 10, 178
France, 21, 22, 23, 24, 26
Friedman, Milton, 124
From, Al, 170

Gallup, George, 12
Gearan, Mark, 157
General Agreement on Tariffs and Trade,
    163
George Bush's War (Smith), 149
Gergen, David, 79, 82, 95, 96, 99, 107,
    109, 120, 121, 123, 125, 169, 177
Germany, 17, 23
Ghostwriters, 9, 129
Gilder, Josh, 98
Gilpatric, Roswell, 60
Goldwater, Barry, 104
Gorbachev, Mikhail, 149
Gore, Al, 161, 170
Governing
  public relations professionals in, 175
  speaking as, 154
Government, 11–12, 178
Gramm, Philip, 165
Great Britain, 41
  see also England
Great Society, 37
Greece, 41, 42, 43, 44
Greenberg, Stan, 164
Greenspan, Alan, 121, 123

Grew, Joseph, 33
Gromyko, Andrei, 59
Gulf of Tonkin Resolution, 88

Hagerty, James, 51
Haig, Alexander, 82, 118
Haldeman, H. R., 77, 78, 81, 82, 83, 84,
    85, 87, 89, 91, 93, 99
Hamilton, Alexander, 8
Hammarskjöld, Dag, 50
Hard Choices (Vance), 138
Harding, Warren, 9
Harlow, Bryce, 81
Harper's Weekly, 7
Hart, Roderick, 177
Hartmann, Robert, 118–19, 120, 121,
    122, 123–24, 125, 126, 127
Hastings, George, 9
Helms, Richard, 89, 90
Helsinki Final Act, 147
Hepburn Act, 2, 3
Hersey, John, 119, 120
Hertsgaard, Mark, 104
Hertzberg, Hendrik, 128, 129–31, 132–
    33, 134, 137, 138–39, 141, 142
Hitler, Adolf, 17, 21, 22, 24, 26, 32, 34,
    149, 150
Holland, 24
Hoover, Herbert, 9, 61
Hopkins, Harry, 14–15, 16, 18, 25, 27,
    30, 32, 33–34, 40
House, Edward, 19
Huebner, Lee, 81
Hughes, Emmet, 46, 47, 48–49, 53, 95
Hussein, Saddam, 148, 149, 150, 151

Ickes, Harold, 170
Image, 177, 178
  Nixon, 76–77, 78, 95, 115
  speechmaking and, 80–81
Image-age presidential speeches, 115
Image making, 99, 177
Imperial Presidency, The (Schlesinger), 87
Initial Action Plan, 96, 169
Internationalism(ists), 17, 18–19, 20, 27,
    33, 37
Iran-Contra operation, 110–14
Iraq, 148–53

Isolationism(ists), 17–18, 19, 20, 23–24, 25, 27, 33–34, 42
Israeli-Palestine Peace Accord, 162
Issues, shaping public understanding of, 174
Italy, 17, 26

Jackson, Andrew, 3, 8
Jackson, C. D., 46, 47, 48–49, 50–51, 53–54
Jackson-Lincolnites, 1
Jamieson, Kathleen Hall, 110
Janka, Leslie, 99–100
Japan, 17
Jefferson, Thomas, 5, 8–9, 158
Johnson, Andrew, 8
Johnson, Lyndon Baines, 36–37, 56, 63, 70, 77, 80, 84, 87, 88
    speech on U.S. policy in Vietnam, 63–75
Joint Chiefs of Staff, 89, 102, 103, 135
Jones, Joseph, 42–43, 44
Jordan, Hamilton, 131

Kamasaki, Charles, 172
Katzenbach, Nicholas, 73
Keating, Kenneth, 56
Kelly, John, 149
Kennan, George, 39, 40, 42, 136
Kennedy, John Fitzgerald, 36–37, 54–63, 66, 70, 74, 77, 80, 92, 129, 130–31, 155, 158
Kennedy, Robert, 56–57, 59–60, 64–65
Kennedy, Ted, 131
Kent State University, 94
Keogh, James, 81
Khrushchev, Nikita, 54, 55, 56, 58, 59, 60, 61, 62, 63
King, Martin Luther, Jr., 159
Kissinger, Henry, 76, 82, 86, 89, 90, 92–93, 99
Klein, Herbert, 78–79
Knute Rockne (film), 97
Kusnet, David, 157, 158, 160, 163

Laird, Melvin, 87, 89–90, 91
Lake, Anthony, 157
Laniel, Joseph, 49–50

Leadership, ix, 1, 177, 178
    moral, 160
F. Roosevelt, 11–12, 35
    Wilson, 7
League of Nations, 17
Leahy, William, 40
Lend-Lease, 30–33
Lincoln, Abraham, 3, 9, 11, 158
Lindbergh, Charles, 23
"Line of the day"
    Nixon, 78
    Reagan, 96–97
Liu, Eric, 157
Livingston, Edward, 8
Lodge, Henry Cabot, Jr., 50
Lon Nol, 88, 89, 95
London Economic Conference, 17
Luce, Clare Booth, 34
Luce, Henry, 34
Ludlow, Louis, 20
Ludlow Amendment, 20

MacArthur, Douglas, 45
MacLeish, Archibald, 14
McCarthy, Eugene, 64–65
McCormick, Colonel, 23
McCurry, Michael, 165
McFarlane, Robert, 102, 110, 112
McKinley, William, 9
McNamara, Robert, 56, 58, 60, 65, 68
McPherson, Harry, 64–65, 66–68, 69, 70–73, 74, 81, 143
McVeigh, Timothy, 165, 166–67
Madison, James, 8–9
Manchuria, 17
Marshall, George, 41–42
Marshall, Thomas, 5–6
Martin, Joseph, Jr., 29
Matthews, Christopher, 142, 144
Media, 8
    manipulation of: Reagan, 99–100
Meese, Edwin, 109
Meyer, Allan, 105
Militias, 165–67
Million Man March, 172
Mitchell, John, 91
Moley, Raymond, 15, 16
Molotov, V. M., 50

Monroe, James, 8–9
Monroe Doctrine, 44
Morgenthau, Henry, Jr., 18
Morris, Dick, 164
Mussolini, Benito, 17, 34

Nader, Ralph, 79
National Journal, 85
National Photographic Interpretation Center, 56
National Review, 147
National Security Council, 39, 46, 56, 61, 86, 89, 93, 102, 111, 112, 151, 157
National Student Association, 94
Nesmith, Achsah, 129
Nessen, Ron, 118, 121, 122
Neutrality Act/laws, 20, 21, 22, 23, 30
New Deal, 15, 20, 26, 37
New Frontier, 37
New Right, 104, 131, 132
New York Herald Tribune, 12
New York Herald Tribune Radio Forum, 21
New York Times, 33, 85, 124
New York *World*, 7
Nguyen Van Thieu, 83
Nixon, Richard Milhous, x, 76–96, 114–15, 116, 118, 127, 129, 154, 177
   Invasion of Cambodia Speech, 88–95
   pardoned by Ford, 125
   resignation, 117
   State of the Union Address, 81–82
Nixon staff
   in Ford administration, 124–25
Noonan, Peggy, 101, 108, 144, 152
North, Oliver, 110, 111
North American Free Trade Agreement, 162, 163
Nuclear weapons/war, 46, 47–49, 52, 55, 58, 63, 103
Nye, Gerald, 20, 23

O'Brien, Larry, 61
O'Connor, Basil, 15
O'Donnell, Kenneth, 55
Office of Communications, 78, 80, 96
Office of Public Affairs, 96
Office of Public Liaison, 79, 80, 85, 96
Office of War Information, 16

Oklahoma City bombing, 165–66, 168
Old Executive Office Building, 87, 89, 118, 125
O'Neill, Paul H., 126–27
Operation Candor, 47–48
Operation Wheaties, 48, 49, 50
Oppenheimer, J. Robert, 47
Orben, Robert, 118, 124
Ordeal of Power, The (Hughes), 53
Outlook, 7

Panama Canal, 131–32, 142
Panetta, Leon, 165, 170
Parvin, Landon, 103–4, 105, 113, 114
Peace at any price theory, 21, 27
Peace movement, 85, 88
Pearl Harbor, 59
Pentagon, 46, 61
Perle, Richard, 103
Persian Gulf, 150, 151
Plebiscitary presidency, 8
Podhoretz, John, 117, 147
Poindexter, John, 102, 110, 111, 112
Poland, 23, 106
Policy, 9, 15, 45
   Bush and, 146–51
   effect of drafting process on, 64–75
   and politics, 179
   Reagan's noninterest in, 169
   shaped through articulation, 176
   and speeches, 16, 146–47, 155
   and speechmaking, 46, 81, 83
   speechwriters and, 35, 38, 63, 80–81, 107–8, 116, 118–19, 170, 175
   and speechwriting, 126, 157, 160
Policymaking, 114–15
   Nixon, 92–93
   and speechmaking, 75
   speechwriting and, 37, 44–45, 75
Politics
   and policy, 179
Polls/polling, 12, 177, 178
   Nixon and, 80, 83
   F. Roosevelt and, 12, 18, 27, 28
Pollsters, 100–101, 115, 169, 177
Potsdam Conference, 38–39
Powell, Colin, 149
Powell, Jody, 131, 136, 141

Praetorians, 124, 125
Presidency, x, 3, 117, 176
  Clinton and, 167, 168, 175
  plebiscitary, 8
  T. Roosevelt's model of, 1, 2
  speeches, core of modern, 9–10
  Wilson and, 3, 4
  see also Rhetorical presidency; Virtual presidency
Presidential speech
  divorcing form from content, x
Press conferences
  Bush, 145
  Clinton, 163
  Nixon, 79–80
  Reagan, 112
  F. Roosevelt, 17, 30–32, 79
Price, Raymond, Jr., 77, 78, 81–82, 89, 144
Princeton, Office of Opinion Research, 12
Provost, Steven, 145
Public (the)
  F. Roosevelt leading, 16–17
Public opinion, 7, 177, 178
  Nixon and, 83
  F. Roosevelt and, 12–13, 17, 18, 19, 27
Public Papers of the Presidents of the United States, 8
Public relations, 115, 154, 175
  Nixon, 78, 80, 85, 86, 93, 95
  Reagan, 97

Rafshoon, Gerald, 128, 129, 133, 136, 137, 142
Reagan, Mrs., 114
Reagan, Ronald Wilson, 8, 94, 96–115, 116, 117, 132, 143, 144–45, 148, 177
  Bush and, 146–47
  ceremonial performances, 168
  Challenger Speech, 168
  control-the-agenda strategy, 168–69
  Moscow State University speech, 97–98
  Notre Dame University speech, 97–98
  "Time for Choosing, A" ("The Speech"), 104–5, 154

Reagan administration
  staging of, 100, 104
Rebozo, Bebe, 91
Reckoning with Reagan (Schaller), 113
Reed, Bruce, 157, 170
Regan, Donald, 100, 101, 107
Reid, Helen, 34
Republican National Committee, 118
Republican party, 4, 28–29, 55–56, 114, 171
  and Clinton, 174–75
  takeover of Congress, 163, 174
Reston, James, 55
Rhetorical presidency, xi, 10, 75, 127, 177–78
Rhetorical Presidency, The (Tulis), 3
Richard Nixon Human Interest Program, 80
Ridgeway, Matthew, 70
Rogers, Lindsay, 15
Rogers, William, 86, 87, 89–90
Rome-Berlin Axis, 17
Roosevelt, Franklin Delano, x, xi, 9, 10, 11–35, 36, 37, 40, 60, 92, 97, 129, 154–55, 158, 169, 175, 179
  Arsenal of Democracy fireside chat, 17, 32–33, 35
  Day of Infamy speech, 62
  fireside chats, 11, 17, 19–20, 25–26, 104, 155
  Lend-Lease speech, 44
  press conferences, 17, 30–32, 79
  Quarantine Speech, 17, 19, 20, 34
  speechwriting process, 83
  State of the Union Address, 17, 21–22
Roosevelt, Theodore, xi, 1–2, 3, 4, 7, 8, 9, 11, 77, 86, 147–48, 154, 179
Roper, Elmo, 12
Rosenman, Samuel, 12, 13, 14, 15, 16, 18, 21, 24, 25, 27, 29, 32, 35, 38, 80
Rosner, Jeremy, 157, 158, 161
Rostow, Walt, 69, 71
Rumsfeld, Donald, 118, 119, 120, 121, 127
Rusk, Dean, 66, 68, 69, 71, 73

Safire, William, 81, 84, 87, 89, 95, 142, 144–45, 146

Salinger, Pierre, 61
Schaller, Michael, 113
Schirmer, Kitty, 133
Schlesinger, Arthur, Jr., 32, 62–63, 80, 87
Schneiders, Greg, 137–38
Schwarzkopf, Norman, 149
Scowcroft, Brent, 146, 152
Seidman, William, 121
Selective Service Act, 28
Shakespeare, Frank, 77–78
Sherwood, Robert, 13, 14, 16, 29, 32
Shipley, David, 172–73
Shoen, Doug, 164
Shrum, Robert, 128
Shultz, George, 103, 110, 111–12
Sidey, Hugh, 36, 117
Sihanouk, Norodom, 88
"Silent majority," 84, 85
Simpson, O. J., 172
Sino-Japanese War, 17
Skinner, Samuel, 145, 152
Smith, Craig, 144
Smith, Gerald L. K., 27
Smith, Jean Edward, 149
Snow, Tony, 145, 146, 152
Social Security, 17
Sorenson, Theodore, 54, 56–58, 59–60, 61, 62, 63, 142, 143
Southeast Asia, 65–66, 71, 74, 91
Soviet Union, 37, 39–41, 43, 151
  and Cuban Missile Crisis, 54–56, 58, 59, 61–62, 63
  nuclear weapons, 46, 47–48, 50, 52, 53
  Reagan and, 98–99, 105, 106–7
Spanish Civil War, 17
Speakes, Larry, 97
Speeches, 8–9
  core of modern presidency, 9–10
  image-age, 115
  number of, 178–79
  written, 16
Speechmaking, 3, 114
  Nixon, 80–81, 83, 86, 95–96
  F. Roosevelt, 16, 35
Speechwriters, x, 8, 74–75, 176
  access to president, 53
  Bush, 143–44, 145–46, 151, 152, 153–54, 155

Carter, 128, 129, 131, 134–35, 136, 139–40, 141–42, 143
  Clinton, 157–58, 165, 172–73, 175
  Ford, 120–21, 125–26, 127
  Nixon, 96
  Reagan, 101, 104
  F. Roosevelt, 15–16, 24, 32
  Truman, 38–39, 45
  see also Policy, speechwriters and
Speechwriting, x, 8, 10, 73–75, 155, 177
  Clinton, 157, 169–70
  Ford, 119–24
  Reagan, 107–10
  F. Roosevelt, 13–15
  and policymaking, 37
  pollsters in, 101
Speechwriting Department, 105, 107, 127, 154
  Clinton, 157, 158
Speechwriting Office, 136, 145–46
Spencer, Stuart, 114
Sperling, Gene, 157
"Spin doctors," 152, 177
Stalin, Joseph, 14, 37, 39, 42, 45
Stalinism, 39
State Department, 26, 42, 43, 46, 50, 61, 86, 92, 93, 102
Stephanopoulos, George, 158, 161–62, 170
Stevenson, Adlai, 56
Stewart, Gordon, 129, 134, 139, 140, 141
Stockman, David, 109–10, 144
Strategic Defense Initiative (Star Wars), 102–4, 153
Strauss, Lewis, 47, 48, 49, 50–51, 53
Strong, Robert, 137
Strother, French, 9
Sununu, John, 143, 145
Supreme Court, 20, 171

Taft, Robert, 22
Taft, William Howard, 4, 9, 77
Taft-Buchanan School, 1
Taylor, Maxwell, 59, 70
Teaching by president, 35, 143, 179
  essence of leadership as, 11–12
Teeter, Robert, 152, 153–54
TelePrompTer, 121, 160–62

Television, 8, 78, 80, 176
  Reagan and, 97–98, 100–101, 104–5
Temple, Larry, 72
Tet offensive, 64, 65, 66, 70
Theis, Paul, 118, 119–20
Tower, John, 112, 114
Treleaven, Harry, 77–78
Truman, Harry S, xi, 36–45, 61, 74, 95,
  119, 120, 122, 155, 164
Truman administration, 65, 70
Truman Doctrine, 44, 45, 66
Truman Doctrine speech, 37
Tugwell, Rexford, 15
Tulis, Jeffrey, 3
Tumulty, Joseph, 21
Turkey, 41, 42, 43, 44, 58
Tutwiler, Margaret, 145

United Nations, 62
  General Assembly, 50, 52–53, 162
United States Information Agency, 50, 61

Values rhetoric
  Clinton, 169, 170–71, 172–74
Vance, Cyrus, 70, 135, 136, 137, 138
Vandenburg, Arthur, 42
Vardaman, James, 37
Vietnam Moratorium Committee, 87–88,
  94
Vietnam policy
  Johnson, 63–75
  Nixon, 83–85, 87–95
Vietnam War, 127, 150
Virtual presidency, 76–115
Virtual reality, 177
Voter participation, 178–79

Waldman, Michael, 157, 160, 170
Wallace, George, 85
Washington, George
  Farewell Address, 8
Washington Post, 85, 153
Watergate scandal, 127

Welliver, Judson, 9
West Berlin, 54
Westmoreland, William, 64
Wheeler, Burton, 23
Wheeler, Earle, 65, 70, 73, 90
White, Theodore, 64, 84
White House, 8
  Briefing Room, 79, 145, 175
  Map Room, 14, 37–38, 40
  press corps, 79
  Press Office, 97
White House Mess, 144
Will, George, 153
Williams, John Sharp, 5
Willkie, Wendell, 27–28, 30
Wills, Garry, 110
Wilson, Charles, 48
Wilson, Edith, 6, 7
Wilson, Woodrow, xi, 3–8, 9, 21, 23, 86,
  92, 136, 175, 178
  Inaugural Address before Congress,
  4–8
Winston-Salem Sunday Journal and Sentinel,
  70–71
Wirthlin, Richard, 96, 100–101, 169
Wood, Robert, 26
Woods, Rose Mary, 82, 86
Wooten, Kathy, 124
Word (the)
  decrease in integrity of, 177–78
Words
  and government, 178
  putting policy into, 15
Works Progress Administration, 18
World Disarmament Conference, 17
World War II, 17–18, 20, 22–35
Writing, ix
  as tool of thinking, x, 125
Writing and Research Department, 80,
  118

Zarb, Frank, 121
Ziegler, Ron, 76
Zoellnick, Robert, 145